REGULATING UTILITIES:
A TIME FOR CHANGE?

REGULATING UTILITIES:
A TIME FOR CHANGE?

Stephen Sayer • Dr. Stephen Glaister
George Yarrow • Professor John Vickers
Professor Colin Robinson • Professor John Kay
Dr. Dieter Helm • Dr. Irwin M. Stelzer
Professor M. E. Beesley

Comments by
Sir Bryan Carsberg • I. C. R. Byatt • Bill Wigglesworth
Graeme Odgers • Professor Stephen Littlechild
Sir Christopher Chataway • John Swift
Professor M. E. Beesley • Clare Spottiswoode

Introduced and edited by
Professor M. E. Beesley

Institute of Economic Affairs
in association with the
London Business School
1996

First published in May 1996

by

THE INSTITUTE OF ECONOMIC AFFAIRS
2 Lord North Street, Westminster, London, SW1P 3LB

in association with the
London Business School

IEA Readings 44
All rights reserved

ISSN 0305-814X

ISBN 0-255 36381-8

Printed in Great Britain by
Redwood Press, Trowbridge, Wiltshire

Text set in Times Roman 11 on 12 point

CONTENTS

INTRODUCTION

Michael Beesley
London Business School

IN MY INTRODUCION TO LAST YEAR'S VOLUME IN THIS
SERIES,[1] I noted the increasing questioning of the UK's methods of
regulating utilities, to which regulators were responding. The
challenges have certainly not abated in the year since. The lectures
reprinted in this *Readings* (given in the Autumn of 1995 but revised
and brought up to date by the authors) reflect the depth and variety of
the professional debates which have ensued. One of the largely
unforeseen consequences of privatisation was the quantum leap not
only in professional and public interest in what had been on the whole
quite tranquil public enterprises, but also in information with which
challenges can be mounted. The consumer has learned how to voice his
discontent in a far more informed manner; an army of experts has
replaced the knowledgeable handful of pre-privatisation days, and all
this has been encouraged by regulators themselves. It is a different
world even from that of the late 1980s, when the pioneer utility
regulators, mindful of judicial review, and true to the Government wish
to keep the lawyers out of regulation as far as possible, gave very little
away in their price determinations.

Critics of UK-style deregulation of course give too little weight to the
fact that regulators have had to develop their techniques over time,
from the very imperfect bases handed to them on taking office. Even
less appreciated is that regulated firms themselves have needed time to
develop the management culture which will throw up adequate
responses, including information, to cope with the demands of
privatisation and regulation. These considerations, rightly, have not
silenced the critics. But regulation is a developing profession in itself,
and, paradoxically, has become more able even as the criticisms have
been increasing. That ability will, no doubt, be enhanced by the several
University centres for the study of regulatory issues that have recently
emerged. This volume will, I hope, add to the even livelier and more
informed exchange.

---

[1] M.E. Beesley (ed.), *Utility Regulation: Challenge and Response*, IEA Readings No.42,
London: Institute of Economic Affairs, 1995.

The papers in *Readings No.44* address both the widening scope of regulatory affairs and the current tasks of regulation. In many contributors' minds was doubtless also the prospect of a General Election, at which the possibility of a quite different philosophy of regulation may emerge. On the wider scene, alongside a growth in UK-style utility regulation, general competition policy has been increasingly influenced by the European Union. One of the ongoing questions of UK regulation is the terms on which, and when, utility regulators should yield their individual powers to influence competitive behaviour to the general competition authorities.

These developments lead naturally to the question: What impact will the European Union have on UK utility regulation? **Mr Stephen Sayer** reminds us of the complexities of trying to answer such a question, giving a comprehensive, annotated review. The application of Articles 85 and 86 to utilities is much influenced by the exceptions preserving member-states' positions where utilities have been granted special or exclusive rights, which is normally the case. So the issue is much bound up with the parallel EU efforts to liberalise the utilities, in which the UK has been regarded as the front runner. The upshot is that even in the most advanced case (Telecoms), progress towards a Single Market in which European competition law would fully apply has been limited. If UK regulators cannot yet, even if they wish, resign in favour of Articles 85 and 86, the question naturally arises of the strengthening of the UK law to cope with the exceptional monopoly power involved.

Sir Bryan Carsberg, from the chair, took up these issues, giving his preferred solutions, which involve prohibitions on certain forms of behaviour; but both he and Mr Sayer are doubtful about the practicality of adopting Article 86's doctrine of abuse of monopoly power.

Three speakers take up further longstanding, unsolved problems in regulation. **Dr Stephen Glaister** sees the basic propensity of utility incentives to invest too heavily as particularly manifest in water. He points specifically to the need to justify expenditure to support security standards, which involves the National River Authority as well as Ofwat, when customers do not face direct financial disciplines. In effect, he says, the present system results in taxes on consumers they are largely powerless to avoid even with the Regulator's help. He assesses proposals involving insurance premia, profit regulation and improved measurement of consumer preferences for quality, seeing some hope of progress in the last.

Mr Ian Byatt agrees on the need for these measurements better to underpin pricing decisions, but pins his hopes more on other measures, such as installing more meters when most needed, and peak pricing. The papers vividly illustrate the regulators' task in bringing good principles to bear on an inherited position.

The inherited price structure in utilities, often inefficient, has thrown up many proposals to measure, and specifically to fund, social obligations, to allow the rebalancing of prices and removal of cross-subsidy. **Mr George Yarrow** deals with social obligations in Telecoms. He reviews the several meanings of what has been a very elastic concept. He is sceptical of the claims of universal service provisions, and the alleged network externalities underlying it, and in particular increased penetration rates. He favours direct income supplements rather than Oftel involvement in 'low income' telephone concessions. Laying licence obligations on BT to meet social objectives is, he argues, inconsistent with competition. He would prefer to deregulate, and shift what social obligations remain away from Oftel; their pursuit by Oftel is possibly even counter-productive.

Mr Bill Wigglesworth, while agreeing with the speaker's thrust, and with the judgement that the cost of universal service has been exaggerated, again brings the regulator's legal inheritance well to the fore. Explaining the approaches of successive Directors General in some detail, he points out how limited in practice the effect of general industry obligations for funding has been on competitive developments so far. He particularly supports the idea of competitive tendering among operators to supply whatever social services are to be funded.

Professor John Vickers concurs with the view that cross-subsidy is inhibiting to effective competition but he brings into question another regulatory aim, that of fixing the incumbent prices and other terms to encourage entrants. He doubts whether, after a decade of managed competition, regulators (or for that matter the general UK competition laws) will achieve their competitive goals. He foresees the need for emphasis on divestment rather than on regulating conduct, and action to deter anti-competitive behaviour. This re-inforces the case for a stronger competitive policy framework, perhaps directed especially to utilities.

Mr Graeme Odgers recounts his dealings, when Managing Director of British Telecoms, with Sir Bryan Carsberg. He felt considerable pressure at that time, but is now convinced that British Telecoms much benefitted by it. Competition in telecoms is still, however, inadequate; and he endorses John Vickers's view that competitive rivalry should be such as to promote efficiency. Any rivalry will not do; it should be subject to the efficiency test.

Disagreement on this last view characterises an important distinction between those who hold neo-classical beliefs and those who are of the Austrian persuasion. **Professor Colin Robinson** would doubtless reject the notion that any regulator can make the prediction about what will, and what will not, be efficient in the event. But in the area he covers, electricity, this has hardly been an issue. For him electricity provides the test-bed for a far wider set of reasons not to pin one's faith in regulation, a position he argues from a wide range and depth of knowledge about the fuel industries as a whole. The principal reason, as he sees it, is that privatisation, though correct in principle, was a political act, with many imperfections from the competitive viewpoint. The main danger now is that regulation, which has attempted to repair the flawed start, will become repoliticised – just as the market for corporate control and rivalry is becoming more effective, and a genuine (Austrian) discovery process has just begun.

Professor Stephen Littlechild agrees with many of Professor Robinson's conclusions about privatisation being preferable, with all its faults, to what went before. He is considerably more optimistic about the competitive progress in generation and supply; and differs strongly about how consumers have fared since 1988. As he implies, the underlying difficulty in such judgements is the counter-factual: it all depends on what one's model of a non-privatised world yields.

Criticism of how RPI-X regulation, UK style, is working has, in the last year, begun to throw up many ideas for its development or reform. **Professor John Kay** gives his reasons why some of the most widely canvassed reforms are wide of the mark. He thinks that the demands from the utilities for more accountability by the regulators stem from their belief that this would work to their own advantage, but that this, if true, is a strategy which invites more short-term political influence. For him, regulation has succeeded in pressing on the incumbents, but has raised more acutely the problem of the utilities' legitimacy in the eyes of the public. Profit-sharing proposals are likewise flawed. Legitimacy requires adoption of the idea of a 'customer corporation', giving customers clear priority among the interests served.

Sir Christopher Chataway disagrees with important aspects of John Kay's analysis. Shareholders have not done uniformly well across the utilities; the RPI-X mechanism has performed much better than he allows. The central proposition of a 'customer corporation', he thinks, relies too much on assuming away the disciplines managers should face; regulatory risk would sharply increase, and the perceived imbalance between shareholders and consumers would not be corrected.

Dr Dieter Helm addresses the question of possible weaknesses in the structures being put in place to accompany rail privatisation. He believes that the original design – calling for franchising over the rail infrastructure involving over 70 companies – is not sustainable. His thesis is that commercial incentives will directly, or indirectly, cause a reversion to integrated modes of production; and with the large subsidies that will be required it is still unclear what their relation with the investment will be. **John Swift, QC**, thinks that the privatisation system is workable and will yield important economies. But he agrees with Dieter Helm in the continuing role of the government, in particular, how it uses its funding powers to underpin the structure it wishes to see. He thinks this should be a function of a long-term bi-partisan political decision.

Dr Irwin Stelzer mounts a root-and-branch criticism of the UK regulatory system, in contrast with the American. In particular, the closed procedure, single regulators, and the refusal to control profits were mistakes, though British regulators are able and fair-minded. But the principal American lessons are that vertical integration should be avoided; competition is critical; open procedures discipline regulators; and the political survival of regulation depends on *not* leaving profit as a free variable. In particular, regulation must not lead to overloading a competition policy with notions of predicting competitive effects. Competition is desirable for its own sake; regulatory rules should focus on attempts to stifle competition. I pointed out that the framers of the licences which accompanied privatisation were very conscious of the dangers both of regulatory capture and of the weaknesses in general competition law in the UK; and that the US system never had to confront the question of privatising state-run firms. The confrontation of US Anti-Trust with State regulators will yield further useful insights. I also suggested that the learning process in UK regulatory affairs is liable to be underestimated.

Alongside these speculations about the reform of UK-style regulation, the system is performing its duty of fixing price controls and other critical regulatory matters. Some of our chairpersons were indeed in this position when lectures were given. My own lecture on British Gas and RPI-X occurred at a time when a major price-fixing episode was in full swing – the prices to be set by the newly-separated TransCo. Previous regulatory decisions have to be taken fully into account on these occasions. The great precedent in this case was the

MMC's verdicts in the gas references of 1993, on which I had served when a Commission member. I thought I detected in TransCo's reaction to Ofgas's consultation document a rejection of what I thought of as a cardinal feature of the MMC's approach to RPI-X, namely its emphasis on the forward-looking cash flow as the basis for judgement, alongside other reasons, for possible modifications of RPI-X. Thus, it seemed important to lay out the reasons for according it so much attention.

Clare Spottiswoode took the point on the importance of the cashflow approach, but argued the need for some difference in emphasis, including the possibility of incorporating profit sharing in the control, especially in view of the implications of take-or-pay contracts. She was strongly in favour of disclosure of information bearing on a monopoly position, which might extend to the thinking behind schemes to split British Gas's assets.[2]

Looking back over the lecture series since they started in 1991, it is pleasing to note how often the contributors have been in the van of developing ideas about UK-style regulation of utilities and competition policy. I hope the tradition will be maintained in the 1996 series, in October and November. We have decided to preserve the 1995 format in that academics will give the papers, and the regulators will take the chair; in this way, discussion need not be trammelled by ongoing regulatory business, as the papers in the 1995 series clearly show.

London Business School   **M.E.B.**
April 1996

---

[2] Since the lecture British Gas has announced its intention to float a separate trading company, which, *inter alia*, will have considerable gas holdings.

THE AUTHORS

Michael Beesley is a founding Professor of Economics, now Emeritus, at the London Business School. Lecturer in Commerce at the University of Birmingham, then Reader in Economics at the LSE, he became the Department of Transport's Chief Economist for a spell in the 1960s. His recent work has centred on the issues of deregulation and privatisation in telecoms, transport, water and electricity, and he is currently Economic Adviser to OFGAS and OFFER. Much of his work to 1991 in this area was summed up in *Privatisation, Regulation and Deregulation* (Routledge with the IEA, 1992).

His independent economic study of *Liberalisation of the Use of British Telecommunications' Network* was published in April 1981 by HMSO and he has since been active as an advisor to the Government in telecoms, the deregulation of buses and the privatisation of the water industry. For the IEA, of which he is a Managing Trustee, he wrote (with Bruce Laidlaw) *The Future of Telecommunications* (Research Monograph 42, 1989) and (with S.C. Littlechild) 'The Regulation of Privatised Monopolies in the United Kingdom', in *Regulators and the Market* (IEA Readings No.35, 1991). He contributed to and edited the IEA's *Markets and the Media* (IEA Readings No. 43, 1996), and he has edited all three of the previous volumes in this lecture series.

He was appointed CBE in the Birthday Honours List, 1985; from 1988 to 1994 he was a member of the Monopolies and Mergers Commission.

Ian Byatt was appointed as the first Director General of Water Services on 1 August 1989. He is an economist and an expert on the regulation of public utilities. His previous post was as Deputy Chief Economic Adviser to the Treasury (1978-89). He was born in 1932 and educated at Kirkham Grammar School and at St Edmund Hall and Nuffield College, Oxford. He also studied at Harvard University as a Commonwealth Fund Fellow. He has lectured in economics at both Durham University (1958-62) and the London School of Economics (1964-67).

He joined the Civil Service in 1967 as Senior Economic Adviser to the Department of Education and Science. His career in the Civil Service also included spells at the Ministry of Housing and Local

Government and the Department of Environment, before joining the Treasury in 1972. In 1986 he chaired the Advisory Committee on Accounting for Economic Costs and Changing Prices.

His publications include *The British Electrical Industry 1875-1914* (1979). For the IEA, he contributed a chapter, 'OFWAT: Regulation of Water and Sewerage', to *Regulators and the Market* (IEA Readings No.35, 1991), and another, 'Water: The Periodic Review Process', to *Utility Regulation: Challenge and Response* (IEA Readings No.42, 1995).

Sir Bryan Carsberg took up his post as Secretary-General of the International Accounting Standards Committee on 22 May 1995. He held public office over the previous 11 years, first as the first Director General of Telecommunications from 1984 and more recently as Director General of Fair Trading.

Educated at Berkhamsted School and the London School of Economics, Sir Bryan qualified as a chartered accountant and became a member of the Institute of Chartered Accountants in England and Wales in 1960. He gained an MSc (Econ.) with distinction through part-time study at the London School of Economics in 1967. Between 1969 and 1981 Sir Bryan was Professor in the Department of Accounting and Business Finance at the University of Manchester. He was the Dean of its Faculty of Economic and Social Studies, 1977-78; and he was Arthur Andersen Professor of Accounting at the London School of Economics, 1981-84. In 1974 he was a visiting Professor at the University of California (Berkeley). From 1978 to 1981 he was Assistant Director of the US Financial Accounting Standards Board. Sir Bryan was a member of the UK Accounting Standards Board, 1990-94, and was its deputy chairman between 1990 and 1992.

In May 1988 Sir Bryan was presented with the Chartered Accountants Founding Society's Centenary Award in recognition of his services to society through his work at OFTEL. He was awarded a knighthood in January 1989. In December 1992 Sir Bryan was presented with the Bleau award for his work in the field of telecommunications.

Sir Bryan is the author or co-author of 11 publications on accounting, economics and finance. For the IEA, he has contributed to three IEA Readings: No.35, *Regulators and the Market* (1991); No.40, *Major Issues in Regulation* (1993); and No.42, *Utility Regulation: Challenge and Response* (1995). Sir Bryan also delivered the 1995 Wincott

Memorial Lecture, *Competition Regulation the British Way: Jaguar or Dinosaur?* (IEA Occasional Paper No. 97, February 1996).

The Rt. Hon. Sir Christopher Chataway's career has been divided between the public and private sectors. After reading PPE at Magdalen College, Oxford, and four years with ITN and the BBC, he was a Member of Parliament for North Lewisham (1959-66) and Chichester (1969-74). He was a junior Education Minister in the Macmillan Government (1962-64) and Minister in the Heath Administration (Minister of Posts and Telecommunications, 1970-72; Minister for Industrial Development, DTI, 1972-74; appointed PC in 1970). From 1974 he was for 15 years Managing Director of Orion Royal Bank. He has been a non-executive Chairman or Director of a number of companies since 1974. He became Chairman of the Civil Aviation Authority in June 1991. Sir Christopher contributed a chapter, 'The Charter Airline Industry: A Case History of Successful Deregulation', to *Utility Regulation: Challenge and Response* (IEA Readings No. 42, 1995).

Stephen Glaister, PhD, is Cassel Reader in Economic Geography with special reference to Transport at the London School of Economics. He was a member of the Government's Advisory Committee on Trunk Road Assessment and he has been Specialist Advisor to the Parliamentary Select Committee on Transport. He was a non-executive director of London Regional Transport from 1984 until 1993. He has acted as advisor to the Department of Transport on bus deregulation, and he developed models for the Department for the cost-benefit assessment of urban public transport subsidies. He has worked on urban transport evaluation for the World Bank. In December 1991 he published *Transport Options for London*, and in March 1993, *Meeting the Transport Needs of the City*, both with Tony Travers. For the IEA, he wrote (with Tony Travers) *New Directions for British Railways?* (Current Controversies No.5, June 1993), and a chapter, 'The Regulation of Britain's Privatised Railways', in *Regulating Utilities: The Way Forward* (IEA Readings No. 41, 1994). He has contributed widely to the journals and to books on transport. He is Managing Editor of the *Journal of Transport Economics and Policy*.

Dieter Helm is a director of Oxford Economic Research Associates Ltd. and a Fellow in Economics at New College, Oxford. His previous appointments include Research Fellow in Economics and Management, New College, Oxford, 1981-83, Lecturer in Economics, Queen's College, Oxford, 1983-86, Senior Research Fellow, Centre for Business Strategy, London Business School, 1987-88. He is a Research Associate of the Institute for Fiscal Studies, and was the founding Managing Editor (now an Associate Editor) of the *Oxford Review of Economic Policy*. He contributed to *Regulating Utilities: The Way Forward* (IEA Readings No.41, 1994). He is Editor of *Energy Utilities*.

John Kay is Visiting Professor of Economics at the London Business School, and co-founder of London Economics. He was previously Research Director of the Institute for Fiscal Studies, and Fellow of St John's College, Oxford. He is the author or editor of several books, including (with Mervyn King) *British Taxation System* (1978); *Foundations of Corporate Success* (1993); and (with Colin Mayer and David Thompson) (eds.) *Privatisation and Regulation – The UK Experience* (1986). For the IEA, he contributed 'The Forms of Regulation', in *Financial Regulation – or Over-Regulation?* (IEA Readings No.27, 1988), and 'Regulating Networks', in *Regulating Utilities: The Way Forward* (IEA Readings No.41, 1994).

Stephen Littlechild was appointed the first Director General of Electricity Supply on 1 September 1989. He has been Professor of Commerce, University of Birmingham, since 1975. He was formerly Professor of Applied Economics, University of Aston, 1973-75, and sometime Consultant to the Ministry of Transport, Treasury, World Bank, Electricity Council, American Telephone & Telegraph Co., and Department of Energy.

He is author or co-author of *Operational Research for Managers* (1977), *Elements of Telecommunication Economics* (1979), and *Energy Strategies for the UK* (1982). For the IEA, he wrote *The Fallacy of the Mixed Economy* (Hobart Paper 80, 1978, Second edn. 1986), and contributed to *The Taming of Government* (IEA Readings 21, 1979) and *Agenda for Social Democracy* (Hobart Paperback 15, 1983). More recently, he contributed a chapter, 'Competition in Electricity: Retrospect and Prospect', to *Utility Regulation: Challenge and Response* (IEA Readings No. 42, 1995*)*. He has been a Member of the IEA Advisory Council since 1982. He was commissioned by the Department of Industry to consider proposals to regulate the profitability of British Telecom. His reports, *Regulation of British*

Telecommunications' Profitability, and *Economic Regulation of Privatised Water Authorities*, were published in 1983 and 1986.

Graeme Odgers was appointed Chairman of the Monopolies and Mergers Commission in April 1993, having been a part-time member of the Commission from the previous January. He was born and educated in South Africa, read engineering at the University of Cambridge and gained an MBA at Harvard Graduate School of Business Administration in 1959. He worked for a period with the International Finance Corporation in Washington, DC, and settled in England in 1962. His varied career has embraced both the public and private sectors. He was Head of the Industrial Development Unit at the DTI in the mid-1970s, Finance Director and then Managing Director of Tarmac PLC, Managing Director of BT, and Chief Executive of Alfred McAlpine PLC. He contributed a chapter, 'MMC: Talking Shop or Decision-Maker?', to *Utility Regulation: Challenge and Response* (IEA Readings No. 42, 1995).

Colin Robinson was educated at the University of Manchester, and then worked for 11 years as a business economist before being appointed to the Chair of Economics at the University of Surrey in 1968. He has been a member of the Electricity Supply Research Council and of the Secretary of State for Energy's Advisory Council for Research and Development in Fuel and Power (ACORD), and is currently on the electricity panel of the Monopolies and Mergers Commission. He has written widely on energy and regulation. His most recent IEA papers are *Energy Policy: Errors, Illusions and Market Realities* (IEA Occasional Paper No.90, October 1993), and 'Gas: What to Do After the MMC Verdict', in *Regulating Utilities: The Way Forward* (IEA Readings No. 41, 1994).

Professor Robinson became a member of the IEA's Advisory Council in 1982 and was appointed its Editorial Director in 1992. He was appointed a Trustee of the Wincott Foundation in 1993. He received the British Institute of Energy Economists' award as 'Economist of the Year 1992'.

Stephen Sayer qualified as a solicitor in 1968, became a partner in Richards Butler in 1974 and works in the London office. He specialises in UK and EC competition law, insurance law, energy law and international commercial law and is head of the firm's Competition Group and Energy Group.

He has extensive practical experience and advises governments as well as commercial enterprises. He has great experience of dealing with governments in various parts of the world as well as with EU and UK regulators, including the Office of Fair Trading, the Monopolies and Mergers Commission and the Department of Trade and Industry.

He has lectured extensively around the world on competition issues, insurance law, energy law and commercial law. He is a contributor to Longman's *Practical Commercial Precedents, Butterworths Joint Ventures with International Partners*, and other publications.

He is a member of the International Bar Association, the Society of English and American Lawyers, the United Kingdom Association for European Law, the Institute of Petroleum and the United Kingdom Oil Lawyers Group. He is a liveryman of the City of London Solicitors Company and a Freeman of the City of London.

Clare Spottiswoode was appointed Director General of Gas Supply (OFGAS) on 1 November 1993, for a term of five years. She graduated in mathematics and economics at the University of Cambridge in 1975, and was awarded a Mellon Fellowship to Yale University where she took a further degree in economics. She began her career as an economist with the Treasury in 1977, leaving in 1980 to start a family and found a business which traded in gifts. Having sold it as a going concern, she started a software company specialising in microcomputer software packages for the financial and corporate sector. She sold this company in 1988, remaining as Managing Director and Chairman until 1990.

Since then she has increased her family whilst holding several part-time appointments, including being a tutor at the London Business School's Centre for Enterprise and a member of the Government's engineering deregulation task force. She contributed a paper, 'Developing Competition: Regulatory Initiatives', to *Utility Regulation: Challenge and Response* (IEA Readings No.42, 1995).

Irwin M. Stelzer is Director of Regulatory Policy Studies at the American Enterprise Institute, where he studies economic and regulatory policy issues. He is US economic and political columnist for *The Sunday Times* (London) and *The Courier Mail* (Australia), a member of the Publication Committee of *The Public Interest*, and an

Honorary Fellow of the Centre for Socio-Legal Studies, Wolfson College, Oxford.

Dr Stelzer founded National Economic Research Associates, Inc. (NERA) in 1961 and served as its President until a few years after its sale in 1983 to Marsh & McLennan. He has also been a Managing Director of the investment banking firm of Rothschild Inc., and Director of the Energy and Environmental Policy Center at Harvard University.

Dr Stelzer has written and lectured on economic and policy developments in the United States and Britain, particularly as they relate to privatisation and competition policy. He is the author of *Selected Antitrust Cases: Landmark Decisions* (7th edition, 1986), and co-author of *The Antitrust Laws: A Primer*, as well as articles for business, professional and popular journals, including *Commentary* and *The Public Interest*. He is consultant to NewsCorp. For the IEA, he contributed a chapter, 'Regulatory Methods: A Case for "Hands Across the Atlantic"', to *Regulators and the Market* (IEA Readings No.35, 1991), and another (with William B. Shew), 'A Policy Framework for the Media Industries', to *Markets and the Media* (IEA Readings No. 43, 1996).

Dr Stelzer received his Bachelor and Master of Arts degrees from New York University and his Doctorate in Economics from Cornell University. He is a member of Phi Beta Kappa.

John Swift, QC, was appointed Rail Regulator and International Rail Regulator (Office of the Rail Regulator) in December 1993, having previously been special adviser on the railway privatisation regulatory framework to the Secretary of State for Transport from January to November 1993.

He was born in 1940 and educated at Birkenhead School and University College, Oxford, where he gained MA with first-class honours in the School of Jurisprudence in 1963. He then gained a Diploma with Distinction at the Johns Hopkins School of Advanced International Studies at Bologna, 1963-64. He became a Barrister at Law in 1965, a QC in 1981, and a Bencher of the Inner Temple in 1992. For the IEA, he contributed a paper, 'Regulatory Relationships Between Key Players in the Restructured Rail Industry', to *Utility Regulation: Challenge and Response* (IEA Readings No.42, 1995).

John Vickers is Drummond Professor of Political Economy at the University of Oxford and a Fellow of All Souls College. After studying

PPE at Oxford (BA, 1979), he worked for a while in the oil industry before returning to Oxford to pursue graduate economics (DPhil., 1985). From 1984 to 1990 he was Roy Harrod Fellow in the Economics of Business and Public Policy at Nuffield College, where he was also investment bursar for two years. He has held visiting positions at Harvard, Princeton, and the London Business School. He has published numerous journal articles on industrial organisation, privatisation, regulation and competition. His books include (with George Yarrow) *Privatisation: An Economic Analysis* (1988) and (with Mark Armstrong and Simon Cowan) *Regulatory Reform* (1994). His current research concerns competition theory and policy.

Bill Wigglesworth advises governments and others on telecommunications regulation. He also lectures on the subject at City University; is adviser to the telecommunications forum of the International Institute of Communications (IIC); and is a board member of UKERNA, the body that manages the advanced network for academic and research institutions in the UK.

He was responsible for setting up Oftel in 1984; and was Deputy Director General of Telecommunications from then until retiring in March 1994. He had acted as Director General from June 1992 to April 1993, pending the appointment of a permanent successor to Sir Bryan Carsberg. Previously, in the DTI, he had responsibilities for competition policy (1975-78), telecommunications liberalisation (1978-82) and policy towards the computer and office equipment industries (1982-83).

He has lectured widely on telecommunications policy issues. Recently published papers include: 'The Current Trends of Telecommunications Issues in the UK', Tokyo, July 1995; 'British Privatisation of Telecommunications: Process and Impact', Seoul, September 1995; and 'The Role of Information in Telecommunications Regulation', Paris, September 1995.

George Yarrow is Fellow and Tutor in Economics, Hertford College, Oxford, and Director of the Regulatory Policy Institute at Oxford. His main academic interests are in the theory of the firm, industrial organisation, and privatisation. His main publications are (with J. Vickers) *Privatization – An Economic Analysis* (1988) and (with Helen Lawton Smith) *Social Security and Friendly Societies: Options for the Future* (1993). He contributed a chapter, 'Does Ownership Matter?', to

Privatisation & Competition: A Market Perspective (IEA Hobart Paperback No.28, 1989).

THE IMPACT OF THE EUROPEAN UNION ON UK UTILITY REGULATION

Stephen Sayer
Richards Butler

Introduction

ONE OF THE EUROPEAN UNION'S PRINCIPAL OBJECTIVES is to achieve a single market in Europe by eliminating all internal barriers preventing the free movement of goods, persons, services and capital. This must be achieved while fulfilling another founding objective, which is to raise the standard of living and quality of life throughout the Community.

One of the means by which the Community is required to achieve its objectives is by establishing a system designed to ensure that competition in the single market is not distorted. Having hitherto largely concentrated on goods and services, the Community's attention has now turned to infrastructure. In this context, access to the utilities, such as electricity, gas, water, telecommunications and transport, is of primary importance to the Community in fulfilling its overall aims and objectives.

It is my intention to provide you with a legal view on the specific issue of Community regulation of competition in the utility markets.

The debate on how competition in the utility markets should be regulated is particularly relevant now for two reasons. *First*, there are the current deliberations of the DTI under the Fair Trading Act in relation to the spate of acquisitions and proposed take-overs in the various parts of the electricity and water markets. *Second*, the privatised utility companies have been extensively criticised for the significant profits which those companies have realised and the apparently generous remuneration packages given to Board directors, when the standard of services received by the customer is said to be less than satisfactory. These events have heightened the debate as to whether there is, or will remain, effective regulation in the relevant markets. I confine my comments to the industries that have already been privatised, with a view to focusing on the issues that are arising now that their regulation is becoming established. The industries are electricity, gas, water and telecommunications, each of which has an independent regulator. Whilst transport is also a utility it has many different characteristics from the industries mentioned above and is therefore outside the scope of this paper.

Forms of Utility Regulation

It is important to reflect on the background to the regulation of the utilities and why it is considered that these industries require specific regulation, over and above the general competition rules which are predominantly implemented by the OFT, the DTI, the MMC and the Restrictive Practices Court. The utilities with which we are concerned are traditionally regarded as 'natural monopolies', that is, industries where the market may only be able to support one supplier and the capital expenditure required and infrastructure itself act as barriers to entry, severely hampering competition. When an enterprise is in this position, there are few incentives for it to be efficient because of the absence of competition. Furthermore, the enterprise is in a position of power in which, without regulation, it can move its prices without reference to market forces.

In the case of utilities, there is also a major concern to protect the security of supply of the resource, upon which the state and its population depend. The concerns over security of supply have been voiced by several member-states to the European Commission in response to its proposals for establishing a single market for each of these utilities. For example, in Ireland the government has been allowed to restrict the quota of imports of electricity in order to protect its own resource, which it would have to resort to in the event that imports ceased to be available. The restrictions were justified on grounds of public policy.[1]

Different member-states employ different methods for the regulation of the utility industries. The majority of member-states in the Community still have predominantly state-owned utilities. Clearly, this creates difficulties for the Community, as not all the member-states are

---

[1] *Campus Oil Ltd -v- Minister for Industry & Energy*, 72/83 [1984]ECR 2727.

prepared to decentralise power by privatisation or to liberate the market to a significant degree. The task faced by the Community is to establish a single market in the face of this reluctance on the part of member-states, whilst at the same time providing adequate safeguards for their concerns over security of supply.

Independent regulation can take two forms. The first attempts to 'mimic the market' by imposing conditions and strict requirements on the monopoly to make it behave as if it were in a competitive market. For example, price capping can be used as a substitute for competitive price pressures, in the absence of actual competition. Alternatively, the regulation can attempt to create an effective competitive market, by implementing measures to promote competition wherever possible. An example of such a measure would be the introduction of 'transparent pricing', allowing potential competitors to see the prices being charged to customers and therefore encouraging those potential competitors to enter the market.

Current Regulation of UK Utilities

First, I will briefly consider the rôle of each of the specialised regulators and their powers and duties within the structure of competition regulation in the UK. Then I will discuss the Community's approach to regulating utilities and how this will affect UK regulation in the future.

In a recent speech, Mr Cruickshank, Director General of OFTEL, observed that traditionally UK competition law is a system of review and not a penal system where anti-competitive behaviour can be punished or damages awarded against an offending party in favour of an injured party.[2] In contrast, under Community law the Commission has the power to impose immense fines for activities carried out in breach of the Community's competition rules. The largest fine imposed to date has been ECU75 million, that is, approximately, £56·25 million.[3]

The Directors General of Electricity Supply, Gas Supply and Telecommunications are appointed by the Secretary of State for Trade and Industry. The Director General of Water Services is appointed by the Secretary of State for Environment. The powers given to the

---

[2] This is not in every case true; damages are available under the Restrictive Trade Practices Act 1976.

[3] 'Tetra pak II', Commission Decision of 24 July 1991, 92/163/EEC.

specialised regulators do not permit them to impose penalties on offending parties, but rather to impose conditions in their licences to operate, or to require information from the party in question, or indeed to refer matters to the MMC for an investigation to be carried out.

The duties imposed on each of the specialised regulators are similar. In respect of electricity, The Electricity Act 1989 gives the Director General of Electricity Supply duties, jointly shared by the Secretary of State, as follows:

- to secure that all reasonable demands for electricity are satisfied;

- to secure that licence holders are able to finance the activities which they are authorised by their licences to carry on;

- to promote competition in the generation and supply of electricity;

- to protect the interests of consumers in respect of the prices and other terms of supply, the continuity of supply and the quality of service provided; and

- to promote efficiency and research in the industry.

The common task set for all the specialised regulators is therefore to protect the interests of the consumer while promoting competition, efficiency and economy in the industries concerned. As we shall see, the Community as a whole faces the same task, but in the broader context of Europe, with all the complexities that surround the introduction of a single market.

General Community Legislation

Which existing provisions of the EC Treaty ('the Treaty') are having, or will have, an impact on the regulation of utilities in the UK? The relevant provisions are principally those concerned with competition, state aids and free movement of goods.

In considering Community legislation it is necessary, following the Maastricht Treaty, to take into account the principle of subsidiarity. Under this principle, any action by the Community must not go beyond what is necessary to achieve the objectives of the Treaty. Therefore we must begin with, and continually bear in mind, the task which the

Community has, and the objectives which it strives to achieve. The Community must pursue certain activities, including: the strengthening of competitiveness of Community industry; the provision of a system ensuring that competition in the internal market is not distorted; the establishment of a common policy in the sphere of transport and the encouragement of the establishment and development of trans-European networks. These activities must be conducted in accordance with the principle of an open market economy with free competition.[4]

Rules on Competition

Where Community law is applicable, it will prevail over national law. In the context of the rules on competition, existing national law will remain applicable if trade between member-states is not affected. This is an area which, despite case law, lacks definition and is at times politically sensitive.

Articles 85 and 86, much discussed, are the key provisions on competition in the Treaty. The Commission has the necessary powers to apply Articles 85 and 86 and impose fines for breach.[5] In the absence of effective legislation on the establishment of single markets in the utility industries, the Commission can apply the rules on competition to any utility if its behaviour is anti-competitive and affects trade between member-states.

Article 85 prohibits agreements and concerted practices which restrict competition and which may adversely affect trade between member-states. This prohibition may be declared inapplicable where certain conditions are satisfied. These conditions include improvement in the production or distribution of goods and the promotion of technical or economic progress, while allowing consumers a fair share of the resulting benefit.

Article 86 prohibits abuse of a dominant position by one or more undertakings, so far as it may affect trade between member-states.

There are exceptions to the application of Articles 85 and 86 in the case of enterprises in the utility industry with special or exclusive rights granted by the member-state, if the application of the competition rules would obstruct the enterprise from performing the particular activities of economic interest which have been assigned to them. This is an extraordinarily wide exception which may be regarded as significantly

---

[4] Articles 3 and 3a of the EC Treaty, as amended by the Treaty on European Union.

[5] Council Regulation 17/62.

reducing the application of Articles 85 and 86. On the face of it, this exception is limited by provisions which state that any activity must not affect the development of trade to such an extent that it would be contrary to the interests of the Community.

This requires the principle of proportionality to be applied. The activities contrary to the rules on competition must be necessary to achieve the public service tasks assigned to the enterprise. In the Almelo case[6] in 1992 the European Court of Justice (ECJ) held that import restrictions on electricity would only be justified to the extent that they were necessary to enable the enterprise to carry out the public service obligations imposed on it by a member-state.

The interpretation of the exceptions to the rules on competition is the task of the Court of First Instance and the European Court of Justice. However, their remit is limited by the fact that they must wait for decisions by the Commission to be appealed or referred to them. Those courts will have to continue to perform this function until the Council adopts legislation in the utility sectors.

The Commission, in exercising its powers under Articles 85 and 86, has a number of possible courses of action available to it in regulating anti-competitive behaviour in the Community. In recent cases notified to it under Article 85, the Commission has issued so-called 'comfort letters' to telecommunication organisations with special or exclusive rights which have entered into joint ventures.[7] The Commission's concern was to ensure that the arrangements would not enable the telecommunication organisations to use their privileged positions to limit the opportunities for other companies in unrestricted activities. One of the cases involved the Financial Network Association, a joint venture set up between 12 leading telecommunication organisations to provide telecommunication services combining voice, data and image services. The Commission had concerns over cross-subsidisation and bundling of the reserved services (for which it was granted special rights) with non-reserved services (open to competition). These concerns were resolved by way of undertakings given by the organisation.

The issuing of comfort letters provides an enterprise with sufficient security to carry on its operation. Provided the circumstances do not

---

6   *Municipality of Almelo -v- Energiebedrijf Ijsselmij*, C-393/92 [1994]ECR I-1477.

7   'Financial Network Association', Commission Statement dated 15 November 1993 (IP(93)988); and 'PTT Telecom BV, Nederlands Omroepproduktie Bedrijf NV and Intrax BV', Commission Statement dated 25 October 1993 (IP(93)907).

change, the Commission will not usually take any action for breach of the competition rules arising from the subject of the letters. But the enterprise is aware that any change in the circumstances may result in the Commission re-investigating for breach of the rules on competition. The system, even without the help of comprehensive secondary legislation in the utility fields, provides enterprises with strong incentives to conduct their activities in a competitive and efficient manner.

As well as forming the basis for a complaint to the Commission, Articles 85 and 86 create rights for individuals which national courts must protect. The rules on competition may therefore be relied upon in actions for damages or injunctive relief brought in the national courts.

A Regional Electricity Company (REC), for example, may arguably bring an action against the National Grid, a national monopoly, for damages under Article 86 for an abuse of a dominant position affecting trade between member-states, provided the actions of the National Grid were not defensible under the exceptions for enterprises with special or exclusive rights provided in the Treaty.

Article 86 has recently been successfully relied upon to challenge a port owner's decision not to grant the operator of a competing ferry service access to that port.[8] In the same way that a port is an essential facility to a ferry operator, so too a grid is an essential facility to an electricity or gas supplier. The essential facility doctrine originated in the US railroad cases.[9] The Third Party Access system proposed by the Commission to allow for access to electricity and gas grids, is the development of this doctrine in the context of Article 86. Article 86 will therefore have an important rôle to play in opening up an internal market in energy.

State Aids

State aids, in the form of monetary aid or otherwise, can distort competition through the favouring by a member-state of its own industries over industries from other member-states. This is discrimination on the grounds of nationality which is specifically prohibited in the Treaty.[10]

---

[8] 'Sealink/B&I:Holyhead', Commission decision of 4 November 1988; 'Sea Containers/Stena Sealink:Holyhead II', OJ L15, 18.1.1994, p.8.

[9] *United States -v- Terminal Railroad Association*, 224 US 383, 411 (1912).

[10] Article 6 of the EC Treaty as amended by the Treaty on European Union.

The Treaty allows for member-states to grant state aid to protect certain interests. For instance, it may be considered compatible with the common market if the aid concerned is to facilitate the development of certain economic activities or of certain economic areas, so long as it does not adversely affect trading conditions to such an extent that it is contrary to the common interest.[11]

Free Movement of Goods

The third set of existing provisions in the Treaty that may have an impact on the regulation of utilities in the UK are the provisions relating to the free movement of goods. It is fundamental to the operation of a single market that there should be free movement of goods. Articles 30 to 36 prohibit quantitative restrictions, or measures having equivalent effect, on imports and exports between member-states. These Articles only apply to goods. This raises the question of whether electricity and gas are considered as goods or services. The ECJ in the Almelo case,[12] to which I have previously referred, held that electricity constitutes a 'good' for the purposes of the Treaty. The Commission has also stated that the provisions on free movement of goods in the Treaty apply equally to trade in energy, except for coal and nuclear minerals and fuels.[13] Gas therefore also constitutes a 'good'.

One of the most noteworthy effects of the principle of free movement of goods on the electricity and gas sectors, is that a national monopolist in these sectors can no longer maintain exclusive rights to import. Similarly, exporters from other member-states must be free to sell directly in the member-state where the national monopoly exists. A national monopoly in this context includes a privatised monopoly, or even a body through which the government appreciably influences imports or exports between member-states.

The Commission has recently brought cases under Article 169[14] against five member-states for failing to fulfil obligations imposed by the Treaty by maintaining import and export monopolies in France,

---

[11] Article 92 of the EC Treaty as amended by the Treaty on European Union.

[12] See note 5 above.

[13] Agence Europe (EUROPE Document), No. 1757, 29 January 1992, and COM(91) 548 final.

[14] *Commission -v- Ireland*, C156, 1994; *Commission -v- Netherlands*, C157, 1994; *Commission -v- Italy*, C158, 1994; *Commission -v- France*, C159, 1994; *Commission -v- Spain*, C160, 1994. OJ C202, 23.7.94, pp.9-12.

Italy and Spain, and import monopolies in the Netherlands and Ireland. The Commission has claimed that the member-states' actions are not necessary for security of supply. As yet, the European Court has not given judgement in these cases.

Utility Specific Community Legislation

There has been extensive Community legislation implementing the provisions of the Treaty since 1957, covering almost every aspect imaginable. But little has been adopted specifically on regulation of the utility industries. This is due to the complexities of the markets and the concerns expressed by member-states over their national interests. To the extent that the Community has implemented measures to regulate the utilities, its focus has been on the telecommunications industry and, to a lesser extent, electricity and gas. I will now consider the Community legislation already enacted in those industries. As will be seen, the Community legislation has not yet had a significant impact on the UK.

Telecommunications

The telecommunications industry is at the most advanced stage of liberalisation on the path towards a single market. There have been steps taken towards opening up competition in both telecommunications services and telecommunications infrastructure or networks. The supply of telecommunication services has been easier to open up to competition than networks.

A directive has been adopted on competition in the market for telecommunications services (the Telecommunications Services Directive),[15] issued by the Commission. Interestingly, it was made under Article 90 of the Treaty without the need for approval by the Council of Ministers. It addresses the grant by member-states of special or exclusive rights to undertakings to supply telecommunication services. This Directive provides that all exclusive rights for supply of telecommunications services, other than voice telephony, must be withdrawn by member-states before 31 December 1990. Further, member-states must take any measures necessary to ensure that an operator proposing to supply such telecommunications services is entitled to do so. The Directive excluded radio broadcasting and television from its application. It has now been amended to include satellite communications.[16]

---

[15] Commission Directive, 90/388.

[16] Commission Directive 94/46, OJ L268, 19.10.94, p.15.

The Telecommunications Services Directive, as currently amended, has not yet had any impact on the UK because the UK had already opened up access to the telecommunication services market under the Telecommunications Act 1984 which at the same time allowed for the privatisation of BT. The Government did not consider it necessary to take any measures to implement the Telecommunications Services Directive into national law. It would appear that the Commission is of the same mind, as there has not been any indication from the Commission that it considers the UK has failed to fulfil an obligation under the Treaty in this regard. In fact, the UK has been the focus of the Community's attention as being at the leading edge in liberalisation of the telecommunication services and infrastructure. The history of utility regulation in Europe has tended to be that the UK has provided the model for Commission thinking.

In respect of the liberalisation of the infrastructure, as opposed to simply the telecommunication services, there has been a directive on the establishment of the internal market through the implementation of Open Network Provisions (the ONP Framework Directive).[17] The ONP Framework Directive outlines the conditions necessary for open and efficient access to telecommunications networks within and between member-states. The implementation of open network provisions ('ONP') in telecommunications is equivalent to the Third Party Access system currently being considered in relation to electricity, which I will discuss later.

The ONP Framework Directive provides definitions, guiding principles and the essential requirements for the application of ONP, as well as the procedural framework necessary to achieve the objectives in stages. Further, specific Directives will have to be issued to give effect to ONP.

There have been problems in the implementation of the ONP Framework Directive. It required the adoption, before the end of 1992, of two specific Directives covering Leased Lines and Voice Telephony Services respectively. To date, the only specific Directive that has been adopted by the Council is in respect of Leased Lines.[18] This was implemented into national law in the UK in 1993 and amended in 1994.[19]

---

[17] Council Directive 90/387, OJ L192, 24.7.90, p.1.

[18] Council Directive 92/44, OJ L165, 19.6.92, p.27.

[19] SI 1993/2330 The Telecommunications (Leased Lines) Regulations 1993; SI 1994/2251 The Telecommunications (Leased Lines) (Amendment) Regulations 1994.

The other specific Directive which was to have been adopted by 1992, in respect of Voice Telephony,[20] was blocked by the European Parliament on 'comitology' issues revolving around the practice of the Council of appointing committees of national representatives to oversee the Commission in implementing legislation. The proposed Voice Telephony Directive involved such a Council-appointed committee, which was set up under the ONP Framework Directive (the ONP Committee).

The European Parliament is concerned to ensure that it, rather than a Council-appointed committee, is involved in overseeing the Commission, to ensure that the balance of effective decision-making and democratic accountability is maintained. As a result, the proposed Voice Telephony Directive was blocked. It is expected that these institutional barriers will be overcome in one way or another, possibly by the Commission using its sole powers under Article 90 to adopt a Directive, or perhaps in 1996 in the Inter-Governmental Conference to consider the revision of the Maastricht Treaty.

There are proposals for the adoption of two directives applying ONP, one in respect of Packet and Circuit-Switched Data Services[21] and the other in respect of Integrated Services Digital Networks (ISDN).[22] Council Decisions are pending, but as yet, Directives have not been adopted.

The Community has not therefore progressed towards a single market in telecommunications as quickly as it first envisaged.

Electricity and Gas

Development of a single market in the electricity and gas industries is proving even more difficult to achieve than in telecommunications. The difficulty stems from the desire of member-states to retain control over their indigenous energy resources because economic and even political stability can be dependent on security of supply. The Community has taken preliminary measures in the process of liberalisation of the electricity and gas markets. As in the case of the telecommunications market, the effect of these measures on the UK has been limited because of the relatively advanced state of liberalisation the UK market has achieved.

---

[20] 92/C263/02, OJ C263,1992, p.2.

[21] Council Recommendation 92/382, OJ L200, 18.2.92, p.1.

[22] Council Recommendation 92/383, OJ L200, 18.2.92, p.10.

The Council of Energy Ministers has so far adopted in this area one Directive on price transparency and two on transit. The Price Transparency Directive[23] has led to greater transparency of prices charged to industrial end-users of electricity and gas.

The Transit Directives are on gas[24] and electricity[25] respectively. The Gas Transit Directive was implemented in the UK in 1992.[26] It is restricted in its application to the transport of gas between high pressure transmission grids from or to a member-state. Certain requests to an operator of a high pressure transmission grid in a member-state for the transmission of gas must be negotiated by that grid operator. Such a request must be notified to the Commission. Any failure to enter into a gas transit contract must also be notified to the Commission. If the reasons for failing to enter into a gas transit contract are considered by the Commission to be unjustified or insufficient, the Commission may implement the procedures provided for by Community law. Notably, the Directive does not impose an obligation actually to transmit and it seems the only additional obligations in the UK on grid operators are the requirements for notifications to be made to the Commission.

Community Proposals for Telecommunications, Electricity and Gas

The Community is currently considering proposals from the Commission on the development of a single market in the energy sector, electricity in particular, and in telecommunications.

Telecommunications

The European Commission's objectives for total liberalisation of the telecommunications industry are ambitious. They aim to liberalise progressively areas currently under monopoly, such as voice telephony services, while respecting the rules of competition. At the same time they will establish open and non-discriminatory access to all the networks for satellite, mobile and terrestrial telecommunications services, once they are all liberalised. The objectives include extending

---

[23] Council Directive 90/377, OJ L185, 17.7.90, p.16.

[24] Council Directive 91/296 OJ L147, 12.6.91, p.37.

[25] Council Directive 90/547.

[26] SI 1992/1190 The Gas Transit (EEC Requirements) Regulations 1992.

the use of cable-TV networks as an alternative to the existing telecommunications infrastructure. The ultimate goal is to establish an 'information society' in Europe under which information, data and telecommunications will form part of a single market. Deregulation of telecommunications is planned for completion by 1 January 1998. A Green Paper on the liberalisation of the telecommunications infrastructure and cable television networks has been published by the Commission.[27] The liberalisation is to take place in conjunction with liberalisation of voice telephony services, timetabled for the same date.[28]

Voice Telephony Services

As I mentioned earlier, the application of ONP to Voice Telephony services by a proposed Directive was blocked by the European Parliament on constitutional grounds. The proposed Voice Telephony Directive[29] is a significant step in widening the application of ONP. The Council asked the Commission to prepare, before 1 January 1996, the necessary amendments to the Community regulatory framework in order to achieve full liberalisation of all voice telephony services as timetabled.[30]

The Voice Telephony Directive is innovative because it sets up a clear regulatory hierarchy, recognising the principle of subsidiarity. Primary responsibility for compliance with the Community's requirements rests on the parties to the commercial agreements. The second level is the national regulatory authorities (NRAs), upon which are placed responsibilities for implementing the Directive. The NRAs will be responsible for, among other things, ensuring that adequate safeguards are in place for fair access to networks and that conditions for interconnection of public telephone networks throughout the Community are objective, non-discriminatory and guarantee equality of access. Access to the public networks and services may only be refused on the grounds of 'essential requirements'. These are: security of network operations; maintenance of network integrity; interoperability of services in justified cases; and protection of data as appropriate.

---

[27] Part I, COM(94) 440 final; Part II, COM(94) 682 final.

[28] See Council Resolution dated 22 July 1993, 93/C213/01.

[29] See note 20 above.

[30] See note 28 above.

In order to ensure access to the networks, while protecting the essential requirements, the proposed Voice Telephony Directive requires certain systems and procedures to be put in place. One of the requirements is the introduction of transparent cost accounting systems. Another is the right of appeal against the decisions of telecommunications organisations to an NRA, under a detailed national dispute resolution procedure, with recourse to a Community level conciliation procedure involving the ONP Committee.

Infrastructure

In parallel with the proposals for voice telephony services, the Community is debating the liberalisation of the telecommunications infrastructure and of cable television networks. I referred earlier to the Commission's Green Paper in relation to this. Part I of the Green Paper was published in October 1994 and sets out the principles and timetable for liberalising the telecommunications infrastructure together with the cable television networks. Cable television networks have only recently been considered in the context of the liberalisation of the telecommunications market. The Commission intends to adopt a draft Directive, after public consultation has taken place, on the use of cable television networks for the provision of telecommunications services, as an alternative infrastructure to the existing telecommunications infrastructure.[31]

Part II of the Green Paper, published in January 1995, details how the general principles in Part I will be implemented within the timetable envisaged in Part I.

The Green Paper proposes a two-stage process for liberalising the infrastructure. The first stage involves the removal of restrictions on the use of own or third party infrastructure:

- for the delivery of satellite communications services;

- for the provision of mobile communications services;

- for the provision of all terrestrial telecommunications services already liberalised (broadly, all services other than public voice telephony).

---

[31] Commission notice OJ C76,1995, p.6.

The second stage would involve the lifting of exclusive and special rights over the use of own or third party infrastructure for the delivery of public voice telephony services, once those services are liberalised from 1 January 1998.

The existing regulatory system would be replaced by licensing and authorisation schemes created by the member-states. These schemes would provide the necessary safeguards within the framework of the Telecommunications Services Directive and the ONP Framework Directive.

The Commission has already put forward two draft measures in implementation of the Green Paper. The first, unveiled on 14 November 1995, is a draft Directive setting out the principles for licensing new entrants into the telecommunications service market.

The second, known as the 'Interconnection Directive', is aimed at ensuring universal service and the interoperability of telecommunications services throughout the European Union. The draft Directive was considered at a meeting of EU telecommunications Ministers on 27 November 1995. Although the draft Directive was generally well-received, the Ministers decided, because of the particularly important issues raised by the draft, to refer it to the Committee of member-states' Permanent Representatives (COREPER) for further consideration. It is now anticipated that the draft will be finalised by the end of June 1996.

Electricity and Gas

The development of the internal market in the energy sector is not as advanced as that of telecommunications. I will explain the proposals which the Commission has put forward for allowing access to the electricity and gas networks. The Commission's first proposal, the Third Party Access system ('TPA'), was initially rejected. An alternative proposal, the Single Buyer system proposed by the French, was in turn rejected by the Commission. In another attempt to enable agreement to be reached between the member-states, the Commission has made a proposal consisting of a dual approach.

a) Third Party Access

In 1991, the Commission put forward proposals for draft Directives concerning common rules for the internal market in electricity and natural gas.[32] Since that time the Commission has

---

[32] COM(91) 548 final.

focused on the common rules for the internal market in electricity. The rules for gas will be considered after agreement has been reached on electricity.

The 1991 proposals included the Third Party Access system. In its current form, Third Party Access ('TPA') is the right for electricity producers and transmitters to negotiate access to the electricity networks of transmission and distribution companies (the System Operators), so as to be able to conclude supply contracts with large industrial customers and certain other parties. The System Operator may only refuse access where the contract in question would prevent it from carrying out the public service obligations assigned to it by its member-state.

Alongside the TPA are two important concepts:

- the creation of a transparent and non-discriminatory system for granting licences for the production of electricity and the building of electricity lines;

- the 'unbundling' of vertically integrated entities, that is, the separation of the administration and accounting for each of the different activities of production, transmission and distribution.

b) *Single Buyer*

As stated above, the French rejected the amended TPA proposed by the Commission and proposed a different approach to opening up the electricity market to competition, referred to as the Single Buyer system ('SB'). This allows for the national body to maintain its position as the sole distributor of energy within its country, but involves separating the activity of production of electricity from that of distribution. It therefore recognises the agreed principle of ending state monopolies over the import, export and production of electricity. The SB system is preferred by the majority of the member-states, with only the UK and a handful of other member-states in favour of TPA, all of which have opened up their electricity market to varying degrees of competition.

c) *Dual Approach*

The SB system has been rejected by the Commission in its proposed form, as incompatible with the rules on competition and free movement of goods in the Treaty. To overcome this deadlock, the

Commission recently published a Working Paper on alternative models for liberalising the Community electricity market, in which it proposed a dual approach to allow for both Third Party Access and the Single Buyer system, albeit in a modified form.[33] Member-states would be free to choose their preferred system.

Both systems are designed to lead to a directly comparable degree of access to electricity markets and to conform with the provisions of the Treaty. The Commission has expressed the view that it considers the introduction of TPA alone would progress the liberalisation of the electricity market more quickly, but recognises the need for a dual approach.

The modifications that the Commission has proposed to the Single Buyer system in order to make it compatible with the Treaty, are as follows:

- the right of eligible (i.e. large) consumers to contract electricity supplies directly with external producers;

- the obligation for the Single Buyer to buy unlimited quantities of imported electricity under certain objective conditions, with transparency of prices paid by the Single Buyer;

- the Single Buyer, where part of an integrated undertaking, should be fully unbundled in terms of a separation of management and of information flows, between its different activities, especially in terms of production and supply;

- the existence of a parallel procedure for authorisation of independent producers alongside the tendering procedures for new and additional production capacities;

- freedom for eligible consumers to construct and use direct lines for transactions with external producers and domestic independent producers.

The Council of Ministers accepted in June 1995 the dual approach proposed by the Commission in its Working Paper. As a result, the proposals for draft directives are being further amended by the Commission to incorporate this dual approach.

---

[33] SEC(95) 464 final.

d) Trans-European Energy Networks

In Maastricht, the Community had new obligations imposed on it to contribute towards the establishment and development of trans-European networks in the areas of transport, telecommunications and energy infrastructures.[34] The Community aims to promote the interconnection and interoperability of national networks, as well as access to such networks. In this context, the Commission proposed a Decision by the European Parliament and Council of Ministers laying down a series of guidelines on trans-European energy networks together with measures aimed at creating a more favourable context for the energy network.[35] The guidelines emphasise the need for interconnection of transmission networks for electricity and natural gas with third countries having signed the Energy Charter Treaty. These guidelines were approved by the Council in June 1995.

e) European Union Energy Policy

There is at present no obligation on the Community to establish a common energy policy, unlike the position in respect of transport and agriculture. However, in 1994, the Commission produced a Green Paper for a European Union Energy Policy,[36] attempting to make progress towards a single market in the energy sector. It is also possible that an energy chapter may be inserted into the Treaty on European Union following the 1996 Intergovernmental Conference.

The Commission's Green Paper for an Energy Policy aims to establish a free market in energy whilst meeting the requirements of security of supply, public service obligations and environmental protection. It calls for fiscal measures to be taken to create an internal market and to promote greater equality of competition between the various forms of energy. It also seeks the reduction and eventual abolition of state aid in the energy sector, which distorts competition.

---

[34] Articles 129b, 129c, and 129d of EC Treaty, as amended by the Treaty on European Union.

[35] COM(95) 226 final.

[36] Commission of the European Communities, *For a European Union Energy Policy*, Green Paper, COM (94) 659 final 2, February 1995.

18

The Council adopted a resolution on the Green Paper in Summer 1995 and in December 1995 published a White Paper[37] to elaborate concrete proposals. This recent spate of activity on the part of all the European institutions in the energy sector suggests that the Community has reached a time when agreement is finally being reached on the way forward.

Impact of Community Proposals on UK Utility Regulation

Implementation

As the telecommunications infrastructure is gradually liberalised, legislation will have to be enacted in the UK to implement the Community legislation which is forthcoming. Although the UK is already on the road towards liberalisation, the vision of the Community is far greater, encompassing not just existing infrastructure but possibilities for new forms of infrastructure. According to the principle of subsidiarity, the Community intends to give member-states the freedom to implement its regulations in so far as is necessary to achieve the Community's aims.

Liberalising the telecommunications infrastructure is only the first step to be taken towards the Information Society.[38] Certain basic principles derived from the telecommunications experience will assist the debate for the future:

- liberalisation of infrastructures and services must go hand in hand with the implementation of a clear regulatory framework, which can help to mimic competition pending the emergence of genuinely competitive markets;

- effective and independent regulation at the appropriate level will be essential;

- principles at a European level are required, based on the rules in the Treaty, as well as clear criteria for their application in a predictable manner at national level;

- there will be increasing reliance on competition rules;

---

[37] Commission of the European Communities, *An Energy Policy for the European Union*, White Paper, COM (95) 682 final, December 1995.

[38] *Commission's Action Plan on the Information Society*, COM(94)347 final, 17.7.94.

- effective competition in the markets for services should evolve without rigid structural safeguards. Where safeguards have been considered necessary, proportional solutions have been chosen, such as transparent cost-accounting and separate accounting for different parts of a business.

The implications are clear: greater public consultation; increased transparency of commercial activities by public and private enterprises in the market, through the use of transparent pricing and accounting methods and unbundling of different activities of vertically integrated enterprises; and greater responsibility on the NRAs, such as OFTEL, OFFER and OFGAS, to implement the European policies at national level.

Undoubtedly the existing statutory duties imposed on the specialised regulators will need to be amended to reflect the European requirements in the utility industries discussed. The European Union's regulation of competition will be applied to the utilities as it has been applied to other industries subject to certain safeguards. The threat of substantial fines for breach of the rules on competition, together with greater accountability for actions resulting from transparency of pricing and unbundling of accounts, will provide strong incentives for undertakings to compete fairly.

Non-Implementation

A final word of warning for those in privatised organisations.

It is an established principle of European law that a directive which has not been implemented by the due date can be relied upon by an individual in an action for damages against the party to which the Directive is addressed, namely, the member-state itself.[39] This was considered, until recently, to be limited to actions against the state itself or public enterprises.

In the recent unreported High Court case[40] of *Griffin -v- South West Water Services*, the court held that a privatised body was one against which an EC Directive,[41] which had not been implemented by the member-state, was capable of enforcement. As a result of another EC

---

[39] *Foster and others -v- British Gas Plc*, [1991] ICR 84; and *Marshall -v- Southampton & South West Hampshire Area Health Authority*, 152/84 [1986]ECR 723.

[40] *Griffin and others -v- South West Water Services Ltd* (unreported), considered *Foster and others -v- British Gas Plc*, [1991] ICR 84.

[41] 75/129/EEC, OJ L04829.

case,[42] a party injured as a result of an unimplemented directive may therefore have a right to damages against a utility enterprise.

This will be so where the utility enterprise has taken on the public obligations carried out previously by the state and the directive confers identifiable rights on individuals where a causal link between the failure to fulfil obligations under the directive and the damage suffered by the individual is shown. The Griffin case has not yet been considered by an appeal court. It is therefore possible that the decision may be overturned. It nevertheless serves as a reminder to us all that European legislation cannot be ignored.

---

[42] *Francovich and others -v- Italian Republic*, [1991] ECR I-5357.

CHAIRMAN'S COMMENTS

Sir Bryan Carsberg
International Accounting Standards Committee

AMONG THE MATTERS WHICH PARTICULARLY CAUGHT MY INTEREST, I would first mention Mr Sayer's early statement – in an aside to the written text – that it would be preferable to end special regulation and rely entirely on the general competition law. It reminded me of the first Parliamentary debate on telecommunications that I listened to, where Member after Member stood up to say that one of the best signs of success for the telecoms régime would be if I worked myself out of a job. This did not seem such a good idea at the time, although I can look at it now from a more sanguine perspective. Nevertheless, I wonder whether today, at least across the board, we can think that is realistic. In telecommunications, there are many aspects of communications in which there is a reasonable hope, I think, in the provision of services over networks and over the sale of apparatus, although more of that in a minute. But, as one looks at network competition itself today, perhaps we feel we are a long way away from the competition that would make that objective of yours seem achievable.

I share Mr Sayer's wish, of course, because to have so much competition that we could rely on the general competition law would seem to me to be excellent; and we have some good vigorous competition in telecommunications network operation. I am sure that will be sustained. Nevertheless, the feeling has been recently that it has not moved quite as far and quite as fast as one would have wished. There have been signs of retrenchment among the challengers to British Telecom partly, no doubt, because British Telecom has become a formidable competitor. But one wonders whether perhaps people had earlier underestimated the extent of the economies of scale which still actually persist and had thought that we might have more competition than we really shall.

In recounting the consequence of the Maastricht Treaty you did not quite call for European-wide regulation. I was in Munich to give a talk to an excellent telecoms conference organised by Professor Vitter. My task was to say what I thought we had learnt from our experiences so far. Recently I discovered to my delight that Germany is finally catching on, reaching a very interesting state in the development of telecoms liberalisation. It was said that there will be full liberalisation in Germany with effect from the beginning of 1998. It is still, of course, subject to the formulation of statute. Competition will extend to networks in 1998; not just to mobile networks but also to fixed networks. And they are now debating what form regulation and privatisation will take. At the end there was a panel discussion, at which I was chided by one of the panellists, the head of The Netherlands' PTT, for not calling for European regulation. I had thought about it years ago; and it seemed then so beyond the realms of the politically possible that I stopped thinking about it. It is clearly a long step from where we are today for the member-states to be willing to agree to give up the kind of local power they have in areas like the utilities in the interest of Euro-regulation. At one time I had wondered whether one might make progress by having a Convention of national regulators who might at least deal with some issues needing very difficult regulation and perhaps aptly dealt with at the European level. An obvious one to start with is international telephone calls. But it does seem a long time away at present.

You will know, I think, that one of the things that I was calling for towards the end of my time at the Office of Fair Trading, and indeed have been calling for since, was the adoption of the prohibition approach in British competition law. First, I called for something like Article 85 prohibition in relation to restrictive agreements with, no doubt, the provision for exemption that Article 85 also has. This has been discussed for a long time. As you know well, we have a White Paper going back to 1989, in which the Government promised to deal with prohibition. They committed themselves to it in their 1992 Election manifesto but we are still waiting. The Trade and Industry Select Committee has also pressed for it. We all keep pressing. One of the attractions of it for me, of course, is the deterrent effect as compared to the present situation, in which people can do things once, knowing that they can get away with them until they are told to stop. It seems to me to be rather a weak system now.

I am intrigued by the application of the idea of deterrence to the utilities where there is the same problem. They are regulated by rules in the licences rather than the more general competition law, but it is still the case that if they break one of those rules in the licence then the Regulator has to issue an order to tell them to stop it. Then they do face the prospect of penalties. In many cases, a difficulty is that the licence rule is not fully defined, and the Regulator has to define it before it can take effect. An example is the rule against unfair cross-subsidisation in the telecommunications licence. I was intrigued that, earlier this week, Oftel announced that it was once more taking action against unfair cross-subsidisation of BT's apparatus supply business. I am not the only one who will remember that this is the third time of asking. I took action twice on it. The first time we started to get somewhere and then it fell back so I had to take action again. Apparently things improved for a while and now it has fallen back again. I wonder whether perhaps that is an example of an area where things would be better if one had a tighter regulatory régime so that penalties would be faced earlier on.

What we are talking about here is the abuse of dominance rather than the making of restrictive agreements, the field of Article 86 rather than Article 85. How far can one apply the prohibition approach in that situation? You cited the case of the access to the port, the essential facility which is an interesting case, but it is fairly clear-cut if no access is permitted by the regulated firm. What is much more difficult is where access *is* permitted, but there is then dispute about the price. We all know how difficult getting the price exactly right is. And of course that would be one example of difficulty in applying the prohibition approach. So my question is, drawing on your experience, how far do you think we could go in using prohibition of the abuse of a dominant position to deal with these kinds of issues that arise in an extreme fashion in the utilities? Can it be done or do we have to accept that such an approach is not tailored for the particular problems of the utilities?

RESPONSE: MR STEPHEN SAYER

What I was saying is predicated on something said by the Commission itself, namely, that if it is unable to make progress through directives which need the political agreement of ministers in the Council, it will be forced to fall back upon the existing provisions of the Treaty, in particular Article 86. In effect, this is the Commission saying: 'There is a little threat but this is the way we will have to proceed.'

Your question raises very complicated and wide-ranging issues that arise in relation to utilities. I think that you can deal with a part of the spectrum of the problems, but by no means all.

As you say, the example I have given (which in fact is a practical example), of point-blank refusal to allow the facility to be used, was capable of being dealt with. At the other end of the scale, I can see significant problems where Article 86 would be incapable of being applied.

That causes me to look at your comparison between the British system and the prohibition system. It seems to me there are three gradations. There is the British 'soft' situation. Then there is the licensing system which I regard as the middle ground because it requires a breach of the provision of the licence followed by, if you like, a warning notice, followed by an ultimate order: a two-stage process seems to me highly desirable given the complexity of some of the issues that we are facing. The third, and most severe, system is prohibition which seems to me rather draconian in some of the circumstances where the consequences may not be entirely clear to the utility concerned. So I think that you are right – that we need changes in the UK law because restrictive trade practices legislation is out of date and a clumsy way of looking at cartelisation. But I would not want to go all the way to a prohibition system.

2

INCENTIVES IN NATURAL MONOPOLY: THE CASE OF WATER[1]

Stephen Glaister
The London School of Economics

Introduction

THE PERIODIC REVIEW OF THE WATER INDUSTRY is complete and the Regulator has survived his trial-by-MMC.[2] In 1995 we enjoyed a dry spell of weather and the consequent problems generated a vast amount of public comment. Whilst much of it was based on misunderstanding or misinformation, some of it raised very real issues which require to be addressed.

It should be said from the outset that I believe the present system has much to commend it and that I am not intending to argue for its destruction or a return to any pre-existing arrangement. But I do think some fundamental problems need to be dealt with if the system is to survive.

Most observers will agree that the conduct of the Periodic Review was exemplary, both in terms of process and in terms of substantive outcome. The ease with which the outsider can obtain detailed and high quality documentation on each aspect of OFWAT's work is an exercise in open government from which some other parts of the British public services could learn.[3]

---

[1] I am grateful for comments on an earlier draft by Michael Beesley, Christopher Bolt, Ian Byatt and Ralph Turvey.

[2] The Monopolies and Mergers Commission reports on *Portsmouth Water Plc* and *South West Water Services Ltd.*, resulting from these two companies appealing against the Periodic Review, were published in July 1995.

[3] I am most grateful to the library and information services at OFWAT for their ready assistance.

One point of view would be that the system is now through its formative stage and that it can now be expected to settle down into a long maturity. It may be rough and ready and it will involve some rough justice, but then so do all regulated and unregulated markets.

However, it is worth considering the proposition that the political economy of water is such that, sooner or later, something fundamental will have to change. OFWAT has been working to bring the system to a degree of maturity within the confines of the legislation. But some of the attributes of the system amount not so much to rough justice as outright injustice in the eyes of the general public. They will not tolerate the situation indefinitely. Whether, however, change should be in the system of regulation or in another aspect of public administration is debatable.

Summary

There are more severe market failures in water than the other utilities. Market disciplines have had to be largely replaced by regulatory discipline and tax funding. The system of regulation gives the industry every incentive to expand capacity without regard to the costs or benefits of doing so. The considerable costs of investment are funded by what is effectively a direct tax on individuals – yet the democratic accountability which was originally designed to go with the tax has been stripped away and there is no mechanism in place to deal with the important equity issues. The public good attributes of water (emphasised by the rarity of domestic water metering) mean that one cannot ignore the incidence of costs and benefits on different individuals. Insufficient attention has been given to the economics of capacity determination in the presence of quantifiable risk – the weather. A method is presented for analysing the implications of the incidence of costs and benefits on individuals and of risk. As with all public goods, one must treat the interpretation of information gathered on consumers' wishes with particular care. 'Profit sharing' or sliding-scale regulation might offer an alternative as far as price regulation is concerned (if there were metering), but it probably will not offer one for quality regulation.

Water, Sewerage and Market Failures

The traditional issues of public sector economics – and public finance in particular – refuse to go away in the case of this industry, to a much greater degree than is the case with the other privatised utilities. Almost all the classical reasons for market failure are to be found. Some of these cannot be ignored in the way that the present system attempts to ignore them. The reasons for this are as follows:

Externalities

The water industry is riven with externalities. Domestic water consumers pay for the removal of pesticides which are a consequence of profit-seeking behaviour of the agricultural industry and of public subsidies on agricultural output which provide an incentive to their greater use. So water consumers are subsidising farmers in their rôles as water consumers, food consumers and, additionally, as taxpayers.

For-profit companies plan the maintenance of their main distribution and sewerage networks with no regard for the costs caused to traffic by methods of working, bursts and collapses. The Monopolies and Mergers Commission reports that Portsmouth Water experiences between 500 and 700 mains bursts each year (para 5.22). Marvin and Slater (1995) report 6,000 collapses a year in England and Wales, a number of which 'have been expensive to repair and disruptive to traffic'. So water and sewerage service consumers are imposing costs on local economies in order to save on their own expenditures.

Newquay has a resident population of 17,500 but has to fund a sewerage capacity for 100,000 to cater for visitors on holiday from other parts of the world. Residents of the South West pay for the investment to avoid their sewage polluting bathing waters for the benefit of holiday-makers from elsewhere.[4] This benefits particular commercial interests – for instance, the tourist industry – which are not necessarily the same as the domestic households who pay the charges. Much of the long-standing building regulations concerning water supply and sewerage derive from health externalities.

Conversely, some charges do not relate to any service rendered to those who have to pay them: on average, 50 per cent of sewerage costs relate to highway surface water drainage. It seems that domestic householders have to bear these costs purely as a matter of history and expedience. Ian Byatt has suggested that these costs might be better borne by others (see Smith, 1995).

Returns to Scale

The industry is likely to exhibit non-constant returns to scale for a variety of reasons. It has long been recognised that the network effects

---

[4] The rights and wrongs of this clearly depend upon an unheard debate about who holds the property rights to clean bathing waters.

make this the most natural of monopolies and, of course, this is clearly recognised in the regulatory framework. There are likely to be increasing returns to density of supply wherever there are capacities of storage and delivery which depend upon the square of the linear dimensions.[5] On the other hand, OFWAT reckons that long-run marginal costs are increasing with total quantity supplied (that is, the resource costs including bulk transfers and treatment). It follows that any kind of efficient pricing in classical public enterprise terms would be unlikely to result in break-even. Yet, with perfectly good political and administrative justification, it has been decided that the industry must be financially self-contained. Quite what this means in this case is a burden for the Regulator who has to work out sensible pricing policies for an industry where, due to inflation before vesting and under-valuation at vesting, the replacement costs of the assets are alleged to be of the order of 10 times the capital value used for setting price limits.

The issues of effects external to the water industry and the implications of returns to scale are probably of considerable quantitative significance. But I do not consider many of them in detail in this paper. I concentrate on interactions between agents within the industry – though many of the principles are relevant to the analysis of extra-industry issues.

Public Goods and Product Quality

In any case, the greater part of the water is supplied unpriced at the point of consumption and this looks likely to continue for a long time. Figure 1 shows the proportion of all water supplied in England and Wales which is *not* measured. The increase during the 1970s is remarkable. It is the result of generally declining industrial demand and a growth of unmeasured domestic consumption. This shows that the unmeasured market is likely to remain a substantial part of the whole for some time to come, unless the Director General is spectacularly successful in his campaign to encourage water companies to offer attractive terms to domestic consumers for the installation and use of water meters. His aspiration is that 33 per cent of households will be metered by 2014 compared with 6 per cent now and that non-household metering will rise from 73 per cent today to 86 per cent in 20 years' time.[6]

---

5   See the statistical models in OFWAT (1994).

6   Ian Byatt, 'Water: The Periodic Review Process', in *Utility Regulation: Challenge and Response*, IEA Readings No.42, London: Institute of Economic Affairs, 1995, pp.21-30.

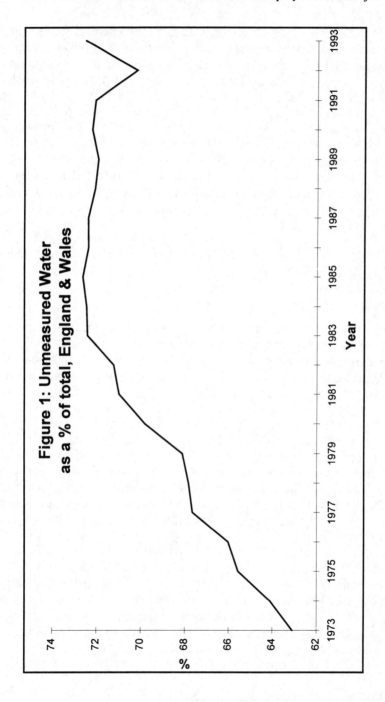

Figure 1: Unmeasured Water as a % of total, England & Wales

As we shall see, there are some fundamental public good characteristics. There are two generic kinds of quality: the chemical composition of water delivered and disposed of, and the security of supply. The consumer is offered no choice in either of the dimensions (although, as I shall argue, she or he could and should be offered choices about security of supply). All have to consume the same qualities yet willingness to pay will vary. And in the absence of metering, for most domestic consumers water is nearly as much a public good as the classic examples of defence and the police service. Amongst other problems this public good characteristic must be expected to create free-rider problems when attempting to divine willingness to pay for quality by means of asking consumers to state their own preferences.

Even if water and sewerage were universally metered overnight, most of the problems identified in this paper would remain – though some of them would certainly be mitigated.

Equity and Taxation

Most of the discussion one sees about the regulated utilities in general, and indeed the legislation, is phrased in terms of '*the* consumer'. This is as if she or he were a single individual, or we were all the same, or it was legitimate to deal in terms of a representative consumer. Because of the technological and institutional factors this seems to be less legitimate in the case of water than in the case of any of the other utilities. To ignore the differences is to ignore a significant part of the important economic and political features of the problem.

As in the case of many public goods, costs are funded by means of a tax. The present rate-based approach has patterns of incidence on specific individuals which the public will not simply ignore even if it is currently legitimate for the Regulator and the water companies to turn a blind eye. This is particularly telling when externally imposed increases in quality standards have to be funded by a direct increase in tax-take, even though not everybody would be willing to pay for them. It is an historical accident that water companies finance a large portion of their activities through a property tax which was designed to be part of a (local) democratic process, but that process has been stripped away. Individuals face the same taxes but they now have no democratic control. If they are being charged for something they do not want, or if they see injustice, there is no local politician they can vote out of office. The only substitute is a dialogue with the 10 Customer Service

Committees and the OFWAT National Customer Council which, at the end of the day, rely on the Director General's interpretation of his duties to '...ensure that the interests of every person who is a customer...are protected as respects the fixing and recovery...of water and drainage charges...' (Water Industry Act 1991, S3).

The companies do not face any *market* discipline in fixing prices, investment and quality. That discipline is an administrative one involving several regulators, of which the Director General has shown his concern to protect the interest of *the* consumer. But one notes some ambiguity about the extent to which he should become involved in issues of equity as between different consumers.

The magnitude of the potential liabilities for consumers is indicated in *the outcome of the Periodic Review* (OFWAT, 1994, p.11):

> '...the average annual household bill may rise by around £17 above inflation by 2000. This compares with the expectation of an increase of £60 in the companies' Market Plans or the possible increase of £36 to £54 which could have resulted from the increases in quality being discussed a year ago.'

Even so, the average conceals some much larger individual changes: average bills in the Southern area are expected to increase by £81 at 1994-95 prices.

In economic efficiency terms there is nothing wrong with geographical variations in charges which are related to geographical variations in costs, though this is bound to lead to complaint when the public has become so used to 'universal service averaging' in utilities such as the mails. Residents of the South West complain that they have a third of the country's coast line and only 3 per cent of the population so that imposing the cost of land-based sewage treatment on them is unfair. Arguably, all one is doing is asking them to treat their sewage in the same way that others have had to in parts of the country which did not have available the cheap but now *socially* costly alternative. Until now they have enjoyed the benefits of fortunate circumstances. But there is a real, if transitional, equity problem if one suddenly insists on burdening today's domestic charge payers with making good the failure of previous generations to invest.

It is clear that equity is a real issue when one looks at the incidence of charges on different groups. OFWAT in *Paying for Quality*, Annex 5 (1993), gives some national figures, and some local estimates are contained in Monopolies and Mergers Commission, *South West Water Services Ltd.* (para.13.51). Although detailed and precise financial analysis was not possible from the available data, South West Water Services Ltd. concluded that:

(a) On average, water bills accounted for some 1·9 per cent of disposable income. Therefore on average, across the region, the level of bills did not account for a significant proportion of customer income...Water bills as a proportion of income in the region were similar to gas and electricity bills, each of which averaged about 2 per cent of household income. Local authority taxation, through the council tax, accounted for about 3 per cent of household income.

(b) There was a significant minority of customers on low incomes. About 20 per cent of households...were on incomes of £7,000 or below...In about 10 per cent of these cases...bills would exceed 10 per cent of income.

(c) ...in the South-West there were many pensioners who enjoyed a relatively secure financial position. Affordability was likely to be a problem for single pensioners mainly dependent on state pensions. 50,000 households in the South West Water Services Ltd. area...were in this position, with incomes of about £3,900 a year...For these customers, water bills would on average account for 7 per cent of income. For about 6,000 customers, water bills would absorb 10 per cent or more of their income.

If one remembers that there is a high concentration of elderly persons living in coastal areas, many of whom are poor, and that by far the largest financial liability for future investment is in respect of sewerage facilities to clean up bathing waters, one can see that there is a serious social problem which nobody has a statutory duty to take account of. In the somewhat analogous case of deregulated and privatised local bus services, explicit provision was made to allow *local authorities* to provide unremunerative services for the benefit of particular groups of individuals by competitive tender for subsidy, financed (in part) by local taxes. There is no such provision in the case of water and sewerage. If this kind of approach were to be tried, great care would have to be taken to avoid adverse effects on incentives. In the bus case this has now been achieved through open competition for service tenders, but there is good evidence that before deregulation, local authority planned and provided bus services exhibited substantially higher unit costs than similar services provided in competitive markets.

Why a Standing Charge?

The question of whether charges based on rates are regressive or not was debated before the system was abolished for the purpose of local government finance. Whatever the outcome of that debate there is an anomaly which makes the system more regressive than it would otherwise be: the standing charge. This is typically a fifth to a third of the average water and sewerage bill, though it is higher or lower than this in particular instances (OFWAT, 1995-96 Report on tariff structure and charges, Table F1.2).

The argument for a two-part tariff is clear enough in the case of the 'normal' utility: it allows the falling average cost utility to recover its full costs without unduly distorting the unit price from the marginal costs of supply (see Armstrong *et al.*, 1994, for a clear exposition). But what is the logic of the standing charge when water is unmetered? Then charges are simply taxes on households and should be considered as such. There are no marginal incentive effects. (Beesley, 1991, makes a similar observation.) For a given total yield, raising the standing charge means that the part variable with rateable value can be reduced: it thus makes the overall tax less progressive – or more regressive. There seems to be no obvious rationale for the imposition of standing charges with unmetered water. It is no more than the perpetuation of an historical accident.

In the case of metered supplies, the concept of a standing charge does have a justification. These should be based on the appropriate cost-drivers – which may well imply that the levels should be different from those inherited from the past.

The Incentives on the Water Companies

The companies providing water and sewerage services are constituted straightforwardly as for-profit enterprises. So we must inquire what behaviour the search for profit will create. There are several different forces at work, all of them acting in the same direction: to encourage the firms to increase the capital intensity of the industry at the expense of variable inputs and, ultimately, at the expense of the water-charges payer.

The Incentive to Expand the Capital Base

In competitive industries profits are made through the exploitation of superior information and the successful exploitation of risk and uncertainty. In the water industry the companies have a particular problem. As many commentators have observed, the degree of uncertainty is low. Most ploys which succeed in producing a super-normal return will sooner or later be spotted by our vigilant Regulator and the rents will be abstracted for the benefit of the consumer. However, there is one bluechip source of gain which should be expected to have a strong and distortionary effect on the companies. A major incentive on the industry is to find ways of expanding the capital base (the Averch-Johnson effect, which is illustrated below).

Whether we like it or not, the system of price determination we have has a large element of rate of return regulation, albeit a forward-looking one (return to be allowed on *future* investment). This is an inevitable consequence of the structure created at privatisation: there is no market discipline on consumer prices because charges are effectively a tax levied on an inelastic tax base. The only way of determining a 'reasonable' charge has been judged to be to allow pass-through of operating costs (with an efficiency discount) plus a return on capital employed. It is notable that the water legislation gives the specific duty to the Regulator to

> '...secure that companies are able (in particular, by securing reasonable returns on their capital) to finance the proper carrying out of the functions of such undertakings' (Water Industry Act 1991, S2).

Whereas to secure that companies will be financially viable is common to the utilities' Privatisation Acts, the bracketed condition about 'reasonable returns' is unique to water.

The consequence is seen in the following simple arithmetic:

cash flow available to create value for shareholders is revenue, net of operating costs and costs of funding return on capital:
$$\pi = R - C - rK.$$

Share price is the present value of this cash flow:
$$P = \pi / r$$

Regulation requires that the return must not exceed some 'fair return', s:
$$(R - C)/K = s.$$

Hence
$$P = \{(s/r) - 1\} K.$$

The implication is clear: over the long term the share price will be directly proportional to the amount of capital employed. The constant of proportionality depends on the ratio of the allowed rate of return to the actual cost of capital. If they are the same then there is no problem: increases in capital employed will be exactly reflected in the share price.

The Regulator and the Monopolies and Mergers Commission have put a great deal of effort into determining the allowed rate of return. It is an impressive body of work and I have no reason to query the outcome. However, the art is inevitably imprecise and my hypothesis is that, given the Director General's duty to secure funding and the likelihood of at least a minimal degree of 'capture' by the industry, there will be a tendency to allow a rate that is slightly too high rather than one which is slightly too low. If the true real cost of capital to the industry is 5 per cent and the allowed rate is 6 per cent, then the ratio is 1·2. So every £1 raised and invested in capital will yield a net capital gain of 20 per cent.

A minority of companies has retained a provision which allows for adjustment if any circumstance arises which has a substantial adverse (or favourable) effect and which (in the case of an adverse effect) could not have been avoided by prudent management action. It is significant that Portsmouth relinquished the 'shipwreck clause', telling the Monopolies and Mergers Commission that it had given it up 'in exchange for an assurance from the Director that this would be reflected in a higher cost of capital at the Periodic Review' (Monopolies and Mergers Commission, *Portsmouth Water Plc*, 1995).

It is for this kind of reason that it has been recognised all along that the investment plans of the industry must be subject to detailed regulatory scrutiny, amongst other things to prevent over-investment at the consumers' expense. But there are many opportunities to exploit this incentive.

The long life and irreversible nature of the physical investments exacerbate the Regulator's problem. Once an investment is approved the rules say that the shareholders must have their return, whether or not the investment turns out to have been what was required. The Regulator's scope for control is thus confined to allowing or disallowing funding in future charges for yet-to-be-made investments; hence the regulatory interest in future cash flows and the relative unimportance of the issue of the valuation of historical assets. The industry will always be pressing to persuade the Regulator of the virtue of future capital projects and the Regulator will always be doing his best to prevent unjustified ones.

Investment for Environmental Protection

In practice, much of the capital investment programme is not determined by the Director General, but by the requirements of the other quality regulators and their regulations. On my hypothesis it would suit the industry very well to have independent guardians of health and the environment insisting on ever-increasing quality standards, because it helps in their crusade for a larger capital stock.

Thus, I would expect to see approval by the industry of raising quality standards – indeed, this is what one finds in many places. For instance, in the evidence to the two recent Monopolies and Mergers Commission inquiries where it is argued by the industry that consumers have been shown to be willing to pay more for increased quality, against the testimony of the consumers themselves and their representative groups, including the ONCC (Ofwat National Consumer Council). And it has been notable that it has been the Director General, with his explicit duty to protect the interests of the consumer, who has led an effective campaign of questioning whether consumers should, in fact, have to bear the financing burdens that the improvements proposed by the outside agencies would imply.[7]

Investment for Customer Services

Another way of inflating the capital base is to install new facilities under such headings as improvements to customer service even when the justification for them in terms of the benefits in relation to the costs is doubtful. The Regulator has expressed concern about several such proposals.

Distorting Choice of Technology

There are opportunities other than investment in quality for inflating the capital base. The pro-consumerist groups express themselves clearly about the obvious need to avoid 'gold-plating'. But the choice of technology as between variable inputs (operating expenditure) and capital is a more subtle issue which it is harder to monitor. The regulatory ideal would be to leave choice of technique as a matter for the industry alone. But the consumer representatives have begun to notice that this cannot be the case, essentially because of the distortionary incentives. There are many opportunities to substitute

---

[7] A good example is recounted in the Monopolies and Mergers Commission report on Portsmouth, concerning the river Hamble scheme, paras. 11.39 – 41.

between operating and capital expenditure. One can use more chemicals in water purification or one can build larger storage reservoirs to give water more time. One can pump or purify difficult local water or one can build long-distance pipes to remote sources. Importantly, one can put effort into maintaining existing pipes, or one can let them leak and put capital into building more collection and purification capacity.[8]

The Motive to Expand Capacity

The incentive to expand capital may explain several other forms of behaviour. To the extent that increased capacity means increased capital investment, the companies have the incentive to push for anything which would imply increased capacity.

The first such incentive is the response to the potential competition for the supply to consumers of more than 250 megalitres, opened up by the possibility of establishing inset appointments (licences enabling the establishment of local water supply companies). Eighteen of the 31 water supply companies have quickly introduced extra tariffs which offer savings to large consumers and, unsurprisingly, most of them become advantageous at about the level of consumption at which competition becomes feasible (see OFWAT, 1995, for details).

This is a normal response to a new competitive threat and one would expect the price paid by large users to fall substantially in order to pre-empt loss of business to alternative suppliers whether or not such alternatives actually appear. Apart from the loss of profit associated with this business – which may well have had a substantial monopoly element – its loss would weaken the case for new investment to expand capacity. The tariff basket approach allows rebalancing of tariffs within the overall average. It follows that by reducing charges to large users as a competitive response, headroom is created to raise revenues from small (that is, domestic) users. Since most of them are not metered, most of them will have to pay higher water rates without affecting their

---

8 The opportunities for substitution between capital and revenue expenditure are illustrated on the Camel Estuary in Cornwall where the National Rivers Authority (NRA) wanted South West Water Services Ltd. to build a primary treated long sea outfall at a cost of £22 million. But South West Water Services Ltd. had wished to build a full treatment works using UV light disinfection instead at a cost of £15 million, which negated the need for an expensive long sea outfall. (Monopolies and Mergers Commission report on South West Water Services Ltd, para.12.98.) This is a counter-example to my proposition: the water company was arguing for the *less* capital-intensive option.

consumption: the overall demand for capacity will rise (subject to the Regulator's strictures on undue discrimination or preference: see OFWAT, 1995).

Then there is the lukewarm attitude that the industry has taken towards the introduction of domestic water meters. The Director General has had to work hard to persuade the firms to offer meters on terms which are at all attractive. This may seem surprising in the light of the evidence now emerging that metering might be expected to reduce peak demand – and hence required capacity – by about 30 per cent.[9] A 'normal' for-profit enterprise which faced a highly peaked demand and received a low and uniform price for its output would be particularly concerned about the high costs of providing the capacity to meet peak demand and it would pursue any opportunity to reduce them. However, in this case, the companies have every incentive to promote peak demand in order to justify the capital investment to meet it, financed by increased taxation.

It is noticeable that in the published literature on the industry there is very little discussion of long-run capacity costs which, according to traditional public enterprise principles should, for efficiency, be charged to peak users. OFWAT has published a good deal of useful data and analysis of costs. But this all seems to concern average costs. There is little analysis of the *structure* of costs: returns to scale and the distinction between average costs and long-run marginal (capacity) costs.

Capacity and Security of Supply in the Presence of Uncertainty

The affair of the drought of 1995 points up several issues which are of general interest. In the public debate very little consideration was given to the investment costs that further ensuring security of supply would imply. There was no real consideration of the magnitude of the costs incurred by consumers in the event that their supply was interrupted. There has been no discussion of the implications of the fact that improvements will have to be funded through taxes which will bear on individuals in a pattern which will not match the pattern of beneficiaries – those with gardens to water and cars to wash.

---

[9] Ian Byatt, 'Water: The Periodic Review', *op. cit.* This lecture contains an interesting early public mention of the important observation that it is the effect of metering on *peak* demand rates which is important for capacity planning, not the 15 per cent effect on *average* demand which has often been quoted in discussions of the costs and benefits of metering.

Any company that could succeed in providing a completely normal water supply during the most severe drought for many decades must either have negligible costs of providing the capacity necessary to cover this eventuality or it must have over-invested in capacity. Such over-investment is a serious matter because it is at the expense of the consumer, not at the expense of the shareholder.

On my hypothesis that firms have an incentive to welcome addition to their capital stock the reaction of commentators and politicians to events over this past summer will be most welcome to them: it will give them a strong hand in arguing that they should be allowed to invest even more in capacity to guarantee security of supply in even more adverse circumstances.

Uncertainty – The Weather

It is striking that the water industry faces an obvious problem of planning investment and charging in the presence of uncertainty of both future supply conditions and future general level of demand. Failures in demand forecasting have had serious consequences for both the industry and the consumer (as they did with electricity), but this issue is not addressed in this paper.

But a portion of the uncertainty facing planners is associated with weather conditions for which probabilities of future 'states of the world' (as the theorists put it) are about as well determined as one could hope for in an economic problem. I have used the word *uncertainty* but, strictly, this is the much more tractable problem of *risk* – the probabilities are known, at least, in the absence of unanticipated climatic change. This is a fairly standard problem in public finance, and indeed in electricity economics. Yet we see little evidence of even the most general consideration of the relevant issues in the public documents on water. Companies have used risk-based planning techniques for their internal purposes, as one would expect. However, the regulatory régime introduces an extra dimension – the incidence of costs and benefits on consumers. It is this I wish to explore. It is ironic that one of the path-breaking books on applied public finance in general, and cost-benefit analysis in particular, was written in the context of water resource planning (Maass *et al.* (1962), *The design of water resource systems*).

The Relationship Between Equity and Efficiency

The question of security of supply brings together several of the important issues: treating valuations of different individuals differently, the implications of the differing incidence of funding of different consumers, the differing values that consumers may place on security of supply, the capital costs of security, and the presence of uncertainty.

Figures 2, 3 and 4 are based on the Family Expenditure Survey for 1988.[10] They indicate that, *on average*, owner-occupiers spent a roughly constant proportion of their outgoings on rates (and, therefore, outgoings on rates increase roughly in proportion to income). But the proportion of all household expenditures accounted for by 'seeds, plants, flowers and horticultural goods' increases with expenditure. This effect is more strongly marked in the case of 'motoring expenditure'. On the whole, gardening and motoring would be classed by economists as luxury goods. This is a superficial analysis, but, taken at face value, it is consistent with the notion that the costs of funding water and sewerage through the rates will fall equiproportionately on all groups, but the benefits of expenditure to increase capacity and reduce the likelihood of hosepipe restrictions will fall relatively heavily on the higher income groups – who, in any case, have a higher willingness to pay.

Economists like to make a clear distinction between the equity effects of policy and the efficiency effects. On the whole, they tend to concentrate on the efficiency side, partly because they feel more able to avoid getting involved in value-judgements and partly because efficiency is easier than equity to analyse. Of course, the *equity* issues are of much more direct interest to the general public. I now want to explore the relationship between equity and efficiency effects.

John Kay (1979) set out a useful framework which can be adapted to the present problem. If it looks complicated that is because it takes care to treat consumers as individuals and not as a single representative.

Efficiency

Adopting Kay's notation, $s(q, Q)$ is the quality (say, security of supply) provided if q in total is consumed and installed capacity is Q. Consumers are indexed by h, and

$$\sum q^h = q.$$

Consumers choose between consuming 'other goods', x^h (a composite numeraire) and water q^h at a price of p (which may be zero). Consumers have an income y^h to spend which Kay assumes to be fixed.

[*continued on p.46*]

---

[10] The last year that rates were used, as distinct from the newer forms of local taxation: the published FES does not distinguish water charges from local taxes.

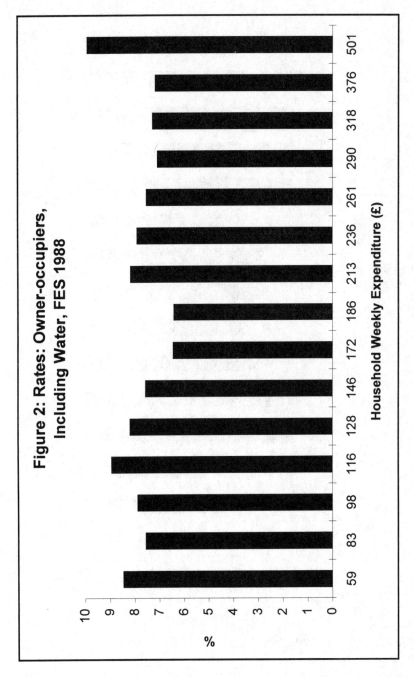

Figure 2: Rates: Owner-occupiers, Including Water, FES 1988

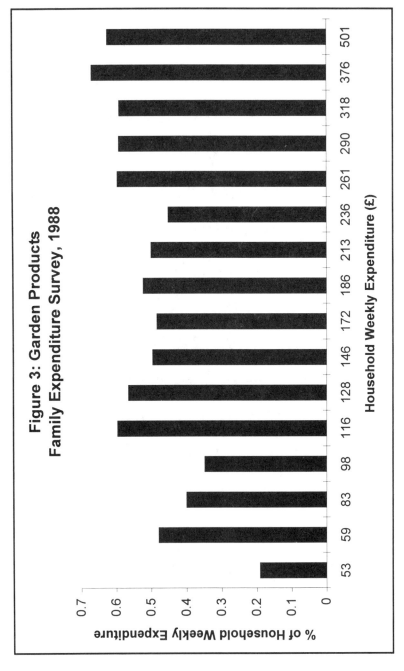

Figure 3: Garden Products
Family Expenditure Survey, 1988

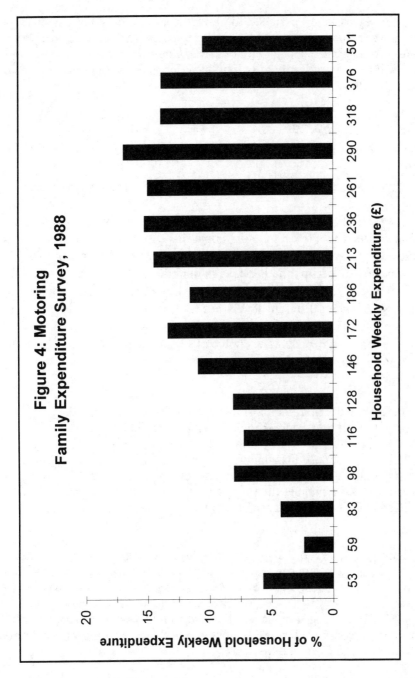

Figure 4: Motoring
Family Expenditure Survey, 1988

Operating costs are assumed to be zero for simplicity but it would be easy to add non-zero marginal operating costs. Kay shows that if price is set to maximise social welfare and *if lump-sum income transfers are available* to 'correct' the distribution of income, then familiar classical results follow:

$$p = \frac{\partial s}{\partial q} \Sigma \left(\frac{\partial x^h}{\partial s} \right)_u$$

This states that price should equal short-run marginal *social* cost. $\left(\dfrac{\partial s}{\partial q} \right)$ is the effect on quality of a change in consumption and $\left(\dfrac{\partial x^h}{\partial s} \right)_u$ is the valuation by individual h of a change in quality, in terms of the numeraire. The interesting point about this expression is that it requires the *summation* of marginal valuations across all consumers. This is characteristic of a public good, as in our context. The point is that only one level of security of supply is offered to all consumers: they cannot choose between different levels at different prices. We will return to this point under the heading of sliding-scale regulation.

The long-run decision, the choice of capacity, requires that

$$- \frac{\partial s}{\partial Q} \Sigma \left(\frac{\partial x^h}{\partial s} \right)_u = \gamma$$

where γ is the marginal cost of capacity. This states that the marginal social benefit of capacity should equal its marginal cost.

This much is standard economic efficiency analysis. But it is not realistic to suppose that lump-sum transfers can be used to spirit away distributional problems. And we cannot ignore the fact that changing capacity will change funding requirements; that in turn will have different financial incidence on different consumers.

Equity

Some people argue that particular individuals have absolute rights in respect of water and sewerage services and that these must be honoured irrespective of costs. However, I believe that if we are to expose the true nature of the choices we face in a methodical fashion, then we have to be willing to make explicit the weight we are prepared to give to one person's welfare as against another's. What follows is a crude framework to facilitate this.

Let β^h measure the *social* benefit of £1 given to individual h. (The standard, efficiency-only treatment guarantees that $\beta^h = 1$ for every individual.) Then the pricing condition becomes

$$p = \frac{\Sigma(1 - \beta^h)x_p^h}{\Sigma \beta^h q_p^h} + \frac{s_q q_p}{\Sigma \beta^h q_p^h} \Sigma \beta^h \left(\frac{\partial x^h}{\partial s}\right)_u.$$

If water is not metered and therefore the price cannot be set, then this is of less interest than the capacity choice condition which is:

$$- s_q \Sigma \beta^h \left(\frac{\partial x^h}{\partial s}\right)_u = \gamma - \Sigma \beta^h y_Q^h.$$

Here y_Q^h is the net effect on individual $h's$ disposable income of financing a unit change in Q. This, in turn will depend upon $h's$ liability through the tax (that is, rating) system and his or her share in the profits from the production of capacity. In a closed economy,

$$\Sigma y_Q^h = 0.$$

A more instructive way of writing the capacity choice condition is

$$\Sigma \beta^h \left\{ -s\left(\frac{\partial x^h}{\partial s}\right)_u + y_Q^h \right\} = \gamma.$$

In words, we must calculate the benefit to each individual of an improvement in capacity *net* of the consequential effect on disposable income. We must then weight this benefit by our view of the social value of the net change in individual welfare. The result is to be compared with the marginal cost of capacity.

If we rewrite the condition using an obvious simplifying notation:

$$\Sigma \beta^h \left\{ \sigma^h + y_Q^h \right\} = \gamma,$$

then one way of looking at it is

$$N\bar{\sigma} = \gamma - N cov(\beta, \sigma) - N cov(\beta, y_Q)$$

where $\bar{\sigma}$ is the *unweighted* mean of the individual valuations and $cov(\beta, \sigma)$ is the covariance of β^h and σ^h over the N individuals. (In deriving this result I have used the normalisation $\bar{\beta} = 1$ and $\Sigma y_Q^h = 0$).

To see the implications of this, suppose there is a range of income groups. Concern for equity will suggest that β^h tends to be larger for the poor. But suppose the poor's valuation of quality tends to be relatively low. Then $cov(\beta,\sigma)$ will be negative. Therefore, at the optimum level of capacity the unweighted average value to consumers of the improvement in quality on the margin should be higher than the marginal cost of capacity. Assuming that this marginal cost is increasing, that implies that optimum capacity should be reduced relative to the case where equity is ignored. (Note that if $\beta^h = 1$ for all h the condition reduces to $\overline{N\sigma} = \gamma$ as before.)

This conclusion may be strengthened or weakened, depending upon how regressive is the funding mechanism used to pay for the investment. If negative values of y_Q^h are associated with high values of β^h, then $cov(\beta,y_Q)$ will be negative and the conclusion will be strengthened. That is, if the poor's net income is reduced more than that of the rich.

Introducing Risk

Now I introduce the additional complication of risk. Suppose that there are several possible 'states of the world' – very dry, dry, ..., very wet – which we will index with θ. Each θ will occur with known probability

$$\pi_\theta, \quad \sum_\theta \pi_\theta = 1.$$

During each possible outcome the consumer will be supplied for a fraction of the time and will consume q_θ^h. Total consumption in θ will be $q_\theta = \sum q_\theta^h$.

The critical concept is the cost to the individual consumer of service failure in state θ, c_θ^h (see Kay, 1979, p.606, for a precise definition). Note that this cost is defined in terms of willingness to pay to avoid disruption, as expressed by the individual. It will be higher for those with high incomes. Any 'social discounting' of high income occurs in the choice of the β 's.

Then the condition for optimum choice of capacity (assuming a zero price and that the quantity of numeraire consumed is constant) can be written

$$\sum_h \beta^h \left\{ \sum_{\theta \in \theta_1} \pi_\theta c_\theta^h \frac{q_\theta^h}{q_\theta} + y_\theta^h \right\} = \gamma.$$

Here θ_1 is the set of all states of the world in which some rationing is required – that is, in which some costs of non-supply are incurred by consumers. This is directly comparable with the expression obtained previously with σ^h defined by

$$\sigma^h = \sum_{\theta \in \theta_I} \pi_\theta c_\theta^h \frac{q_\theta^h}{q_\theta}.$$

This is the expected cost of service failure to consumer h, weighted by the fraction of consumption that he or she accounts for. Once again the condition reads:

$$N\bar{\sigma} = \gamma - Ncov(\beta, \sigma) - Ncov(\beta, y_Q)$$

and the interpretation is exactly similar. Note that the left-hand side is the benefit from more capacity, conventionally measured as the total over all consumers of the *expected* value of the costs they would suffer from disconnection.

Implications

The upshot of all of this is fairly obvious: it is not sensible to invest heavily in the attempt to achieve absolute security of supply – whether it be by being over-zealous in repairing leaks or by over-investing in new physical works – if the valuation of extra security by customers does not match the costs. But this familiar economic efficiency point is doubly reinforced if those who would suffer the largest costs in the event of interruption – perhaps those with large gardens to water and cars to wash – bear a relatively small proportion of the costs.

Compensation and Risk Pooling

The introduction of the correct notion of the costs associated with a risk of insecurity of supply suggests there must be an economic gain from reducing that cost, on the analogy of the economics of insurance. As illustrated by the comment during the 1995 drought, the personal loss caused by loss of supply can be made good by cash compensation. The trick which insurance achieves is that it pools risk so that no individual faces the cost associated with a big loss, in return for which all participants pay a relatively small premium. On average they will pay out a little more than they expect to claim back, but they are better off because the unpleasantness associated with an uncertain future is reduced.

One can, in fact, pool risks across years. Most home owners carry insurance against the possibility that the foundations will be damaged by cracking in dry weather – no doubt there were claims in 1995 as there were after 1976. There is nothing to stop water companies operating a similar scheme. Rather than over-investing in physical capacity, they could charge a uniform premium and pay compensation out of the proceeds if supply fails. Since some unjustified physical investment would be avoided there must, by definition, be a way of arranging such a scheme so that everybody is better off. Interestingly, this suggestion is to be found in Maass's 1962 book, where Robert Dorfman, in his classic early exposition of the treatment of uncertainty in project appraisal, attributes it to H.A. Thomas, Jr.:

> '...specifically for application to the design of water-resource systems. This approach stems from the idea that the net benefits yielded by any installation are the present value of its gross benefits minus the present value of its costs, where the costs include the cost of any uncertainties inherent in the project. The crux of the method is the device for measuring the cost of uncertainty. Imagine that at the time the system is constructed an equalisation fund is established with the understanding that in any year when actual benefits fall short of expected benefits the fund will be used to make up the difference, while in any year when actual benefits exceed expected benefits the excess will be used to replenish the fund...This device converts a risky situation into a fully insured one. The cost of the uncertainty is then just the size of the fund required to obliterate it, and this statement is true whether or not such a fund is actually established.' (Maass *et al.*, 1962, p.150)

The suggestion here is a little more sophisticated than the compensation that was talked of in the Summer of 1995. The cost of insecurity of supply is recognised and insured against by consumers paying insurance premia. In return for this they are relieved of some of the costs of funding investment in excessive physical capacity. If such a scheme were established, the insurance markets would no doubt find beneficial ways of trading these risks, hedging them by bundling them with other risks which are negatively correlated.

Interruptible Tariffs

It is remarkable that few interruptible tariffs exist in water supply. Plainly, the costs of supply rationing are much greater for some commercial enterprises than for others. Yet there is no mechanism offered whereby they can express their willingness to pay more. The introduction of interruptible tariffs for large users would give discounts to those who would suffer the least damage from interruption. In cases where the capacity shortages relate to the distribution network, rather than the collection facilities, interruption could be by time of day, thus allowing a more efficient use of under-used night-time capacity. And once the incentive existed some users would find it worth their while to install their own storage systems so as to be able to sign up to the interruptible tariff, thereby alleviating the peak supply problem.

It would, of course, relieve the pressure to create new peak capacity – because the existing capacity would be more accurately targeted to its high-value users. My hypothesis that water companies have the incentive to take every opportunity to invest capital to increase capacity may explain the absence of interruptible tariffs, when they are a common feature of the other utilities operating under a different set of regulatory incentives.

Similar possibilities exist for metered domestic consumers. One advantage that water has over gas and electricity is that it is relatively easy for the domestic user to store.[11] There is no technical reason why water meters could not be produced which would charge different rates at different times of the day or year, thus giving incentives to reduce peak demands on the systems.

The Regulation of Profits

Much of the public concern that has been voiced recently has been directed at the profits earned by the industry. Some of this comment has been founded on a misunderstanding which essentially confuses the economist's understanding of profit with the accountant's definition, which is the one that is published. Much of the accounting profit is, by agreement with the regulator, surplus of revenues over operating cost which is used to finance capital.

However, it may be the case that some form of profits control becomes expedient, so it is worth considering what that form of regulation could be expected to achieve. Burns, Turvey and Weyman-Jones (1995a) have written about some aspects of the following under the heading of sliding-scale regulation (also see Glaister, 1987, for a treatment of this).

The Something-Related Profits Tax

All sliding-scale type mechanisms work by allowing the firm to maximise profit, but distorting either the marginal revenue or the marginal cost in some way so as to achieve some regulatory objective. This can be expressed in a fairly general way in terms of a 'something-related profits tax'.

---

[11] According to Ralph Turvey the British habit of having large storage tanks in our lofts is a consequence of the standard practice in the past of only providing supply to any one property for a few hours in each day on a rota basis.

Profit (in the accountant's sense) is revenue, R, net of cost, C. Suppose a tax is imposed at a rate $(1 - T(q, Q))$. Here I am assuming that the two regulatory variables of interest are quantity sold (or, equivalently, price) and generic quality. Quality could refer to security of supply, chemical composition or some other attribute.

Hence retained profit is given by

$\pi = (R - C)T(q, Q)$.

Price Regulation

Assume for a moment that quality is fixed by direct regulation, but the firm can maximise net profit with respect to output:

$$\frac{\partial \pi}{\partial q} = (R_q - C_q)T + (R - C)\frac{\partial T}{\partial q}$$

$$= (R_q - C_q)T + \frac{\pi}{q}\tau_q$$

where

$$\tau_q = \frac{\partial T}{\partial q}\frac{q}{T}$$

is the elasticity of the retained profit with respect to output. Hence profit maximisation requires

$$\frac{\partial \pi}{\partial q} = 0 \text{ or } R_q + \frac{\pi}{Tq}\tau_q = C_q .$$

This last equation shows how the marginal revenue, R_q, is distorted as seen by the firm. Since

$$R_q = p(1 - \frac{1}{e_p})$$

where e_p is the price elasticity of demand, we can arrange for the firm to put price close to marginal cost if we make

$$\frac{p}{e_p} = \frac{\pi}{Tq}\tau_q.$$

In other words, we require

$$\tau_q = \frac{R}{(R - C)} \frac{1}{e_p}$$

$$= \frac{1}{\left[1 - \left(\dfrac{C}{R}\right)\right]} \frac{1}{e_p}.$$

Therefore, if we have an approximate idea of the price elasticity of demand, and of the ratio of operating cost to total revenue which would obtain at the optimum, we can compute the corresponding elasticity required for the profit retention function.

Figure 5 shows the calculation for a range of price elasticities and cost:revenue ratios. It will be noted that the required elasticity is fairly insensitive over a reasonably wide range. A value between one and two would do the trick for price elasticities greater than unity or operating costs less than half revenues.

Note that what matters is the *elasticity* of the retained profit rate, not the absolute value of it – removing a lump sum or a constant proportion of profit will not alter profit-maximising incentives. So one could set the average proportion of profit which is to be retained at some 'reasonable' rate.

So, as other authors have noted, there seems to be a fair prospect of using 'sliding-scale' techniques to achieve price regulation. Unfortunately, in the case of the UK water industry this is not of much interest since most water is unpriced. So the interesting issue is quality.

Quality Regulation

The optimality conditions from the firm's point of view are just as before, with Q written for q. In the case of quantity choice the efficiency condition was assumed to be the classical 'price equals marginal cost'. However, in the case of quality the efficiency condition is less familiar.

The conventional consumer surplus measure of overall benefit is

$$\int_p^\infty f(v, Q)dv + R - C(q, Q)$$

where

$$q = f(v, Q)$$

is the demand. So for a social optimum:

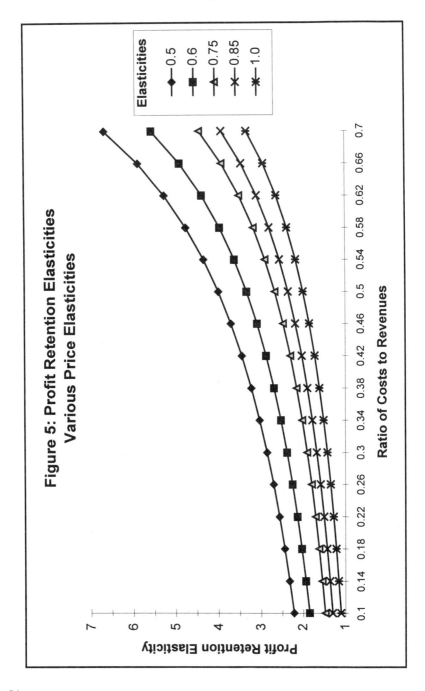

Figure 5: Profit Retention Elasticities
Various Price Elasticities

$$\int_p^\infty \frac{\partial f}{\partial Q}(v,\, Q)dv - R_Q = \frac{\partial C}{\partial Q}(q,\, Q).$$

That is, marginal benefit of quality must equal marginal cost. The evaluation of the first term on the left is an old problem in cost-benefit analysis: in terms of the diagram in Figure 6 it means evaluating the whole of the strip between the two curves. In other words, we need to know the additional willingness to pay for every, intra marginal, unit of water, as a result of the quality improvement, and we must add them all together. So we are concerned with the total additional benefit – or, after dividing by the quantity consumed, the average benefit – whereas the firm is only concerned with the extra benefit on the *marginal* unit. It is only that which it can turn into revenue. This problem was first analysed by Spence (1975).

We now investigate the special conditions which would have to apply to individuals' preferences for a simple regulatory scheme to work.

One obvious possibility is that marginal valuations of quality are constant. Suppose the 'generalised cost' to the consumer of a unit is $p - \omega Q$ where ω is the constant money value of quality, Q. Then demand can be written as

$$q = f(p - \omega Q)$$

and

$$\frac{\partial q}{\partial Q} = -\,\omega\,\frac{\partial q}{\partial p}.$$

Then

$$\int_p^\infty \frac{\partial f}{\partial Q}\,(v - \omega Q)dv = \omega f(p - \omega Q).$$

So for the profit-maximising firm to achieve the efficient result we require

$$\tau_Q = \frac{q\omega Q}{(R - C)}$$

$$= \frac{\omega Q}{\left(p - \dfrac{C}{q}\right)}.$$

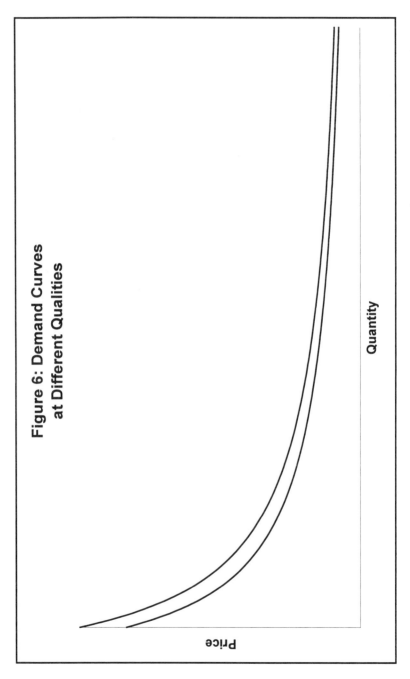

**Figure 6: Demand Curves
at Different Qualities**

Hence the elasticity of the tax retention function should be the ratio of the 'expenditure on quality' to the difference between price and average cost (which must be positive if the firm is to stay in business).

It is possible that some progress in regulation might be possible along these lines. Note that at the very least it would require an estimate to be made of ω, the money value to consumers of quality. (The analogy is with the money value of time savings.) This problem is similar to that faced in road design for unpriced (or rather, under-priced) roads. There the solution is to measure benefits by time saved – valued by observing people's willingness to pay to save time. Individuals do in fact trade in a market for various dimensions of water quality and it may be possible to make progress by studying this revealed behaviour.

However, the basic assumption of constancy of marginal value of quality across all units consumed (and therefore across all consumers) is implausible and assumes away much of the interest. It is difficult to avoid the problem of having to take account of variations in preferences of consumers.

Finding out Consumers' Preferences: The Free-Rider Problem

As Spence (1975, p.425) observes:

> 'A random survey of current users will yield accurate information about the average willingness to pay for service quality. But the fact that average willingness to pay exceeds the cost does not imply that an increase in service quality will be profitable. That the regulatory problem should be informationally complicated in this particular way is simply a reflection of the fact that the price signals are misleading in the unconstrained market. ...'

This is in the context of output that is priced. If, as in the case of unmetered water, it is to be paid for by increases in local taxation, then the money can always be raised (subject to the Regulator being convinced about the veracity of the surveys). The issue becomes one of whether those who are willing to pay will be those who are actually required to pay by the tax system.

For instance, as incomes rise, willingness to pay for improved quality may rise more rapidly than the liability to pay for it through the old rating system. Then those with high incomes will have no discipline on them to prevent them overstating the benefit to them of increasing quality (mainly at other people's expense). Conversely, those at the other end of the spectrum will understate their benefit in the hope of preventing the innovation. Similarly, an individual may overstate the benefits to him of every beach in the country being cleaned up, in the knowledge that only the local costs will fall on her or him: the rest of the country will be paid for by everyone else.

In the case of research in the Southern region, typically some 70 per cent of those surveyed only wished to see specific service improvements if they could be delivered at minimal cost to customers. Southern CSC (Customer Service Committee) was not convinced that this strong customer message had been fully taken into account by the companies when they had developed their Market Plans (Monopolies and Mergers Commission, *Portsmouth*, para.12.6):

> 'The Market Plans had implied Ks that would have...resulted in some of those on low incomes paying over 10 per cent of their disposable income in water and sewerage bills by the year 2000. ...There are high proportions of pensioner households concentrated along the coast. ...Portsmouth had reflected customers' general unwillingness to incur higher bills...by making no proposals to improve levels of service. However Southern CSC said that there was a fine line between expenditure which was deemed to be asset maintenance, and that which enhanced the assets, ability to deliver services or increased security margins. ...'

Portsmouth wished to work with considerable supply capacity security margins, with new supply sources developed well ahead of any increase in demand, even though security was already high by national standards (Monopolies and Mergers Commission, *Portsmouth*, paras.12.18 to 12.21).

Portsmouth Water saw this differently:

> 'Opinion polls had indicated that customers expected to see continuing improvements in service. Companies would face heightened expectations of levels of service without the necessary resources to deliver them.' (para.12.108)

The Director General is sensitive to this issue:

> 'The Director said that, since they affected all customers, decisions about the appropriate trade-off between quality and price had, for the most part, to reflect the views of all customers. Customers had different views, and a judgement had to be made' (South West Water Services Ltd., para.10.13).

> '...As for the company's claims that a "sufficient" number of customers were willing to pay for improved services, the Director said that South

West Water Services Ltd. had submitted two sets of evidence of customer views. Neither had justified burdening the generality of consumers with higher charges to cover the costs of discretionary enhancements in an area already subject to the highest water and sewerage charges, and having some of the poorest people in the country' (para.10.15).

Appendices 5.1 and 5.2 of the Monopolies and Mergers Commission report on South West Water Services Ltd. give a general impression of the consumer survey work the company has been involved with. It is that the surveys tend to be simple direct questions about how much customers would be willing to pay for this or that. It has been found in the transport field – and in the 'contingent valuation' literature more generally – that one can obtain reliable information only if respondents are forced into simulating real choices. The technique of 'stated preference analysis' has been developed to achieve this. A special issue of the *Journal of Transport Economics and Policy* is devoted to this (Bates, 1988).

Beesley (1991) notes the potential of hypothetical choice studies. He also suggests 'implicit values of water derived from house price comparisons' and asks 'can anything be gleaned from willingness to pay for complements to water use?'. One might add the possibility that one could now make progress by observing willingness to pay revealed by actual trading behaviour in purchasing bottled water and increasing private storage capacities in the case of industrial users.

Conclusion

History has landed the Regulator with the continuing task of setting taxes to fund the provision of a public good. Forces, such as outside pressures to improve the environment and incentives on the industry itself to invest, conspire to press for substantial increases in these taxes – which the Regulator has worked hard to resist. I have illustrated some of the principles that might be appropriate to a more rational appraisal of these taxes, suggesting that more consideration than in the past should be given to how we value the benefits to consumers of quality improvement attributable to capacity investment, and how these interact with the incidence of the burden of paying for them.

The Regulator does not have the support of the local democratic process which originally partnered the rating system. Nor does he suffer the interference that might have brought. The issue is whether the Regulator should move to fill this vacuum or whether the problems of equity should be either ignored or recognised and dealt with by some other legitimate agency such as local authorities or the general social security system which might operate some system of user-side subsidy.

Before jumping to the conclusion that the regulatory system should be fundamentally changed a very strong argument would, in my view, have to be made to show how a new system would avoid 'letting the politicians back in' to the day-to-day running of the industry, thereby jeopardising the considerable efficiency benefits which the current, privatised system can continue to offer.

Whatever happens, a better informed debate is needed on ways of dealing with the vagaries of the weather, before we unthinkingly concede to the industry an opportunity to over-invest at a cost which few of us would gladly pay.

References

Armstrong, M., S. Cowan, and J. Vickers (1994): *Regulatory Reform*, Cambridge,Mass.: The MIT Press.

Bates, J.J. (ed.) (1988): 'Stated preference methods in transport research', *Journal of Transport Economics and Policy*, Special Issue, January.

Beesley, M.E. (1991): 'Price Regulation and Competition', in *Lectures on Regulation*, London Business School.

Burns, P., R. Turvey, and T.G. Weyman-Jones (1995a): *Sliding scale regulation of monopoly enterprises*, Centre for Regulated Industries.

Burns, P., R. Turvey R., T.G. Weyman-Jones (1995b): *General properties of sliding scale regulation*, Centre for Regulated Industries.

Byatt, I. (1994): 'Water: The Periodic Review', in *Utility Regulation: Challenge and Response*, IEA Readings No.42, London: Institute of Economic Affairs.

Glaister, S. (1987): 'Regulation Through Output Related Profits Tax', *Journal of Industrial Economics*, Vol.XXXV, No.3, March.

Kay, J. (1979): 'Uncertainty, Congestion and Peak Load Pricing', *Review of Economic Studies*, Vol.XLVI, No.4.

Maass, A., *et al.* (1962): *The design of water resource systems*, London: Macmillan.

Marvin, S., and S. Slater (1995): *Holes in the Road*, Report to the Rees Jeffreys Road Fund, May.

Monopolies and Mergers Commission (1995): *Portsmouth Water Plc*, June, London: HMSO.

Monopolies and Mergers Commission (1995): *South West Water Services Ltd.*, June, London: HMSO.

OFWAT (1995): *Competition in the Water Industry: inset appointments and their regulation.*

OFWAT (1993): *Paying for Quality: the political perspective.*

OFWAT (1994): *Future charges for water and sewerage services: the outcome of the Periodic Review.*

Smith, J. (1995): 'Water services 1994 – a watershed year', *Regulatory Review 1995*, Centre for Regulated Industries.

Spence, M. (1975): 'Monopoly, quality and regulation', *Bell Journal of Economics*, Vol.6.

CHAIRMAN'S COMMENTS

I.C.R. Byatt
Office of Water Services

WATER IS AN INDUSTRY little touched by economics and it is a pleasure to listen to a paper applying economic principles to issues of costs, consumer choice and pricing. One of the valuable consequences of privatisation has been to focus more attention on the industry by those not traditionally concerned with it. Stephen Glaister shows how useful this can be.

I read him as arguing for change to deal with:

- some of the inequities and inefficiencies of the present pricing system;
- the tendency to over-investment.

I will take each in turn.

Pricing Policies

I agree with him that charging on the basis of a property tax without (local) democratic accountability is asking for trouble in the long run, although in the short term very convenient for water companies. Some of them want, indeed, to switch to what they consider a more acceptable tax base, the Council Tax – although not accompanied by any accountability to local authorities or by the many concessions made to particular groups.

I also agree that there is a considerable degree of 'publicness' – as the public finance experts would put it – about water, especially on the waste water side although extending to the quality of drinking water. Pricing techniques have, however, a greater rôle to play as far as the private attributes of water are concerned. I hope that one of the useful effects of this summer's drought – which has been as much, or more, a matter of demand rather than of supply – will be to concentrate people's minds on pricing issues.

Pricing policies must be properly linked with the cost structure of the industry where we observe:

- economics of density (but not scale) in distribution but where population density is exogenous;

- rising marginal costs of developing new resources (a Ricardian world);

- steeply rising marginal costs of higher quality;

- a situation where the accounting costs established at privatisation and used in price setting are massively below the resource costs of increasing either quality or quantity;

- cost allocation, especially on the sewerage side, presents many technical problems.

Marginal costs are well *above* average costs.

There is, therefore, a strong case for pricing policies which can deal with the quantitative if not the qualitative aspects of the supply of and demand for water services. This is what Stephen Glaister is telling us, and I agree with him.

The directions which I believe are the more fruitful are:

- Establishing tariffs for customers taking measured supplies which are fair in relation to what would be paid for unmeasured supplies (we have largely achieved this but will take full account of changes in estimates of unmeasured consumption).

- Pressing ahead with installing meters in areas where household demand, especially for garden watering, is rising.

- Developing peak tariffs to cope with hot and dry spells and with the seasonal factors which plague customers in the South West as a result of the influx of tourists.

- Development of policies to compensate customers – but not those using hosepipes and sprinklers at zero cost – who experience shortages and poor pressure. Companies would then have incentives to manage resources better.

- Using revenue from measured tariffs, rather than higher water charges – that is, taxation – to augment supplies when market signals are favourable.

- Increasing competition to influence tariffs for large business users not needing to use the local distribution system.

Investment

I agree with Stephen Glaister that there are incentives to over-investment. There are also incentives under price cap regulation to exaggerate the need for investment ahead of a price review.

There are strong political pressures for high investment in *quality*. Better (or at least *some*) cost-benefit analysis is desirable and I am glad that a statutory duty to consider costs and benefits has been placed on the Environment Agency. The Commission in Brussels has duties under the Treaty, but we still lack mechanisms for implementing them.

Cost-benefit analysis is only part of the story. The key is public attitudes. The environmental pressure groups prey on public fears and feelings of guilt. The politicians rely on free lunches – on the right, greater efficiency; on the left, lower profits. I hope that OFWAT's work on Paying for Quality will have a long-term effect on the debate and on the outcome. But we need help in 'empowering the customer's wallet'.

Water companies, to their credit, have generally been helpful to their customers in this area. One advantage of privatisation is the quick translation of costs into bills – perhaps the best form of transparency attainable. But I have also noticed activity designed to get quality regulators to sign up for quality improvements. There are some perverse incentives, which need to be counter-balanced by strong and continued customer pressure to keep prices down.

So far, the pressures for over-investment in *quantity* have been less obvious – except for a string of unproven assertions about fixed costs and demand elasticities. The apparently rising demand for water will, however, lead to pressure for more resources. Here I hope environmentalists and economists will continue to agree on the need for the greater use of pricing mechanisms.

3

DEALING WITH SOCIAL OBLIGATIONS IN TELECOMS

George Yarrow

Regulatory Policy Institute,
University of Oxford

Introduction

THE IMPOSITION OF VARIOUS TYPES OF SOCIAL OBLIGATIONS on suppliers is a familiar feature of public policy in network industries. Indeed, one traditional view of social obligations (broadly defined) is that they are part of a wider regulatory bargain which links them to monopoly rights awarded to the relevant supplier. For example, a requirement that telecoms services be provided to all customers in a particular area at the same, regulated price, irrespective of any differences in supply costs among those customers, was traditionally accompanied by the granting of a monopoly franchise to prevent the desired cross-subsidisation being undermined by competing operators.

The development of competitive telecoms markets over the past decade has, however, undermined the links between social obligations and monopoly rights, and it has given rise to a necessary re-examination of public policy goals for the industry and of alternative ways of pursuing those goals. In this context, perhaps the two central questions are:

- What are the appropriate social policy objectives in a competitive telecoms market?

- How are those objectives best achieved?

In respect of the first, it appears that the social objectives currently being pursued in the UK are something of a rag-bag: they include both conventional universal service aims and much more specific goals relating to particular groups in the community. I will argue that, given the present state of the market, at least some existing social objectives – of which the promotion of ever increasing telephone penetration rates is perhaps the most significant – would be better abandoned.

In respect of the second question, diversity of objectives suggests that it might be appropriate to rely on a range of different policy instruments. I will, however, also argue that there are strong reasons for believing that an industry-specific regulator such as Oftel is not the best institution to be entrusted with the formulation and implementation of social objectives.

Social Obligations in Practice

In considering policy objectives, a useful starting point is the Oftel consultative document, *A Framework for Effective Competition* (December 1994), which sets out the various obligations that have been imposed on British Telecom via its licence conditions. These include:

- the requirement to meet all reasonable demands for basic telephone service, including in rural areas (conditions 1 and 2);

- the requirement to continue to provide public call boxes, unless certain criteria are satisfied and consultation has been carried out (condition 11);

- the prohibition of the use of prices or other terms and conditions to discriminate unduly against certain persons or groups, including customers in rural areas (condition 17);

- the requirement to provide a residential low user scheme (condition 24D);

- requirements to provide:

  > special telephones for the hearing impaired to meet reasonable demand (condition 32),
  >
  > text relay services for deaf people (condition 31A),
  >
  > facilities for hearing impaired people in public call boxes (condition 33),
  >
  > priority fault repair services for long-term sick and disabled people (condition 10),
  >
  > free directory information services for the blind and disabled (condition 3); and

- the requirement to provide free public emergency call services.

A number of these specific requirements can be grouped together under the general heading of universal service obligations, where universal service is interpreted as *provision that is made available to all on similar terms*. Other of the requirements, however, are directed at meeting special needs, and these tend to imply provision on *dissimilar* terms.

Irrespective of the precise classification of the various requirements, the list set out above invites the immediate question: Why, in an increasingly competitive market-place, should licence conditions contain social obligations at all? Competitive suppliers of other products (which may be equally important to the well-being of the rural population or the disabled or the poor) are not typically encumbered by such obligations, and it is far from obvious why telecoms services are nowadays much different.

In raising this question, I do not suggest that the public policy objectives underlying BT's licence conditions are necessarily misguided. Rather the point is that the objectives might well be better met in other ways. Measures to help the poor, the sick and the disabled are normally entrusted to social security policy, and, going back to first principles, it is rather odd to find them placed in the hands of a policy body concerned with a specific industry.

Before further considering the question of how *best* to deal with social policy objectives in a competitive telecoms market, I will first briefly outline why it might be that Oftel currently plays such a significant rôle in these areas.

The Genesis of Regulation

Universal service obligations (USOs) developed initially in the growth phases of the major network industries when whole localities and communities were first being connected. The politics of the early development stages need not detain us here; suffice to say that policy-makers at the time of BT's privatisation had to deal with a telecoms industry characterised by a typical combination of monopoly and systematic cross-subsidisation. As is generally well understood, perceived political constraints slowed the rate at which post-privatisation tariff structures could be rebalanced and, given also that competition took some time to develop, preservation of at least some USOs was an unsurprising outcome.

It might, however, have been anticipated that the significance of USOs would decline over time as competition increased and as average telecoms prices fell relative to average incomes (allowing tariff rebalancing to occur without damaging the real incomes of major user groups). Against this expectation the actual imposition of *additional* social obligations might be viewed as surprising, but it is, in fact, a particular example of a familiar story in the economics of regulation.

One aspect of the process by which new obligations are generated is what I will call *regulatory opportunism*, a term that can refer to the behaviour of both legislators and industry regulators. To illustrate, as it is being developed, telecoms legislation concerned with issues such as privatisation and regulation of prices is vulnerable to amendment in ways that are designed to favour particular interest groups and that may be quite different in spirit from the central intent of the legislation. The underlying principle at work here is that politicians can win favour by delivering highly visible benefits to particular groups when the costs of regulation are thinly spread and are not transparent.

Once regulatory agencies are established, regulators themselves may be able to use their considerable discretionary powers to extend the scope of USOs and of other social obligations. The opportunities to do so are limited by the procedures for changing licence conditions, and in particular by the ability of the regulated firm to take disputed matters to the Monopolies and Mergers Commission (MMC). Initially, however, privatised utilities were fearful of MMC references – among other things because the scope of any reference might be much wider than the issue in dispute – and the intended checks and balances in the system failed to operate effectively.[1]

Flexible Definition of Universal Service

The scope for regulatory opportunism is apparent from the flexible way in which universal service can be defined. In the consultative document, *A Framework for Effective Competition*, Oftel suggested that existing USO policy embodied three governing principles:

- *Geographic accessibility*: basic telephony service should be available to all who reasonably request it, regardless of where they live.

---

[1] There are now encouraging signs of more active oversight of regulatory decisions by the MMC, although both the procedures and the institutional set-up leave substantial scope for improvement.

- *Access should be affordable*: basic telephony service should be reasonably available for customers who have difficulty in paying the standard price.

- *Access should be equitable*: reasonable measures should be put in place to give customers with special needs or disabilities access to basic services.

These are combined in Oftel's working definition of universal service:

> *'Affordable access to basic voice telephony or its equivalent for all those reasonably requesting it, regardless of where they live.'*[2]

There is a natural inclination to agree with propositions so heavily qualified by implied tests of reasonableness, but it should be noted that the second and third of the above propositions or principles represent major extensions to – or, perhaps more accurately, major deviations from – the traditional view of universal service (service available to all *on similar terms*, irrespective of location and cost). Thus:

- Use of the affordability principle takes the regulator into the realms of policy towards income redistribution – one way or another, implicit taxes are levied on some part of the industry in order to redistribute resources to the poor.

- Use of the notion of equitable access implies that the regulator takes responsibility for defining both special needs and the means by which they should be met, and (again) for raising the necessary finance via implicit taxation on other parts of the industry.

As implied earlier, the goals here may be laudable but the methods of achieving them are highly questionable. In *Effective Competition: Framework for Action*, it is stated that *'Oftel does not believe it is possible to specify in detail the meaning of "affordable" and "reasonable" in the universal service definition'* (para.4.8). These are indeed difficult issues, and the subsequent sentence in the document goes on to state that the operational criterion that is to be used in this context is the level of penetration of telecoms services. This is, however, something of a cop-out, since there is nothing desirable about increased penetration that brings benefits smaller than its costs.

---

2   See Director General of Telecommunications, *Effective Competition: Framework for Action*, Oftel, July 1995.

In general, the relief of poverty and public provision for special needs are much better handled by the Department of Social Security (DSS), which can look at the positions of the relevant individuals and groups in their entirety, and not just at their positions as buyers in the market for telecoms services. Such a re-assignment of responsibility would also have the advantage that the resources required for redistribution would have to be raised via general taxation, thereby establishing clear lines of accountability for relevant policy decisions, first to Parliament and then to the electorate. In contrast, accountability for taxation and redistribution via industry regulation is highly problematic.

A further problem with the *status quo* – and one that affects even the traditional approach to USOs – lies in the definition of what comprises a basic telephony service. Oftel's proposed definition, set out in *Effective Competition: Framework for Action*, is:

> '*Individual access to the telecommunications network via switches capable of providing voice telephony, with free services of itemised billing and selective call barring, and some supplementary services available (such as call diversion and call waiting).*' (para.4.13)

The concept of a basic service is, therefore, clearly an elastic one that will vary with technology and costs. A few years ago a telecoms regulator would not have thought about including services such as call diversion and call waiting in the definition. In the future there could be pressure to include ISDN or wideband services. Some recent discussion concerns the possibility of imposing additional obligations in respect of levels of service provided to schools and other educational establishments (thereby appropriating some aspects of education policy to Oftel).

What is going on here is constant regulatory re-assessment of the costs and benefits of providing alternative levels of universal, basic service. As technology develops and as the costs of certain enhancements to service levels fall (often dramatically), the improvements are gradually reclassified as basic. That is, the regulator makes an assessment of the trade-offs between the costs and benefits of the various services, seeks to impose a minimum level of service throughout the market, and determines how the costs of the enforced minimum shall be borne.

Once again, the contrast with normal practice in competitive markets is apparent: in other markets consumers themselves determine the level of service they require. As well as tending to reduce diversity of outcomes, the risk inherent in a system of regulatory adjudication is that incorrect assessments will be made of customers' valuations of benefits and of the costs of meeting USOs. It is difficult to see, for example, what great contribution to social policy objectives would be made by universal provision of free itemised billing and of call diversion and call waiting. These may well be services that would emerge as standard as a result of a combination of falling costs and competition among telecoms operators, but no significant market failures appear to be involved and the case for regulatory involvement is a weak one.

Rationales for Universal Service

At this point it may be useful to look a little more closely at the underlying arguments in favour of regulatory intervention in the name of universal service provision. These arguments can be divided into those concerned with efficiency and those concerned with equity. In general, assignment of policy responsibility to an industry-specific regulator is more easily justified on efficiency than on equity grounds (the regulator tends to be specifically concerned with efficient supply in the relevant industry whereas other parts of government have responsibilities in respect of groups such as the poor, the sick, and the disabled).

Of the obligations listed in the previous section (above, p.68), it can be noted that measures to promote the provision of free emergency telephone services and of public call boxes can be justified on efficiency grounds. These services have certain of the characteristics of public goods: they are jointly consumed by a great many people and it is important that there be no barriers to their use by anyone in need. Arguably, the market might be expected to under-supply such services, in which case policy intervention can have the potential to enhance efficiency in resource allocation.

Given, however, that call boxes and emergency services tend to serve particular communities, in competitive telecoms markets the most sensible arrangement would appear to be for policy responsibility to rest with bodies such as local authorities and the Department of Transport (for telephones along trunk roads). These bodies could then negotiate with telecoms suppliers for the level of provision deemed most suitable for the relevant community.

Other possible efficiency arguments in favour of some forms of universal service objective rest upon the educational value of connection to a telecoms network, efficient access to the internet from schools being a much discussed recent example. I will not examine this issue in any detail here, but note simply that, whatever the merits of the efficiency arguments, they do not appear to lead to a case for Oftel involvement. These are matters that could be left to normal market negotiations between education authorities – who are in the best position to assess the costs and benefits of alternative uses of their resources – and telecoms suppliers.

Network Externalities

The classic argument for measures to raise household penetration rates in telecoms is based upon the existence of network externalities. That is, when a household is connected to a network benefits will be conferred upon other users of the network, who will then be able to communicate with the new subscriber.

There are a number of immediate, general points that can be made about this type of argument. *First*, the existence of an externality does not in itself provide a justification for regulatory action. Externalities are endemic in economic life and their existence acts as an incentive mechanism for the development of more efficient contractual and institutional arrangements. To illustrate, when the manager of a company takes actions that improve the performance of a company, benefits are typically conferred on the shareholders of the company. This external effect encourages the development of more effective performance-related remuneration schemes – which tend to reduce, but not to eliminate, the externality – and its existence is not usually taken as *prima facie* evidence that managerial effort should be regulated or subsidised!

Second, the size of the externality can easily be exaggerated. In a well-functioning system of network charging, the owner of the relevant capital will collect revenues from *incoming* as well as outgoing calls. That is, at least part of the benefits conferred on other users will be captured by the provider of access facilities, and it will therefore not constitute an externality at all. On the other hand, if network pricing arrangements fail to allow the access provider to appropriate incremental revenues effectively, then the obvious remedy is to work on reducing the pricing inefficiencies (rather than introducing a new objective, 'universal service').

To illustrate, suppose an access provider calculates that a new connection would lead to a profit contribution of π_0 on outgoing calls and a profit of π_i on incoming calls, for a cost c. Such a provider could offer access at a price down to $c - \pi_i$ and still make a positive profit on the transaction, and such below-cost pricing is common in other markets where initial capital investments are required in order to produce a continuing service. Even if network pricing is distorted so that, for example, the access provider cannot capture revenue from the incoming call, private arrangements may well internalise much of the externality. For example, those family members who would most want to be in contact with an elderly relative could themselves pay part or all of the latter's connection charge.

Third, residual network externalities can be expected to decline in importance as telephone penetration rates reach high levels. In such circumstances households not connected will tend to be those which would generate only light use of the facilities, and therefore those whose connection would add relatively little benefit.[3] Moreover, where penetration rates are already high, unconnected households will generally lie in close proximity to a connected household: a neighbour's phone (as well as a local call box) could serve as a substitute for direct access in respect of those occasional calls that are of high value (for example, emergency calls of various types). In this context it can be important to remember that because a household is not itself connected to the network does not mean that it does not have access to that network: joint-consumption of facilities can often be an efficient economic arrangement.

Fourth, the existence of network externalities does not in any case establish a case for a policy of encouraging ever higher penetration rates. Rather, ignoring all other complications for the moment, the implication is that penetration should be encouraged up to the point where the marginal benefits equal the marginal costs. Whether this occurs at, say, 85 or 90 or 95 per cent penetration is a matter for determination, and the issue can be settled only by quantitative assessment.

In summary, the network externalities case for regulatory intervention to promote universal service is far from compelling. The existence of an externality does not establish a *prima facie* case for intervention; the size of the externalities may not be large, particularly in developed telecoms systems; there exist alternative methods of correcting externalities; and, even where intervention might be justified, the optimal policy may well be to aim at penetration rates that fall significantly below 100 per cent.

---

[3] It may be worth emphasising that I am considering only efficiency issues here. Questions relating to ability to pay are discussed later.

Distributional Concerns

Much of recent Oftel activity in respect of social obligations has focused on the position of low-income households in general and on the issue of affordability in particular. One interpretation of this behaviour is that the concern stems from a universal service objective that is itself derived from other principles (such as the promotion of efficiency or of basic rights). If, for example, the aim is to increase penetration to close to 100 per cent, then the encouragement of, say, light-user schemes can be seen as a means to this end. On the other hand, ensuring that telecoms services are available to low-income households could be interpreted as an objective in its own right, and it is this approach that I will comment upon here.

To the extent that the social objective is to raise the real incomes of the poor, the case for Oftel involvement is clearly a very weak one and redistribution of income through the tax and benefits system is a much preferable option. The policy aim is, however, usually taken to be the slightly different one of equalising access to telephone services, which can be viewed as a form of redistribution in kind.

The debate concerning redistribution of cash versus redistribution in kind is a well-rehearsed one. Redistribution of cash allows individuals to dispose of their resources in the way that, in their own view, contributes maximally to their welfare. For example, if a household believes that additional resources would be better used in improving the fabric of the home than in connecting to the telephone network, it would be free to exercise that choice. On the other hand, telephone connection might be deemed to be a 'merit' good, meaning that someone in authority has decided that households should consume this particular commodity irrespective of the choices that would be made by the households themselves. Alternatively, telephone connection might be deemed to be a basic right of all members of society (although in this case the rhetoric tends to suggest that connection should be provided free of any charges).

While the merit good approach is the one that best accords with existing policy, there is some reluctance to acknowledge the paternalistic judgements upon which it rests. Thus, research by Oftel has indicated that around two million households in the UK are currently without telephones and that approximately two-thirds of these have said that they would like a telephone connection. Noting that the principal reason these latter households give for not having a connection is cost, Oftel reasoning tends to assume that the research results establish a case for regulatory action to increase penetration rates.

The fact, however, that a person says that he or she has not purchased a commodity because it is too expensive tells us only that he or she has decided to spend his or her disposable income on other commodities. Or, in other words, it tells us that the perceived value of the connection was less than the cost. This hardly provides a sound justification for a policy of ensuring that such persons are provided with telephone connections.

In any event, acceptance of either the merit good or the basic rights position does not imply that the best approach is for these matters to be handled by Oftel. If redistribution in kind is a policy objective, there is a strong argument for assigning responsibility to a part of government which is able to balance the costs and benefits against the costs and benefits of other forms of redistribution or of other types of government activity. As an industry-specific regulator, Oftel simply does not have the capacity to make such evaluations.

Neither does Oftel have access to the range of policy instruments available to, say, the DSS. By way of illustration of the resulting problems, consider the current light-user scheme which provides rebates on line rentals for low-volume users. The correlation between call volume and income is far from perfect: many low-volume users will not be low-income households and many low-income households will not be low-volume users. For example, Oftel analysis of the Family Expenditure Survey indicates that only 34 per cent of households in the lowest two income deciles are currently eligible for the current light-user scheme, while BT research indicates that about 57 per cent of customers on the scheme have an annual income in excess of £10,000 per annum. And although there are likely to be changes to the light-user scheme in the future, the fact remains that other parts of government can have recourse to economic instruments that are better suited to meeting such objectives (see 'Paying for Social Obligations', below, pp.79-82).

Similar conclusions also follow in respect of special services for the disabled. Here the issue is that special equipment or facilities may be required, thus raising the cost of communicating by telephone. Cost-based pricing could then lead to relatively low penetration rates among the disabled.

To the extent that the problem is one of lack of income, however, the obvious remedy is to increase the resources allocated to the disabled via the social security system. This could either be in cash, leaving individuals to decide whether or not the additional income would be best spent on telecoms services, or, on the basis of the merit goods argument, in kind. In the latter case, vouchers allocated to the disabled, and financed through general taxation as part of a wider redistributive policy, would both enable the beneficiary to exercise choice among competing providers and facilitate monitoring of redistributive policies by those who ultimately pay.

The Costs of Meeting Social Objectives

No matter which public policy body is responsible for determining social objectives, it is important to have good information about the costs of meeting them. As explained above, the definition of what constitutes universal service is one that, in practice, is likely to vary over time. If new services of general interest become available at low cost, or if existing services fall rapidly in price, they may well be adopted as basic services for the purpose of specifying a minimum level of (universal) provision. A danger associated with this flexibility in definition is that services will be included in the basic minimum that are, in fact, expensive to provide and for which very many households would not be willing to pay if charged a price based on the cost of provision.

Recent Oftel studies have estimated that the costs of providing universal service, as currently defined, are relatively modest (less than £100 million, which is small in relation to the total turnover of the industry). There are a number of reasons for believing that this conclusion is broadly correct. For example, in considering whether or not a particular account is uneconomic the following benefits are among those that should be taken into account:

- the revenues from outgoing calls;

- the revenues from incoming calls;

- marketing benefits deriving from the account; and

- avoidance of disconnection and reconnection costs.

In respect of households that are already physically connected to the network, the avoidable costs of connection will tend to be relatively low, implying that even modest benefits may render an account financially attractive. And for new lines the relevant investment calculations should take account of the fact that the wiring-up of premises will potentially generate an income stream that will last for many years into the future. Thus, although the immediate level of revenues might be relatively low, positive returns could accrue from future growth caused by factors such as increasing income or the replacement of a low-volume user by a higher-volume user at the relevant premises.

Growth prospects are particularly important in view of the prospects for using telephone wires for an ever greater number of purposes (for example, video on demand, computer communication, television), and hence for generating a larger income stream. Indeed, given technological advance, connecting a particular household to the network can be seen as opening up potential future demand for a whole range of different services.

This last point is much more than just a theoretical possibility. The bundling together of cable television and telecoms services has led to a situation in which a significant number of the new telecoms accounts of cable-TV operators comprises households that did not previously have a telephone connection. That is, opportunities for more intensive use of the connecting wire have served to increase telephone penetration rates.

One inference that might be drawn from the proposition that the cost of providing something approximating universal service is relatively low is that the industry regulator can impose USOs on BT, and possibly on other telecoms operators, safe in the knowledge that little commercial damage will be inflicted thereby. My own inference would, however, be somewhat different: given the points about the value of connections to the suppliers of telecoms services and about the costs of maintaining existing connections, it is likely that market competition will itself continue to lead to increasing penetration rates, rendering regulation superfluous. Further, given that continued Oftel interest in the level of telecoms penetration risks both the introduction of excessively costly USOs and other, unnecessary regulatory costs, there is a strong case for deregulation in this area.

Paying for Social Obligations

As explained at the outset, the traditional way of dealing with social objectives in general, and with universal service objectives in particular, was to place USOs on an incumbent enterprise that was simultaneously allocated monopoly rights to enable it to sustain the desired cross-subsidies. The approach still persists to some extent in the form of the specific obligations placed upon BT through the company's licence conditions. It is, however, inappropriate in a competitive environment and Oftel has therefore been engaged in the process of searching for alternative methods of implementing and financing policies to meet social objectives. In this last section I will briefly consider some of the alternative ways forward.

Rough Justice

The simplest approach is to impose social obligations on all substantial telecoms operators, and not just on BT, leaving the companies concerned to bear whatever costs are incurred as a result. It is least objectionable when the costs of meeting the social objectives are relatively small, but, since the definition of basic services might possibly be extended to incorporate much more costly options, rough justice has major weaknesses as a general approach to the problem. Moreover, the ability of a telecoms regulator simply to impose social obligations on operators in this way tends to encourage over-regulation, since the regulator is not necessarily held directly accountable for the costs of increasing the stringency of the obligations (costs that may in any case be non-transparent and subject to significant uncertainty).

Interconnect Pricing

Under this approach the costs of meeting USOs are included in charges made for interconnection to a network operator's facilities. In effect, this is the basis of the current arrangements in which the cost of part of BT's USOs is, in principle, shared with other operators through their access deficit contributions (ADCs). As the market develops and as tariff structures change, ADCs will be eliminated, but it would nevertheless be feasible to organise transfers of resources between operators to fund the costs of USOs by means of interconnection agreements.

Although, as noted above, efficient interconnect pricing can reduce externalities and can thereby contribute to greater penetration rates, it is more problematic to use interconnect tariff structures to meet distributional policy objectives. The approach lacks transparency, is likely to be excessively complicated, and would risk the introduction of potentially serious inefficiencies into interconnect pricing.

An Industry Fund

What appears to be the most popular approach to dealing with social obligations in increasingly competitive telecoms markets relies on the establishment of an industry fund, whose revenues would be derived from operators on the basis of some measure of their economic size (variables suggested include market share, gross profits, and net transmission revenues) and which would be used to finance unprofitable activities in the industry.

This option might incorporate *pay or play* options, whereby financial contributions to the fund are made only to the extent that the relevant operator does not contribute to the meeting of social objectives at a level commensurate with its size. It could also encompass *competitive tendering*, whereby certain uneconomic services are defined and competitive bids are invited for the supply of these services.

Such a fund could be administered and managed by Oftel itself or by some new institution, but either way a substantial drawback of the approach is that it leaves most decision-making authority with industry bodies. Choices about the social objectives themselves, the level of finance required to meet them, the means of raising that finance, and the methods of allocating the finance would all be taken by agencies within a general framework that lacks accountability. There would likely be controversies among operators about the divisions of costs and revenues, and the arrangements could become much more complex and costly to administer than is justified by the magnitudes of the underlying problems.

Deregulation

My own favoured solution would be deregulation, by which I mean

- a reduced emphasis on social objectives; and

- the transfer of responsibility for setting and meeting any social objectives that are retained away from Oftel.

Thus, for example, to the extent that it is considered desirable as a matter of public policy to promote certain unprofitable telecoms services among the population or among particular groups of the population, public bodies such as local authorities or the DSS would purchase those services, or would provide others with the means to purchase the services, from telecoms providers (just as they would purchase other goods and services supplied in competitive markets).

To illustrate, the provision of public call boxes in a given locality could be subsidised by the local authority to the extent considered desirable by that body, taking account of alternative uses of local government finance. Similarly, given the policy objective of supporting telecoms facilities for the disabled, subsidies might be provided by the DSS in the form of, say, vouchers that could be used to purchase telecoms services. In both cases, matters would be resolved by means of market transactions in which there would be a genuine purchaser of services exercising choice in a competitive market. This stands in contrast to the industry fund idea, in which choices are made by industry bureaucracies.

Deregulation would place responsibility for social objectives in the hands of parts of government that are concerned with the overall welfare of the relevant groups, and not just welfare derived from the consumption of telecoms services. This would facilitate the proper evaluation of the telecoms policy measures against alternative uses of scarce resources, and would help ensure that the raising of the necessary tax revenues was explicit, transparent, and subject to reasonable accountability.

Conclusions

Social objectives in telecoms, particularly in the form of universal service objectives, have traditionally provided a rationale for regulatory interventions that, among other things, have served to suppress competition and to remove choice from final consumers. Whatever the merits of this approach in the past, when telecoms networks are well developed the suppression of competition is more likely to hinder increased market penetration than to promote it. The reasons for this are that (i) the most powerful factors making for increased penetration, and hence for closer approximations to universal service, are falling real prices and an ever-increasing range of services provided via the network, and (ii) competition is the best means of securing price reductions and encouraging innovative services.

This suggests that the zealous pursuit of social objectives by Oftel is likely to be superfluous, and possibly even counter-productive. Competition and the innovation that it encourages are more likely to increase market penetration and to meet the needs of the poor and the disabled than are bureaucratic and interventionist schemes.

Other arguments also tend to support the view that Oftel should not act as a social policy-making body. An industry-specific regulator is simply not in the best position to determine the most effective overall means of raising revenues and of spending them in ways that contribute maximally to the aggregate level of welfare of particular sections of the community. Nor is the system of regulatory accountability appropriate for monitoring the conduct of what are, in effect, taxation and spending policies. Finally, the allocation of powers in these matters to an industry-specific regulatory body invites excessive intervention via regulatory opportunism: power tends to be used because (i) it is available to be used, and (ii) there will always be groups pressing for it to be used in the furtherance of their own interests.

CHAIRMAN'S COMMENTS

Bill Wigglesworth
Consultant
(formerly Office of Telecommunications)

I STRONGLY AGREE WITH GEORGE YARROW'S CONCLUSION. In the end, I am sure, liberalisation, followed by deregulation and the improved network pricing that will go with it, does provide the best prospect of solving the problems of meeting social objectives at least cost. With telecommunications we are fortunate that developments in modern technology appear likely to allow the achievement of that benign outcome through the creation of a fully competitive market and the process of exploration of the best ways of doing things that results from that.

However, as a practical regulator, there are inevitably differences in approach between us, and these are my main theme.

Constraints and Objectives

To begin with, some general points. The world of telecommunications deregulation as you described it sounded all rather ideal, as though all concerned were unconstrained in the approach they could adopt to the issues at stake. But in practice one finds that there are many constraints.

First, the regulator has a remit laid down in the Telecommunications Act 1984, which can be changed only by amending legislation. That remit reflects the political concerns there were at the time of BT privatisation about ensuring that various social needs would be met by the newly privatised company. So the duties of the Director General include the requirement to ensure that telecommunications services are provided throughout the UK and that those providing can finance them; and to promote the interests of users generally and with particular reference to disabled and elderly people and those living in rural areas.

Second, the network operators' activities are governed by Section 8 of the 1984 Act which, in particular, requires public network operators not to show undue preference to, or exercise undue discrimination against, individual customers or classes of customers, including people in rural areas. Although these provisions are rather general, they do nonetheless inevitably influence the actions of the operators concerned in ways that would not necessarily be the way they would behave in unconstrained market conditions.

The BT licence, the main regulatory document affecting not only the incumbent monopolist but also other network operators, which is in practice only alterable, against the wishes of the licensee, by decision of the Monopolies and Mergers Commission, contains more specific social obligations. These include the universal service obligation, the precise definition of which is in effect left to the Director General to determine; a specific provision prohibiting undue preference and undue discrimination; and various more specific social obligations.

The non-discrimination provision has been interpreted by successive Directors General as embracing the geographic averaging of prices. That is to say, the regulator has served notice that geographic de-averaging would be regarded as entailing undue discrimination against certain users. But the main reason for this has not been so much the original consumer protection intention as the need to prevent anti-competitive behaviour. If the incumbent was able to reduce prices where it faced competition, but to maintain or increase prices where it did not, effective market entry would be made much more difficult. On these grounds the maintenance of geographically averaged prices remains an important element in promoting competition, quite apart from its social benefits for rural customers, and so on.

The regulatory arrangements to which I have been referring represented considerable progress at the time in defining the obligations, on the main network operator in particular, which had previously been concealed in the internal decisions of the nationalised industry and its sponsoring department, with no clear or defined social remit. To that extent they were an advance towards a more rational approach to regulation.

Third, looking at consumer protection issues more generally, there is no way in which these could be entirely ignored. If there was no Oftel then they would be solely a matter for the Office of Fair Trading, instead of being a joint responsibility as at present. We have, in any case, seen a number of important instances of a specific need for consumer protection. For example, Oftel's intervention to require BT to accelerate the provision of itemised billing, as the network was converted to digital operation, in order to ensure that users knew exactly what services they had bought. It also proved necessary for the regulator to apply the principles of 'incentive regulation' to the maintenance and improvement of quality of service as a counterbalance to the pressure to reduce prices. Quality of service had proved too difficult a subject to be dealt with when the BT licence was under discussion with government and the BT licence was therefore silent about it.

Then there is the more general issue of acceptability of the régime. I personally took the view that, for the introduction of competition to be generally acceptable to users, it was necessary, in effect, to deliver a guarantee that there would be no general increase in telecommunications prices in real terms for any significant class of user. In general this has been achieved. The BT low-user scheme and, latterly, its light-user scheme have helped, most recently, by protecting the 20 per cent or so lowest users of BT's network. So that, over the last 10 years, the costs of telecommunication services have declined sufficiently fast for it to be possible to make significant adjustments in relative prices, to bring prices in line with costs, and to bring prices down, on average, by over 40 per cent in real terms, while at the same time ensuring that virtually no users have had to pay more, in real terms, for their services. I would argue that this has played an important part in the popular acceptance of the emergence of a strongly competitive régime in UK telecommunications.

From the practical point of view, perhaps the most important consideration is to ensure regulatory transparency. If everyone is quite clear what the regulator is doing and why, eventually a 'first best' solution is likely to be adopted. An example of this I remember from the past was the approach to Scottish Highlands and Islands aerodromes. A considerable cross-subsidy to support the operation of these aerodromes had originally been effectively hidden in departmental accounts. With the setting up of the Civil Aviation Authority the extent of the cross-subsidy and the source of the funds were made clear. Within eight years it had been decided to adopt the economically correct approach of support from the taxpayer, as part of regional support by the Scottish Office. The important thing was that informed opinion was able to identify the nature of the subsidy and eventually reflect on the best way of providing it.

While on the subject of taxation, I should point out that telephone users are now a rather good proxy for taxpayers generally. Although not universally true, it is roughly the case that the larger taxpayers use telecommunications services more extensively. So, where the regulator considers it unlikely that anything will happen if an identified social need in telecommunications is left to government to finance, it may be more legitimate than would otherwise be the case to seek to ensure that the industry meets the need. A case in point was the Oftel decision in 1992, following extensive public consultation, to require BT to provide funding for the telephone exchange for profoundly deaf people being run by the Royal National Institute for the Deaf (RNID) (known as 'Typetalk') as part of its universal service obligation. Eventually, developed terminals are likely to meet this need much more efficiently. But, until then, BT financial support was judged essential to place this service on a permanently secure footing, since government finance was in practice not available.

Finally, under this general heading, one might ask how far a degree of regulatory intervention in support of social objectives really matters. If the end-point is a fully competitive market, does the odd detour on the way really matter, so long as reasonable progress towards the final objective is maintained? One example that comes to mind is the Government's decision not to impose business separation on BT's apparatus supply business but to allow it to continue to be integrated, in operational terms, in BT's network business. One argument that carried weight at the time, I remember, was that the 'lady up the glen' would not be supplied with telephone equipment economically unless that business could be combined with the provision of telephone service to her. Ten years later we have a fully competitive apparatus market and no one has any difficulty obtaining the telephone equipment they want. In fact, recently, I heard from one particularly successful small firm in this business that the secret of their success was 'never to go into London', where they found the cost of doing business too high. The market has provided effective solutions to social needs, on a more effective basis than they were provided before.

I think one might argue from this that it is better to let the transition from monopoly to competition proceed reasonably smoothly, with minimum disruption to users, rather than trying to adopt too ideal an economic approach at too early a stage.

Externalities, Access Deficit Contributions and Paying for Universal Service

Turning to more specific issues, *first*, I have never been too happy with the discussion on externalities in telecommunications. The lack of origin and destination information on telephone calls is one weakness, since the value of receiving a call is not directly reflected in the pricing arrangements. But that such a value does exist is clear from the rapid development of the 800 series of numbers in the United States, where I understand that over 50 per cent of calls from residential users to commercial users are now paid for by the recipients. The lack of capacity charging and the absence of a 'load factor' in telecommunications charging, in order to reflect the higher cost of handling extra traffic at peak hours, is a further gap, although I agree that commercial pricing in a competitive environment should cover costs (and may perhaps lead to the development of a tariff that reflects capacity costs, if this turns out to be commercially desirable).

Second, in relation to access deficit contributions (ADCs), I think one should be clear about the background. These were essentially a transitional arrangement that was necessary, first, because there was uncertainty about the accounting numbers relating to the 'loss' by BT in providing access in the local network; and, second, because there was concern that prices in conditions of effective competition might be considerably reduced, for example, through the deployment of cost-reduced radio technology in the local loop. It was therefore felt to be preferable to hold the position, through continued control of the rate of rebalancing towards fixed charges, until competition could provide sufficient constraint.

We were, in any case, doubtful about the extent to which arrangements for payment of ADCs would need to be applied before increased competition had created a situation in which the Director General could lift the restriction on the rate of re-balancing of BT's fixed charges, at which time the ADCs arrangements would cease. In practice, indeed, the Director General has judged it appropriate to waive ADCs by new market entrants, with the single exception of part of Mercury's international call revenues which, I think it must be accepted on any analysis, have been extremely profitable. So the actual impact has been limited.

It seems to me that this was a legitimate approach, given the adverse reaction that unconstrained rebalancing might have provoked. But I do acknowledge, of course, that ADCs were a clumsy instrument, which was developed at great speed and which it would have been nice to be able to improve upon. I do very much agree that it has been distressing to see the European Commission expressing the wish to emulate this approach, while we in the UK have been hoping that it will turn out no more than a tiresome temporary expedient, the need for which will soon disappear.

Third, I was pleased to hear that the concept of competitive tendering for the provision of services to meet social objectives was approved in principle. My own inclination has been strongly towards the view that this is probably the best approach where 'public good' services need financial support, for example in areas where the provision of universal service appears non-commercial or in the provision of loss-making rural telephone boxes, and so on. This does seem to me a sensible way to bring the benefits of competition and creative commercial thinking to this area while quantifying the precise extent to which financial support may be necessary. Whether the bill is met from an industry-wide levy or from taxation, as the economists would no doubt advise, is, perhaps, a second order issue.

Finally, on the overall regulatory impact of the cost of universal service, I strongly agree that this has been exaggerated. The absolute numbers are not large and are likely to diminish provided, that is, we are talking about a conventional telephone service. Of course, if we were to indulge in dreams of a universal broadband service, in the absence of overwhelming overall demand, issues of an entirely different order of magnitude would arise; and the creation of a functioning market could be at real risk.

4

COMPETITION AND REGULATION: THE UK EXPERIENCE[1]

John Vickers
All Souls College, University of Oxford

Introduction

IN HIS 1983 REPORT ON PRICE CONTROLS FOR BT, Stephen Littlechild wrote:

> 'Competition is by far the most effective means of protection against monopoly. Vigilance against anti-competitive practices is also important. Profit regulation is merely a "stop-gap" until sufficient competition develops.'[2]

Not only is the 'stop-gap' still with us more than a decade later,[3] but it has grown, and the subject of monopoly price and profit control is now more than ever at the centre of public debate about the utilities. In this paper, however, I want to discuss some policy issues that arise in the transition towards more competitive utility industries. Now that we are in the second decade of their privatisation, it seems to me these questions of competition policy for utility industries are at least as important, difficult and interesting as the ageing chestnut of monopoly price and profit control.

---

[1] This paper is based on joint work with Robin Nuttall, to whom I am indebted. Themes discussed in the lecture are analysed more fully in our paper, Nuttall and Vickers (1996). The research is part of the Competition Policy project at Oxford University funded by ESRC and OFT (grant L114251038) under the ESRC's Contracts and Competition initiative. All views expressed in this paper are entirely my own responsibility, however, and should not be associated with anyone else.

[2] Littlechild (1983, p.1).

[3] See Armstrong, Cowan and Vickers (1994) for an analysis of utility regulation in the UK from 1984-94.

The remarks that follow address five questions:

1. How, if at all, are competition policy problems in the utilities different from those facing competition policy in general?

2. What is the UK framework for competition policy for the utilities? How does it work?

3. In that framework, what is (or should be) meant by the central concept of 'effective competition'?

4. How has policy dealt with major competition problems and cases that have arisen under the headings of

   - divestiture and merger;
   - dominant firm pricing behaviour (in input as well as output markets); and
   - entry barriers and entry assistance?

5. What broad lessons can be drawn from this experience?

I intend to say almost nothing on whether reform to strengthen UK competition law as a whole is desirable. Suffice it to say that some of what follows is 'second-best analysis'.

How Are Competition Policy Problems in Utilities Different?

Competition policy problems in the utilities differ from those facing general competition policy, at least in degree, for three broad reasons.

The *first* is their *history of statutory monopoly*. Unless broken up by structural reforms, privatised utilities have generally inherited dominant positions in relation to consumers and sometimes input suppliers. In the presence of consumer switching costs (and perhaps long-term contracts with input suppliers), inherited dominance is unlikely to be eroded quickly. Protected monopoly also facilitated extensive cross-subsidies – another legacy of the nationalised monopoly era with important implications for competition policy today.

The *second* set of reasons concerns *technology*. Parts of the utility industries remain naturally monopolistic – that is, technology is such that supply by a single firm is cost efficient. Naturally monopolistic activities are often related to activities which, by themselves, are not naturally monopolistic, but which arguably have economies of scope with the former. And at the consumer end, the technology (for example, of metering or numbering) may be such that changing supplier is costly.

Third, there are important *interactions between competition and regulation*:

- they are substitutes insofar as sufficient competition might enable regulation (and its inevitable imperfections) to diminish;

- they are complements insofar as competition can enhance the effectiveness of regulation, for example by reducing asymmetries of information; and

- regulation can distort competition by its effects on the incentives and opportunities of the regulated firms.

I shall return to these broad themes later.

The UK Competition Policy Framework for Utilities[4]

Utilities are subject to (i) general competition law (EU as well as UK), and (ii) competition policy conditions in the licences granted to them under the regulatory statutes.

Competition Law

The Director General of Fair trading (DGFT) can make many (but not all) kinds of monopoly reference to the MMC under the 1973 Fair Trading Act and regulators generally have concurrent powers with the DGFT in respect of their industries. The Secretary of State has wider powers to make monopoly references (this greater width was needed to make the 1992 gas reference). If the MMC finds that a monopoly situation operates against the public interest, it will recommend remedies, but these are for the Secretary of State to decide. Decisions whether to refer (non-water) mergers to the MMC, and decisions on action following adverse public interest findings by the MMC, also lie with the Secretary of State. He need not follow the advice of regulators or the DGFT on referrals, or MMC recommendations to stop or attach conditions to mergers. The 1991 Water Industry Act obliges the Secretary of State to refer substantial mergers in that industry, and requires the MMC to consider whether merger would deprive the regulator of valuable comparative performance information. Anti-

---

4   See Freeman and Whish (eds.) (1991-95) for an authoritative and detailed coverage of the legal framework.

competitive practices may be referred to the MMC by the DGFT, with regulators having concurrent powers in their industries, under the 1980 Competition Act.

Structure of Regulated Industries

Before considering the regulatory statutes it is important to note that the Government took major competition policy decisions for the utilities when determining their structures before privatisation. The contrast between the mid-1980s privatisations of BT and British Gas, which eschewed structural reform, and the 1990s privatisations of electricity and rail, which entail forms of vertical, horizontal and regional restructuring, is striking. In the former cases, regulation of dominant firm conduct has sought to simulate restructuring *ex post*.

Regulatory Acts – Duties

The Secretary of State and industry regulators have primary duties to secure that reasonable demands are met and that operators can finance their activities. In electricity and in gas (since 1992), the promotion of effective competition is also a primary duty. There are various further duties, including the important duty to maintain and promote effective competition in telecommunications.

Granting Licences

Liberalisation policy is ultimately determined by government. Licences are granted by the Secretary of State after consultation with the regulator, or by the regulator with the authorisation of the Secretary of State. The extent of liberalisation has grown over time, landmarks being the 1991 ending of the telecoms duopoly policy and the phased reductions in the scope of monopoly over electricity and gas customers (legislation being required for the latter).

Competition Conditions in Licences

The utilities have various licence conditions relating to competition policy and its enforcement, for example concerning:

- separate accounts for separate businesses;

- prohibition of undue discrimination;

- prohibition of cross-subsidy;

- prohibition of some types of anti-competitive practice;

- access charges and interconnection arrangements.

Other licence conditions – for example, price controls and universal service obligations – can also have important implications for competition policy. Oftel (1995) has recently proposed a licence condition containing a general prohibition on anti-competitive behaviour by dominant (or colluding) telecommunications operators, and the associated deletion of a number of detailed conditions in BT's licence.

Modifying Licences

As well as having to monitor and enforce licence conditions, the regulator may seek to modify them. This can be done either by agreement with the licensee or after a successful reference to the MMC. Some price control references have been made to the MMC in water, electricity and gas, but the only licence modification case concerning competition so far is the 1995 number portability case in telecommunications. Competition conditions in licences have otherwise been modified or introduced without the need for referral to the MMC.

What is Effective Competition?

Regulators – and indeed Parliament in revising legislation – have tended to stress the objective of effective competition in policy towards the utilities. More generally, it is the element of the 'public interest' (as described in the 1973 Fair Trading Act) to which the MMC has most regard. It is important to be clear what is meant by 'effective competition', and I would suggest the following.

Competition is rivalry between two or more parties for something that cannot be obtained by all.[5] To be 'effective', the rivalry must be real – not token or sham or one-sided. It must exert a strong influence upon the behaviour of all firms. But even vigorous rivalry is not enough for effective competition. The rivalry must also tend to promote economic efficiency – which it does by aligning prices with costs, by increasing pressures for cost reduction, by selecting more efficient firms from less efficient firms, by promoting innovation, and

---

[5] See Vickers (1995) for a fuller analysis of the various meanings of the term 'competition', and its economic consequences.

(important in our context) by diminishing the inevitable imperfections of regulation.

Competition is not an end in itself. Promoting economic efficiency is what effective competition is effective at doing. In short: effective competition is rivalry that promotes economic efficiency.

In much of the economy, effective competition is naturally self-sustaining. The history and technology of the utilities, however, make effective competition difficult, and sometimes impossible, to achieve. Effective competition is a logical impossibility in severe natural monopoly conditions (though there is sometimes the possibility of competition *for* the market). Where competition would promote efficiency, it might be thwarted by barriers to entry or anti-competitive behaviour by the dominant incumbent. On the other hand, there is the possibility of inefficient competition ('cream-skimming' and so on) if regulation has distorting effects. Thus, even outside the natural monopoly elements of the utility industries, there are dangers that competition might be either non-existent or inefficient. Even if equipped with adequate powers, the utility regulator following his or her duty to promote effective – that is, real and efficiency-enhancing – competition faces no easy task.

Competition Policy Questions in the Utilities

This section considers three aspects of competition policy in the utilities – divestiture and merger policy, dominant firm pricing behaviour, and entry barriers and entry assistance.

Divestiture and Merger Policy

Structural policy has three dimensions – horizontal, vertical and regional. In (otherwise) unregulated industries, horizontal mergers can reduce competition; on the other hand, they might have scale economy benefits. Vertical mergers can lead to a distortion of competition, with consequent inefficiencies, at one level of production if there is some market power at the other; but they might bring scope economy benefits; and conversely for demergers.

How does the presence of regulation affect these arguments? To address this question we need to consider the sources of regulatory 'failure' – asymmetric information, limited commitment powers, and vulnerability to capture.

Insofar as competition and regulation are substitutes, regulatory failures, which inevitably exist, justify some extra caution about horizontal merger. It might be worth tolerating a marginal sacrifice of scale economies if that avoids direct and indirect costs of regulation. This point becomes stronger when conduct regulation – for example, to check abuse of market power, and so on – is of questionable effectiveness. There are also some complementarities between policies – competition, by providing comparative performance information, can improve the effectiveness of regulation where it is still needed. It helps bridge the asymmetric information gap.

The conclusion that regulatory imperfections tend to weigh against merger, or in favour of divestiture, seems to apply in the vertical case too. A vertically integrated firm that dominates one level of production has an obvious profit incentive to distort downstream competition by raising rivals' costs and discriminating in favour of its own downstream unit. With vertical separation, on the other hand, the playing field is automatically level. If conduct regulation were perfect and costless, the anti-competitive behaviour problem could be solved without resort to structural remedies. But generally it is not so. In practice, it is virtually impossible to avoid the playing field tilting one way or the other, and inefficiency follows. Half-way measures such as 'internal separation' might alleviate the problem somewhat, but not totally, and they might sometimes jeopardise the economies of scope that were the justification for integration.

A further problem arises if the downstream unit is allowed to pass its input costs through to consumers. Vertical integration then undermines cost-reduction incentives and makes it attractive to acquire overpriced supplies from the upstream unit. Obliging the downstream unit to purchase economically might or might not overcome this problem. Again, the principle holds that imperfect conduct regulation strengthens the case for structure regulation.

Regional separation has merit insofar as it yields valuable comparative performance information for regulation. Conversely, conglomerate mergers and diversification by utilities have the danger that information relevant for regulation is lost or deteriorates in quality (for example, share prices become less informative about regulated activities). It does not follow that such mergers should be prevented – after all, we have seen how helpfully *informative* takeover bids for utilities can be – but there is a good case for making them conditional on the utility businesses continuing to be separately listed companies. Thus the acquiring firm would have a majority of the shares, and hence control, of the utility, but a minority of its shares would be independently owned and the utility's shares would still be traded on the stock market. The advantage of this proposal is that it would avoid the information loss that normally results from merger. It may be objected that minority interests are vulnerable to exploitation by the majority owner – for example, via cross-subsidy. But regulation is supposed to stop that in any event, and its effectiveness in doing so might be enhanced by the private incentive that minority interests have to prevent exploitation.

At the time of their privatisations, BT and British Gas remained intact as integrated nationwide firms, separate regional water companies were floated, and the electricity supply industry experienced measures of horizontal, vertical and regional separation (ditto rail). The gas industry has shown most clearly the problems that can arise with vertical integration. The limited effectiveness of attempts by the MMC (1988), Ofgas and OFT to reconcile competition with vertical integration – even including the rather blunt instrument of market share quotas – led the MMC in 1993 to declare that British Gas's dual rôle as both supplier and transporter

> 'gives rise to an inherent conflict of interest which makes it impossible to provide the necessary conditions for self-sustaining competition'.[6]

It remains to be seen whether the current measures of internal separation will overcome this problem.[7] Be that as it may, I think there is a persuasive case that the public interest – and quite possibly the commercial interests of British Gas – would have been better served by vertical separation before privatisation. The benefit of hindsight reinforces, but was perhaps not necessary to reach this conclusion.

Separation did happen in electricity, despite the fact that it was technically more difficult than it would have been in gas. I believe that this was broadly the right policy, but its implementation has been flawed. *First*, horizontal separation did not go far enough. In the circumstances of the industry, the duopoly policy for generation, which became a triopoly policy once the nuclear stations were withdrawn from privatisation, was not consistent with the theory of competitive bidding that justified the efficiency properties of the pool.[8] As a result, more regulation of generation has been required than would have been

---

6   MMC (1993, para. 1.6).

7   Not so! In February 1996 (after this paper was written), British Gas announced a proposal for complete separation between its transportation and trading activities in the Spring of 1997.

8   Green and Newbery (1992).

necessary. Perhaps more entry has resulted too, which might or might not be a good thing. Perhaps regrettably, the English/Welsh and Scottish nuclear companies are to be horizontally merged for privatisation.

Second, and partly to promote more competition in generation, considerable vertical integration – notably between RECs and 'independent' generators – was allowed after all, despite cost pass-through provisions. An important issue here is how effectively economic purchasing obligations can be monitored and enforced. The takeover bids for RECs by National Power and PowerGen threaten to undermine vertical separation rather more comprehensively. The MMC investigation of these bids should consider whether interactions with regulation, as well as horizontal concentration, give rise to public interest concerns about vertical integration.[9]

The key aspect of structural policy in the water industry is regional. The legislation explicitly recognises the danger that intra-industry mergers might reduce the effectiveness of regulation by diminishing comparative performance information (and referral to the MMC is non-discretionary, as perhaps it should be for some other kinds of utility merger). Conglomerate mergers can also worsen information quality – a problem which the separate listing proposal might ameliorate. The policy approach in some cases (for instance, the 1995 takeover of Northumbian Water by Lyonnaise des Eaux) has been to clear water mergers subject to price reduction conditions. A problem facing merger control, like other kinds of regulation, is the asymmetric information disadvantage of the regulator(s) relative to the commercial parties (despite which the onus of proof in the UK is pro-merger). It is therefore difficult to judge whether synergy benefits outweigh possible detriments to the effectiveness of competition or regulation. Making clearance conditional on a payment by the firms to consumers – for which price regulation is a handy vehicle – has the effect of putting purported synergy benefits to at least some sort of commercial test.

In telecoms, like gas (but unlike AT&T in the United States), restructuring was not pursued at the time of privatisation. It has been partially simulated more recently, however, and BT may not broadcast entertainment to homes over its telecoms network. The main

---

[9] Editor's note: The MMC recommended approval of these bids but the President of the Board of Trade vetoed them. (See Colin Robinson, 'Profit, Discovery and the Rôle of Entry: The Case of Electricity', below, Chapter 5, pp.109-140.)

competition policy issues in telecoms have concerned conduct, not structure, regulation.

Dominant Firm Pricing Behaviour

The general *level* of utility prices is constrained by price cap regulation. The *structure* of prices – that is, price relativities – depends on several factors, including (i) the pattern inherited from the nationalised era, (ii) incentives arising from the nature of the regulated price index, and (iii) regulatory constraints such as controls on the rate of 'rebalancing' and undue discrimination conditions in licences.

Under nationalisation, relative prices sometimes became considerably out of line with relative costs. Given the need to finance fixed costs, Ramsey optimal prices would not generally imply equal mark-ups – that is, that price ratios should equal incremental cost ratios – but Ramsey pricing is not a plausible explanation of the pricing patterns that existed. Rather, they came about chiefly for two reasons. The first is inertia. For example, in telecoms the cost of calls (especially long-distance) was falling sharply relative to that of local access, but before the mid-1980s relative prices did not adjust correspondingly. Economic forces were held at bay by monopoly protection, and given the pattern of business/residential usage, there was no political incentive for rebalancing. This leads to the second factor – cross-subsidy – which in some cases was a conscious policy decision (as with geographically uniform pricing), and in other cases arose by default as demand and supply conditions evolved. Again, it should be noted that, in the absence of explicit taxes and subsidies, market power is necessary to sustain cross-subsidy.

Tensions between (implicit) subsidy policy and competition policy have been important in several industries. Uniform nationwide pricing constrains liberalisation of the letter post. Implicit subsidies to coal evaporated in 1992-93 as competition developed in the electricity industry. And rebalancing by BT has been contentious for a decade.

There are conflicting worries in the latter case. First, BT might have incentives to 'rebalance' beyond the point justified by cost movements in order to thwart emerging competition, especially if regulation works so that a price cut in a competitive market can be partly recouped by a price rise in a captive market. On the other hand, BT might be constrained by regulation from rebalancing that would in practice be economically efficient, with the result that inefficient entry might occur. These points have been central to debates (academic as well as commercial) on the interconnection pricing question, which concerns the prices BT charges rivals for a key *input* (local access) that it has monopolised in the past.

Baumol and Willig argue for the so-called efficient component pricing rule (ECPR),[10] which seems at first sight to be cost-based and to avoid the need for elasticity information. But Laffont and Tirole (1994) show the optimality of extended Ramsey pricing (possibly adjusted for effort incentive effects), in which elasticities are prominent. Armstrong, Doyle and Vickers (1995) claim that the ECPR and Ramsey approaches are fundamentally very similar provided the notion of 'opportunity cost' in the ECPR is properly analysed. In particular, the ECPR does require elasticity information except in simple special cases (which tend to be used to explain the ECPR).

Finally, it should be noted that all the analytical approaches just mentioned are essentially static and ahistorical. But the dynamic properties of competition against a background of inherited monopoly should, one would think, be central to the debate. How should these properties be analysed? How should they influence policy decisions? The answer to the first of these questions is unclear. I believe – not as an act of Austrian faith but on grounds of British casual empiricism – that the dynamic process of competition has immensely valuable incentive properties (provided it is not distorted), but these have not yet been satisfactorily captured by economic theory.

Nevertheless, cross-subsidy policies are a poor way to promote whatever dynamic benefits competition may bring. *First*, the entry assistance that cross-subsidy may bring to the implicitly taxed activity means entry hindrance in the implicitly subsidised activity. *Second*, implicit cross-subsidy policies are prone to error and lobbying, both of which entail considerable resource costs. *Third*, taxes and subsidies should and can be explicit, and hence neutral for competition. *Fourth*, subject to availability, other instruments (for example, levies to finance universal service obligations) are usually better ways of promoting effective competition.

Entry Barriers and Entry Assistance

By 1998 virtually all *legal* barriers to entry into utility industry activities that are not naturally monopolistic will have been removed. Experience has taught, however, that legalisation of entry is by no means sufficient for effective liberalisation, since numerous *economic*

---

[10] For a summary of this view see, for example, Baumol and Sidak (1994).

barriers to entry may remain. Where these involve access to network services whose supply is naturally monopolistic, separation policies have attractions. But there are other important sources of barriers to entry.

As domestic liberalisation advances, possible barriers arising from what may be termed 'privileged access to consumers' are especially topical. Consumer switching costs – that is, the costs to consumers of changing their supplier – are a feature of many industries. However, the utilities differ from unregulated industries in at least two respects.

First, some incumbent advantage arising from switching costs might be a legitimate reward for innovation, for example in the computer industry. But the privatised utilities' incumbent positions are primarily the result of history, not Schumpeterian victory in the innovative struggle.

Second, price regulation affects switching cost analysis. On the other hand, part of the eventual aim of liberalisation is presumably to withdraw regulation, and the consequences of switching costs for efficiency – for instance, by selecting between firms of differing efficiency – are likely to matter in any event.

The policy problem is that consumer switching costs cannot be removed without some cost. The installation of adequate metering is not free, and neither is number portability in telecoms. Portability allows users to retain their numbers when changing operator (at a fixed address). BT having rejected Oftel's proposals for allocating the costs of portability between operators, the matter was referred to the MMC. The MMC (1995) reported that portability was necessary to promote effective competition and that its continued absence was against the public interest. It proposed an amendment to BT's licence that would allow BT to recover from other operators only a proportion of its costs of providing portability.

Finally, I want to comment briefly on another possible source of barrier to entry – prospective or actual anti-competitive behaviour by a dominant incumbent. It is here that the question of the effectiveness of UK competition policy inevitably arises. The basic issue is whether anti-competitive behaviour is deterred or, failing that, whether it can be stopped in its tracks. (I cannot see, by the way, why this issue is sometimes linked with institutional matters such as whether the OFT and the MMC should merge.) Some might argue that this is a non-problem – that we should not worry since the incentive and opportunity for anti-competitive conduct rarely arise. I think that such an argument is wrong in general, and especially so in the utility industries, where there would surely be ample incentive and opportunity for anti-competitive behaviour in the absence of policy intervention.

The question is what form that intervention should take. In some respects regulation (price controls, and so on) and competition policy are substitutes. In parts of the utility industries it would seem desirable over the next decade to shift, at least at the margin, from regulation towards competition policy. But UK competition law does not have the deterrent or preventative attributes that one might wish for. An unfortunate consequence of this rather light-handed approach to competition policy is that the heavier hand of regulation may have to stay in place for longer than would otherwise be necessary. Or that structure regulation – that is, a break-up of the dominant incumbent – might be called for to remedy shortcomings of regulation of anti-competitive conduct.

There are two escape routes from this impasse. One is reform of UK competition law as a whole. The other, which Oftel (1995) is proposing for telecommunications, is to introduce a licence condition that generally prohibits dominant firm (or collusive) behaviour that has the object or effect of preventing, restricting or distorting competition in the industry.

Both these routes raise legal and institutional questions on which I do not wish to comment here. But two basic economic points seem worth repeated emphasis. *First*, the incentive to engage in anti-competitive conduct depends on the probability of being found out, the delay in being told to desist if discovered, and the penalty for conviction. UK competition policy is not strong on these fronts. *Second*, insofar as the two policy approaches are substitutes, weak competition policy means more regulation, and possibly more structure regulation, than stronger competition policy would allow. As things stand, therefore, the withdrawal of regulation might be subject to delay.

Conclusions

The first decade of utility privatisation has been one of managed competition – managed by entry restrictions, market share limits, and so on. It is an open question whether the second decade will see the development of effective, self-sustaining competition. What are the main lessons for competition policy from the first decade? What policies henceforth would best promote the prospects for effective competition in parts of the utilities?

Here are five suggested lessons from the past:

1. The inevitable imperfections of conduct regulation create a strong argument for restructuring – that is, divesting ownership of separable natural monopoly networks. For reasons of regulatory risk, restructuring is best done before privatisation.

2. Making competitive entry legal does not make it effective. Accompanying competition policy to deter and to stop anti-competitive behaviour is required.

3. Regulatory policy (or the lack of it) towards pricing structure can seriously distort competition. Perversely, regulation can encourage anti-competitive behaviour. On the other hand, it can prevent pro-competitive behaviour by the incumbent.

4. Cross-subsidy policies and effective competition are generally in conflict. Sustaining cross-subsidy means limiting competition and/or the risk of inefficient competition.

5. Market shares, being endogenous and unpredictable in a properly functioning competitive market, are a dubious target for policy purposes.

And here are five suggestions for the future:

1. Be clear that effective competition means competition that is efficiency-enhancing as well as real. It is not to be equated with the interests of competitors, though positive externalities that they bring – for example, by lessening the need for monopoly regulation – should not be ignored.

2. Maintain a (rebuttable) presumption in favour of structural separation of natural monopoly elements – if not by divestiture then at least by merger control.

3. In the absence of structural separation, seek to decouple regulation of monopolised and competitive activities so that behaviour in the latter is not distorted by incentives arising from the former.

4. In particular, separate subsidy policy, which should be explicit in any event, from competition policy.

5. Establish a competition policy framework – for the utilities if not more generally – that unearths, deters and prevents dominant firm conduct that might undermine effective competition.

It would be a shame if, unnecessarily, regulation became a permanent stop-gap.

References

Armstrong, M., S. Cowan, and J. Vickers (1994): *Regulatory Reform: Economic Analysis and British Experience*, Cambridge, MA: MIT Press.

Armstrong, M., C. Doyle, and J. Vickers (1995): 'The access pricing problem: a synthesis', *Journal of Industrial Economics*, forthcoming.

Baumol, W., and J.G. Sidak (1994): *Toward Competition in Local Telephony*, Cambridge, MA: MIT Press.

Freeman, P., and R. Whish (eds.) (1991-1995): *Butterworths Competition Law*, London: Butterworths.

Green, R., and D. Newbery (1992): 'Competition in the British electricity spot market', *Journal of Political Economy*, Vol.100(5), pp.929-53.

Laffont, J.-J., and J. Tirole (1994): 'Access pricing and competition', *European Economic Review*, Vol.38, pp.1,673-1,710.

Littlechild, S. (1983): *Regulation of British Telecommunications' Profitability*, London: HMSO.

Monopolies and Mergers Commission (1988): *Gas*, Cm.500, London: HMSO.

Monopolies and Mergers Commission (1993): *Gas: Volume 1 of reports under the Fair Trading Act 1973*, Cm.2314, London: HMSO.

Monopolies and Mergers Commission (1995): *Telephone Number Portability*, London: HMSO.

Nuttall, R., and J. Vickers (1996): 'Competition Policy in Regulated Utility Industries in Britain', Institute of Economics and Statistics Discussion Paper No.178, University of Oxford.

Oftel (1995): *Fair Trading in Telecommunications*, London: Oftel.

Vickers, J. (1995): 'Concepts of Competition', *Oxford Economic Papers*, Vol.47, pp.1-23.

CHAIRMAN'S COMMENTS

Graeme Odgers
Monopolies and Mergers Commission

WHEN I WAS MANAGING DIRECTOR AT TARMAC DURING THE 1980s and my firm was competing for a big road, airport or other contract, I used to dream about doing my competitors in – Costain, McAlpine, Laing or whomever. I will not describe the methods used. Some years later when I was Managing Director of British Telecom I used to dream, not about doing Mercury or AT & T in, but of doing Bryan Carsberg in! Once again I will not describe the method.

This dreaming experience leads me to conclude that in some measure at least regulation was working – it was acting as an effective substitute for competition. Bryan Carsberg was doing two particular things that produced my nocturnal response:

- He was insisting on BT charging what seemed to me at the time unreasonably low prices – the formula was RPI-3½, RPI-4½ – later on it even moved to RPI-7½.

- He appeared to me to be tipping the playing field unduly in favour of Mercury so that that company was creaming off our most profitable business – our large business customers.

What caused me so much anxiety at the time was that, while Bryan was making these demands on us, BT was facing up to huge problems:

- An annual £4 billion investment programme – in digital exchanges, optical fibre networks, mobile networks, and so on.

- Major trade union and employee problems.

- Quality of management problems.

- Customer relations problems.

- Governmental pressures – we were the flagship of privatisation.

In the face of these pressures you can understand why it was that Bryan Carsberg's squeeze led me to dream of doing him in!

Looking back now from an external perspective, I regard the privatisation of BT as a triumph. The company still has many faults and I doubt that it will ever be loved. There continue to be difficulties with the regulator. But:

- BT is delivering a quality service;
- compared to a decade ago, prices represent value for money;
- there is a strong infrastructure;
- management is competent;
- the company is a world player in terms of efficiency, strategic presence, international competitiveness.

So one asks the question: Has *regulation* been successful in the case of BT? Has it delivered the goods? At the same time it is relevant to ask: What of competition over that period since privatisation? The answer to this latter question must be: 'There has been some competition and it is growing, but in the broad sense it is still inadequate. BT has remained dominant.'

I would like to go back to what John Vickers was saying about effective competition. He said that competition is rivalry between two or more parties for something that cannot be obtained by all. To be 'effective', the rivalry must be real. It must exert a strong influence upon the behaviour of all firms. But even vigorous rivalry is not enough for *effective* competition. The rivalry must also promote economic efficiency. Competition is not an end in itself. Promoting economic efficiency is what effective competition is effective at doing. In short: effective competition is rivalry that promotes economic efficiency.

The objective clearly is economic efficiency: in the case of BT there is not yet effective rivalry across the board. Yet despite this, I think one could say that there has been real promotion of economic efficiency.

I do not have comparable direct experience of other utilities. But I suspect that to some degree what has happened in telecoms has also happened in most other privatised utilities. There have been major improvements in efficiency, major improvements in competitiveness, despite a lack of meaningful rivalry between companies. So regulation has delivered *some* goods. John Vickers is implying: 'Not enough. It could have been better.' He is making suggestions for the future, so let us debate them.

5

PROFIT, DISCOVERY AND THE RÔLE OF ENTRY: THE CASE OF ELECTRICITY

Colin Robinson
University of Surrey;
Institute of Economic Affairs

Introduction

THERE ARE THREE KEY WORDS IN THE TITLE OF THIS PAPER – profit, discovery and entry – and I will add a fourth key idea – government failure. My argument will be that in electricity, as in other privatisations, a good idea has been very imperfectly executed[1] so that competitive forces have been constrained by government failure. Thus opportunities to bring early benefits to consumers through a competitive process have been neglected. Nevertheless, some economic benefits have been realised and more are in prospect if politicians can restrain themselves from interfering as the market evolves.

Because memories are so short, I begin by reviewing the problems which existed under state ownership before 1990. The paper then discusses the characteristics of the privatised electricity market before moving on to the difficulties which have arisen in regulation. Next it discusses the benefits of electricity privatisation. Finally, it draws some conclusions and looks ahead to whether we can expect increasing liberalisation, or whether there will be a reversion to political interference either from the British government or from Brussels.

A Reminder about Nationalisation

Nationalisation in 1947 continued a trend towards increasing government control of the electricity supply industry, originating in its

---

[1] Colin Robinson, 'Privatising the Energy Industries: The Lessons to be Learned', *Metroeconomica*, Vol.XLIII, Nos.1-2, February-June 1992.

early days in the 19th century. Regulation by government tightened in the interwar years, as it did in other British industries. By the time of the first post-war Attlee government, it seemed a small step to full-scale state ownership and there was widespread agreement that electricity, like other 'commanding heights', should be nationalised.[2]

After several minor re-organisations, the Electricity Act of 1957 established a structure in which the Central Electricity Generating Board (CEGB) – responsible for bulk transmission as well as generation and in control of most of the industry's investment – was the dominant force. Twelve Area Boards took electricity from the CEGB's bulk supply points, then distributed and supplied it within their designated areas. An Electricity Council, consisting of three representatives of the CEGB, the 12 Area Board Chairmen and six independent members appointed by the Minister, had somewhat vague policy-making functions.

In Scotland, two vertically integrated boards – the South of Scotland Electricity Board (SSEB) and the (smaller) North of Scotland Hydro Electric Board (NSHEB) – generated, transported and supplied electricity to consumers in their respective areas.

In common with other British nationalised industries, electricity was beset with the problems inherent when competition is absent both from the product market and the capital market and when decisions are politicised. Essentially, those problems were as follows:

- Because entry to the industry was prohibited, consumers lacked the power of exit. Consequently the corporations in the industry had little incentive to take consumers' interests into account.

- Because the industry was outside the market for corporate control, there was no takeover threat to stimulate efficiency improvements. The ultimate 'owners' of the business were members of the voting public with no transferable property rights.

- The industry's monopoly in the product market translated into considerable bargaining power for its unions which appeared to secure very favourable arrangements for their members.

- The politicisation of decision-making meant that managerial objectives were confused by uncertainty over whether 'commercial'

---

[2] The history of British electricity supply up to the late-1960s is described in R. Kelf-Cohen, *Twenty Years of Nationalisation: The British Experience*, London: Macmillan, 1969, Chap.4.

or 'public service' objectives should be given priority. Both investment programmes and prices were influenced (and at times controlled) by governments with short time-horizons. For example, in the 1970s, a Labour Government persuaded the industry to hold down its prices in an effort to reduce the general rate of consumer price inflation; in the 1980s, a Conservative Government made the industry increase prices to reduce public borrowing.

A succession of White Papers on the nationalised industries (in 1961, 1967 and 1978), which dealt with economic and financial targets and relations with government, did little to help.[3] Well-meaning pronouncements, such as those in the 1967 White Paper – the injunction to price on the basis of long-run marginal cost and to adopt test rates of discount similar to those used for low-risk private sector projects – were over-ridden by the political calculus, by a lack of will in the nationalised corporations and by the practical difficulties of applying such concepts.

Moreover, to governments which believed in 'industrial' and 'energy' policies, the temptation to use one nationalised energy industry to prop up others was just too much to resist. Because the own-price elasticity of demand for electricity is very low, the industry is potentially a substantial revenue raiser for government. Instead of taxing electricity openly (which would have been very unpopular, as the recent fuss about VAT on fuel demonstrates), governments manipulated the industry's choices of inputs such as fuels and equipment; electricity costs therefore increased and the costs of protection fell on electricity consumers as well as taxpayers.

Hence the electricity supply industry became the principal support system for the nationalised British coal industry.[4] From 1957 onwards, as British coalmining went into decline, governments began to shelter the industry from competition: the dominant method of protection came to be government pressure on the nationalised electricity industry to burn more coal than it would freely have chosen. From 1979 onwards, previous arrangements were formalised into a series of government-

---

[3] David Heald, 'The Economic and Financial Control of UK Nationalised Industries', *Economic Journal*, Vol.90, No.358, June 1980.

[4] Colin Robinson and Eileen Marshall, *Can Coal Be Saved?*, Hobart Paper No.105, London: Institute of Economic Affairs, 1985; Colin Robinson, 'Coal Policy in Britain', *Economic Review*, March 1985, and *Energy Trends and the Development of Energy Policy in the United Kingdom*, Surrey Energy Economics Discussion Papers No.61, February 1992.

brokered 'Joint Understandings' under which the nationalised electricity supply industry agreed to take nearly all its coal (at that time almost 90 million tonnes a year) from the nationalised coal industry.

The electricity supply industry was also used to support two programmes of British-designed nuclear power stations, the first (Magnox reactors) beginning in 1955 and the second (Advanced Gas Cooled Reactors) beginning in 1965. It provided more general support for British industry, for example through its 'Buy British' policy for generating plant. Under nationalisation, the electricity industry was not so much a commercial enterprise as an instrument of government energy policy and government industrial policy.[5]

The Electricity Privatisation Scheme

It was this heavily-politicised régime – subsequently revealed, not surprisingly, to be grossly inefficient – which the privatised market replaced. In outline, the changes in England and Wales on privatisation were as follows:[6]

- Generation and transmission were separated, despite dire warnings from the CEGB about the economic and technical consequences of doing so. The separation was not quite 'clean' because two pumped storage plants were left in the National Grid Company – they were divested as First Hydro and purchased by Mission Energy of the USA in December 1995.

- The generation side of the CEGB was divided into two fossil fuel generators. Nuclear plant, after a failed attempt in 1989 to privatise, went into two state-owned nuclear companies (one in Scotland), both now due for privatisation. Protective arrangements for nuclear were made, originally up to 1998.

- The 12 Area Boards were turned into 12 RECs, distributing and supplying electricity.

- To permit competition in supply to develop, the captive market of the RECs was to be reduced by stages up to April 1998 when all consumers would be allowed to choose their supplier.

---

[5] Colin Robinson, 'Liberalising the Energy Industries', *Proceedings of the Manchester Statistical Society*, March 1988.

[6] *Privatising Electricity*, Cm.322, London: HMSO, February 1988. See also *Privatisation of the Scottish Electricity Industry*, Cm.327, London: HMSO, March 1988.

- An independent regulatory office was established, whose Director General had, *inter alia*, a clearly-specified duty (shared with the Secretary of State) '...to promote competition in the generation and supply of electricity'. Price regulation was by an RPI-X mechanism with the initial values of X set by government.

The privatisation scheme for Scotland entailed less disturbance of pre-existing arrangements than in England and Wales. Two vertically-integrated private companies were established, one (Scottish Power) based on the SSEB and the other (Hydro Electric) based on the NSHEB. The nuclear stations built by the SSEB were transferred to Scottish Nuclear and their output was protected under a Nuclear Energy Agreement, originally due to last until 2005.

Differences from Nationalisation

In addition to the structural changes at the time of privatisation, the privatised electricity market differs from the nationalised industry in three fundamental respects:[7]

- entry is now permitted to both the generation and supply businesses whereas previously it was prohibited by the state;

- the electricity companies have private shareholders, instead of being owned by government;

- regulation is by an independent body with a duty to promote competition instead of being conducted behind closed doors, with unclear rules, by politicians, civil servants and industry managers.

In principle, such changes should be beneficial. Actual and threatened entry should bring increased rivalry in generation and supply, leading to increased efficiency pressures and lower costs which, in a competitive market, would be passed on to consumers in the form of reduced prices and better standards of service. Entry into the market for corporate control should also enhance efficiency pressures and reduce the incentives which existed under nationalisation to concentrate resources on political lobbying: the industry's decisions about which fuels to use, which investments to make, whether to purchase British or overseas equipment and services and what prices to charge should no

---

[7] Characteristics of the privatised market are explained in John Vickers and George Yarrow, 'The British Electricity Experiment', *Economic Policy*, April 1991.

longer be subject to government influence. Regulation should be confined to natural monopoly networks and based on clearly defined rules.

Plainly, however, the present electricity market falls well short of the idealised picture I have just sketched.

Government Failure and Electricity Privatisation

Competition was bound to take time to find roots in the British electricity market. After all, the industry had been nationalised for over 40 years and, before that, was supervised by government. Competitive habits have to be formed and market participants have to learn to substitute contractual relationships for the old co-operative relationships within firms.

However, the reason why many of the potential beneficial results of privatisation and market liberalisation are so far unrealised is not just that insufficient time has elapsed. The underlying problem is government failure to establish at the time of privatisation conditions in which a competitive process would flourish and in which regulation would be confined to networks which, given present technology, are 'naturally monopolistic'.[8] The main elements of government failure are analysed below.

Generation

Market Power

Whatever the privatisation scheme, incumbent generators would have had some advantages over entrants. In addition to the usual 'advantage' of having plant with sunk costs, they possessed sites linked into the transmission and distribution systems; moreover, as descendants of the nationalised industry they could take advantage of that industry's near-monopoly of information about all matters relating to electricity generation in Britain.[9]

---

[8] Colin Robinson, *Energy Policy: Errors, Illusions and Market Realities*, Occasional Paper No.90, London: Institute of Economic Affairs, 1993.

[9] Colin Robinson and Allen Sykes, 'Privatising Electricity Supply', Memorandum 48 in *The Structure, Regulation and Economic Consequences of Electricity Supply in the Private Sector*, Third Report of the House of Commons Energy Committee, Session 1987-88, HC307-II, London: HMSO, 1988, and Colin Robinson, Memorandum, in *Consequences of Electricity Privatisation*, Report of the House of Commons Energy Committee, Session 1991-92, HC 113-III, London: HMSO, 1992. The significance of information monopolies is discussed in

But the duopoly structure of generation gave considerable additional power to the two major generators. Though the own-price elasticity of demand for electricity is low, since the product is homogeneous the price elasticity of demand for the product of any generator is very high. Producers have an incentive to take advantage of the inelasticity of the market demand curve by suppressing competition among themselves. With only a few producers (National Power, PowerGen and later Nuclear Electric), one would expect that initially there would be fairly muted competition but that competitive forces would strengthen as entry occurred.

Entry and Constraints on Competition

Given that entry to the market was freed, the initial structure might thus appear of only transient importance: duopoly power would seem unlikely to persist because of a Schumpeterian gale of creative destruction[10] in the course of which entrants, attracted by the profits of incumbents, would compete away those profits to the benefit of consumers. But a number of severe constraints on competition have so far shielded the major generators from the rivalry of entrants. Some of these constraints are unintended consequences of the duopoly and others result (also unintentionally) from past government actions.

Fuel Use, Entry and the 'Dash for Gas'

One of the most significant changes consequent on privatisation was relaxation of the political constraints on generator fuel choice which had existed for over 30 years.

Because, under nationalisation, governments ensured that the industry burned British coal and constructed British-designed nuclear power stations, the CEGB's fuel mix at the time of privatisation consisted largely of coal, with a substantial additional element of nuclear power. To maintain support for British coal and nuclear power, successive governments operated a *de facto* ban on the use of natural gas in power stations, starting in the mid-1960s when gas was found in the southern North Sea,[11] it was subsequently reinforced by a similar

---

George Yarrow, 'Does Ownership Matter?', in *Privatisation and Competition: A Market Prospectus*, Hobart Paperback No.28, London: Institute of Economic Affairs, 1989, pp.52-69.

[10] Joseph Schumpeter, *Capitalism, Socialism and Democracy*, London: Allen and Unwin, 5th Edition, 1976, especially Chap. VII.

[11] Colin Robinson, 'Gas After the MMC Verdict', in *Regulating Utilities: The Way Forward*, IEA Readings No.41, Institute of Economic Affairs, 1994, p.4, and *Utilities Law Review*, Vol.6, Issue 1, Spring 1995.

move by the European Community. Because of these prohibitions, there was considerable pent-up demand for gas as a generation fuel by the time of electricity privatisation in Britain.

On privatisation, with government constraints on fuel use relaxed, the two major generators in England and Wales immediately began to diversity away from a fuel mix which they perceived to be costly and excessively polluting relative to the alternatives. About three-quarters of their plant capacity was coal-fired or dual-fired (coal and oil), with the rest mainly oil, as Table 1 shows. Their fuel mix was an incumbent disadvantage which offset some of their advantages. They no longer had any nuclear stations, though the output of those stations had to be taken by the RECs and had a share of about 17 per cent of pooled output in 1990 (Table 2).

For a time the generators' diversification moves were severely hampered by government insistence that they sign contracts with British Coal for the first three years of privatisation (up to March 1993) to take substantial amounts of coal – 70 million tonnes a year reducing to 65 million tonnes. The extra costs incurred by the generators in signing these contracts were passed on via the RECs to consumers in the franchise market. But the generators were still able to lay plans to build new Combined Cycle Gas Turbine (CCGT) stations, to be commissioned post-1993, which appeared the cheapest form of baseload generation, which had short construction times (two to three years) compared with coal or nuclear stations, and which also offered advantages in meeting EC sulphur emission targets.

From 1993 onwards, the coal contracts were reduced – to 40 million tonnes in 1993/94 and to 30 million tonnes a year for the next four years – and constraints on fuel choice were much diminished. Though British-mined coal was still protected by the contracts, as I have explained elsewhere there were hidden elements of bias against coal in the new market.[12]

At the same time, entrants to the generation industry appeared, all choosing to build CCGT stations. The resulting 'dash for gas' was on a considerable scale. By early 1995, National Power and PowerGen had 6,300 MW of CCGT stations either commissioned or under construction. As well as their wish to diversify away from coal, the two generators may have been making a pre-emptive strike at potential entrants by building, and announcing plans to build, CCGT stations.

---

[12] Robinson, *Energy Policy, op. cit.*

TABLE 1
National Power and Powergen Power Stations at Vesting Day:
by Type of Fuel

Type of Fuel	National Power GWso	National Power % of Total	PowerGen GWso	PowerGen % of Total
COAL	19·5	66	11·6	62
COAL/OIL	2·6	9	1·9	10
OIL	5·9	20	4·0	21
GAS TURBINE	1·6	5	1·2	6
HYDRO	0·1	–	0·1	1
TOTAL	29·7	100	18·8	100

Source: CEGB Statistical Yearbook, 1988-89, Table 11B.

TABLE 2
Generator Market Shares of Pooled Output

	1990/91 per cent	1993/94 per cent	Oct. 1993 – Sep. 1994 per cent
National Power	45·5	35·0	34·2
PowerGen	28·4	26·1	25·3
Nuclear Electric	17·4	23·2	23·3
Inter-connectors and Pumped Storage*	7·7	8·4	8·8
New entrants	0·0	6·2	7·3
Others**	1·0	1·1	1·1
TOTAL	100·0	100·0	100·0

* ScottishPower and Hydro-Electric (via the Scottish Inter-connector), EdF (via the French Inter-connector) and NGC Pumped Storage.

** Mainly BNFL, AEA and renewables.

Source: S.C. Littlechild, 'Competition in Electricity: Retrospect and Prospect', in *Utility Regulation: Challenge and Response*, IEA Readings No. 42, Institute of Economic Affairs, 1995.

117

Whatever the reasons, by early 1995 entrants had commissioned or under construction a little more CCGT plant than National Power and PowerGen – about 6,900 MW (over 10 per cent of pooled generation capacity in England and Wales).[13] One consequence of the 'dash for gas' was to accelerate the decline of the British coal industry.[14]

As a result of new entry (and also an increase in Nuclear Electric's market share), as Stephen Littlechild explained last year,[15] there has been a substantial decline in the shares of National Power and PowerGen of pooled output. In 1990-91, as Table 2 shows, National Power's market share was over 45 per cent and PowerGen's share was 28 per cent: but in the year ending September 1994 those shares were down to 34 per cent and 25 per cent respectively. Nuclear Electric, which has been successful in increasing the output of its AGRs, increased its share from 17 to 23 per cent over the same period. New entrants accounted for about 7½ per cent of pooled output in the 12 months ending September 1994 and that share was tending towards 10 per cent with the commissioning of capacity under construction.

The Pool and its Effects

Given this volume of entry in a relatively short period, it might seem that the market power of the major generators would inevitably be curbed. But, despite the reduction in their market share, the impact on their ability to set prices has been minimal, for the reasons Stephen Littlechild gave last year.[16] The electricity pooling system in England and Wales, established by the privatisation scheme but descended from the 'merit order' operated by the CEGB, has concentrated their influence on a crucial segment of the market to such an extent that they continue to be price-makers. Incidentally, the pooling régime contains another peculiar hangover from nationalisation: the Value of Lost Load (VOLL) mechanism implies a central judgement about the value to consumers of lost load rather than those consumers being allowed to decide for themselves.

---

[13] S.C. Littlechild, 'Competition in Electricity: Retrospect and Prospect', in *Utility Regulation: Challenge and Response*, IEA Readings No.42, London: Institute of Economic Affairs, 1995.

[14] Colin Robinson, 'Privatisation: Saving the British Coal Industry?', *Energia*, 3/95, September 1995.

[15] Littlechild, *op. cit.*

[16] Littlechild, *op. cit.*

The pooling system has combined with other characteristics of the privatised electricity market to preserve the market power of National Power and PowerGen. If entry to the generation industry consisted of a diversified mix of plants in terms of load factor – some operating on baseload, some mid-merit plant and some peaking plant – System Marginal Price (SMP) would be set in rivalrous conditions. However, in practice National Power and PowerGen have set SMP almost all the time because of the lack of competition outside the baseload power market.

Entrant/REC Relationships

But *why* is there minimal competition outside the baseload market? The reasons are complex but they are traceable back to establishment of the duopoly, to avoiding action taken by the RECs, and to the characteristics of contracting under the privatised régime which are themselves rooted in the history of development of the North Sea.

Most entrants are associated with one or more RECs which have formed close equity or long-term contractual relationships with them[17] because the RECs have wished to diversify sources of electricity supplied to them, avoiding dependence on a duopoly in generation. Thus the presence of a generation duopoly has had more significance than the direct constraints it places on competition in generation. It has led also to the REC/entrant relationships just described: had the CEGB been split into more generators, the RECs would have had less incentive to diversify in this way.[18]

These contractual relationships have in turn influenced the development of competition as between baseload and non-baseload. The long-term contracts which the entrants have with RECs are mirrored by the long-term contracts entrants have signed to take gas from North Sea fields. These contracts are 'take-or-pay', as most North Sea gas contracts have been since 1968 when British offshore gas first began to flow: take-or-pay contracts with high minimum bills are a characteristic of the monopolised and monopsonised gas market which existed until recently as a matter of government policy.[19]

---

[17] Dieter Helm, 'Regulating the Transition to a Competitive Electricity Market', *Regulating Utilities: The Way Forward, op. cit.*

[18] Robinson, *Energy Policy, op. cit.*

[19] See note 11.

Because they have take-or-pay contracts with relatively high minimum bills, entrant generators find a large element of their gas purchase costs is fixed. Thus the marginal cost of gas to them is close to zero and they have a powerful incentive to maximise their gas sales by bidding into the pool at whatever price will secure baseload operation. Thus despite the large volume of entry, all the entrants' plant runs on baseload. None competes with mid-merit and peaking plant. Nuclear stations also run on baseload. All non-baseload plant (left over from the days of nationalisation), apart from pumped storage, is still owned by National Power and PowerGen. Consequently, SMP has been set about 85 per cent of the time by those two companies (in most of the other 15 per cent, the pumped storage stations until recently owned by NGC have set it).

Unintended Consequences and the Development of Competition

To summarise, the British government's privatisation scheme for electricity generation resulted in a stream of unintended consequences.

First, in order to placate the management of the CEGB and to make nuclear privatisation easier (though in the event that privatisation did not take place in 1990), the government established a duopoly in generation.

Second, because of past government action there was a huge pent-up demand for gas which meant that any new entrants would build gas-fired plant, buying their gas in a market where (again because of past government actions) take-or-pay contracts were the norm.

Third, the RECs, concerned at the perceived market power of the duopolists, decided to circumvent it and so teamed up with new entrants on long-term contracts.

Fourth, because of the take-or-pay contracts and the long-term contractual relationships between the RECs and entrants to generation, all the new plant is on baseload and so competes with existing generators only in that part of the market.

Thus the incumbents retain market power in that crucial segment of the market where, because of the characteristics of the pooling system, prices are set. I imply no criticism of the generators – which have played the game according to rules set for them by government at the time of privatisation – when I say that the market features described have controlled competition, channelling it into areas where it least affects incumbents and has least impact on wholesale prices.

The (unintended) consequences for competition in generation are serious. National Power and PowerGen have kept about 95 per cent of non-baseload output, compared with only 55 per cent of baseload output.[20] So entry to the industry has depressed the major generators' share only of baseload output. Of course, as National Power and PowerGen stations are displaced from baseload they compete with mid-merit and peak plant. But virtually all the plant concerned is owned by the two big generators so, as OFFER concluded, 'The two companies are thus competing only with each other for a critical part of the load curve'.[21]

The Contracts Market

Although most generated electricity is pooled, there are considerable risks to market participants in relying on a spot market such as the pool, particularly in view of the distortions discussed above. Variations may occur not only for the reasons one would expect in any electricity market – that is, according to time of day and season of year and because of unexpected weather or other unpredicted events – but because of the ability of the major generators to affect prices in the pool.[22] If they could not so affect prices it would, of course, have been futile for OFFER to impose its February 1994 price cap on them: the generators would not have been able to adhere to it as they (more or less) have.

Experience has now revealed how large variations in the pool can be and how they tend to be magnified by the Loss of Load Probability (LOLP) and VOLL mechanism. In January 1995, for instance, there were some particularly large fluctuations in pool prices, caused apparently by the temporary closure of two nuclear power stations which affected prices primarily by increasing LOLP. On one day in late January, the pool purchase price (PPP) reached a maximum of over 63 pence per kWh between 17.30 and 18.00 hours with a corresponding pool selling price (PSP) of over 72 pence, as compared with minima in the early hours of the same day of only 0·9 pence. On another day in April 1995, there was a short period during which the purchase price rose above 83 pence per kWh (though there were evidently software problems at the time).[23]

---

[20] Littlechild, *op. cit.*

[21] *Ibid.*

[22] Richard Green and David Newbery, 'Competition in the British Electricity Spot Market', *DAE Working Paper 9108*, Department of Applied Economics, University of Cambridge, March 1991; Robinson, 'Liberalising the Energy Industries', *op. cit.* See also Vickers and Yarrow, *The British Electricity Experiment, op. cit.*

[23] 'Power price reaches record levels', *The Financial Times*, 12 April 1995.

To safeguard against pool price fluctuations, the contracts market in England and Wales, through which most electricity is traded, is a natural development: 'contracts for differences' (CFDs) help protect against the uncertainty of pool prices. The presence of CFDs tends to make generators less concerned about pool prices than they would otherwise be, but they are not always fully contracted and so may be affected at the margin by pool price fluctuations. RECs and large consumers also protect themselves by CFDs but again some may be affected at the margin and some large consumers (such as ICI and other chemical companies)[24] purchase at pool prices. Over a period of years there must, of course, be a relationship between pool and contract prices since consumers have the option of buying at one or the other price.

But in the contracts market (as well as in the pool) competition appears to have been weak: the three big players – National Power, PowerGen and Nuclear Electric – seem to lack incentives to compete vigorously. OFFER's evidence to the Government's 1994-95 nuclear review was forthright about the ineffectiveness of Nuclear Electric as a competitor to the two big privatised generators.[25] It pointed out that Nuclear Electric had contracted a significantly lower proportion of its output than the other two generators: according to OFFER, its 'limited contribution' to the contracts market may have been a 'significant factor in restricting the availability of contracts and maintaining higher prices than would otherwise obtain'.

Efficiency Gains in Generation: Reducing Inputs and Input Prices

Despite the weakness of competition in generation, there is at least some rivalry where there used to be none, and capital market pressures to increase efficiency also exist: as in all the privatised industries, the capital market has proved far more effective than Treasury control ever was. One effect of privatisation has been to stimulate remarkable reductions in costs by National Power and PowerGen. Now they have private shareholders and they find political constraints on fuel choice much reduced, the two generators have moved to cheaper and much less labour-intensive gas-fired generation. They have also negotiated lower prices for the coal they are still burning, now they are no longer forced by political pressures to contract for such large quantities of British-mined coal.

---

24 'Burden of power discomforts chemicals sector', *The Financial Times*, 8 February 1995.

25 Office of Electricity Regulation, *Submission to the Nuclear Review*, October 1994.

TABLE 3
Employment in Electricity Generation

	Vesting day 1990	End March 1995
National Power	17,200	5,100
PowerGen	9,500	3,700
TOTAL	26,700	8,800

Source: National Power Annual Reviews; PowerGen Report and Accounts,
       and Press reports.

The most striking expression of these cost reductions is in the manning economies achieved (revealing the degree of disguised unemployment which existed during the years of nationalisation). National Power and PowerGen reduced their workforces by over two-thirds in the first five years of privatisation (Table 3) and are continuing with reductions, though at a slower rate. By the end of 1996, the combined workforce of the two generators is likely to be little more than a quarter of what it was at vesting.[26] Labour force reductions in the RECs, where capital market pressures have until recently been less intense, were smaller – about 13 per cent on average between 1990 and 1994.

The prices of generation fuels have also fallen compared with the time when they were heavily influenced by government actions to protect British coal and nuclear power. In the first half of 1995, the major generators paid about 26 per cent less for their coal than they did, on average, in 1988. The price of natural gas, which has only been used on any scale in power generation since early 1993, fell by 13 per cent between then and the first half of 1995.

Predictably, given that serious rivalry has yet to develop in generation, a large part of these efficiency gains seems not to have been passed on to consumers. Consumer price trends are analysed below.

Consumer Price Trends

Until recently the results of electricity privatisation in terms of prices were disappointing, even in sectors of the market where consumers had choice and despite the considerable cost reductions mentioned above. A study carried out in 1992 suggested that prices in the early privatisation

---

[26] 'National Power cut its workforce by another 400', *The Times*, 10 January 1996.

period were considerably higher than might have been expected on the basis of pre-privatisation trends.[27] Subsequently, however, prices to most consumers have tended to stabilise or fall.

To place movements in electricity prices in the context of changes in fuel prices in general, Figure 1 illustrates quarterly trends in coal, fuel oil, gas and electricity prices to industry (all expressed in nominal terms and in thermal equivalents) since first quarter 1988 which was when the White Papers on electricity privatisation were published. The Figure ends in second quarter 1995.

Average coal prices to industry were fairly stable up to late 1992, but have fallen significantly since; gas prices fluctuated around an approximately constant trend until they dropped considerably in the first half of 1995; and fuel oil prices (abstracting from the sharp rise at the time of the Iraqi invasion of Kuwait in 1990) have increased substantially, especially in the first half of 1995.

Despite the declining costs of labour and fuel inputs, electricity prices rose significantly over the period as a whole. Comparing second quarter 1988 with second quarter 1995 (to minimise seasonal effects), the increase is about 15 per cent, equivalent to an annual average compound rate of about 2 per cent. The increase in electricity prices was, however, concentrated in the early part of the period. The trend appears to have changed from early 1994 onwards (which was when the competitive market was considerably extended): in second quarter 1995, average electricity prices to industry were 5 per cent lower than in second quarter 1994 and 6 per cent below second quarter 1993.

One specific factor which helps explain the increases in electricity prices relative to gas and coal prices in the early years is the considerable increases just before privatisation. Another is the loss of the QUICS scheme.[28] As the number of industrial consumers able to choose a supplier has increased, the effects of these early increases have been offset.

The companies which suffered most from electricity price increases in the early years of privatisation were very large consumers which lost

---

[27] George Yarrow, *British Electricity Prices Since Privatisation*, Oxford: Regulatory Policy Institute for the Regulatory Policy Research Centre, Hertford College, 1992.

[28] About 4 million tonnes of coal a year was provided to the CEGB by British Coal at around world prices: the benefits of the electricity deemed to be produced from this coal were passed on to about 400 large consumers under the so-called QUICS (Qualifying Industrial Consumers' Scheme).

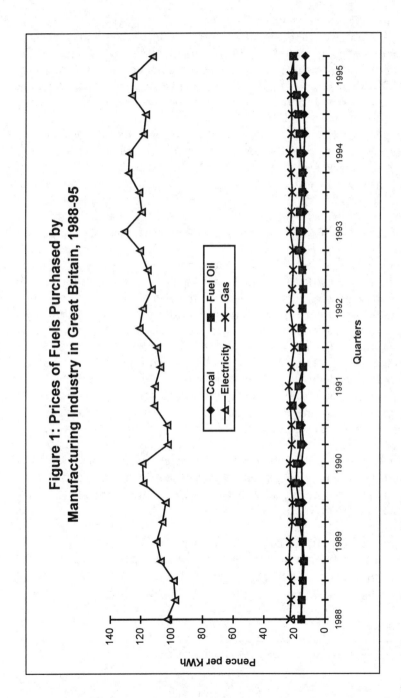

Figure 1: Prices of Fuels Purchased by
Manufacturing Industry in Great Britain, 1988-95

their subsidies; according to DTI statistics[29] (on which Figure 2 is based), 'extra large' consumers were paying 46 per cent more for their electricity in first quarter 1993 than in first quarter 1989 (1989 is as far back as the statistics go). But prices to large consumers subsequently came down: in second quarter 1995, despite the big increases in the early years, extra large consumers were paying only 4 per cent more than in second quarter 1989.

Companies too small (less than 1MW demand) to have a choice of supplier before April 1994 also fared badly before they entered the competitive market: in first quarter 1994 they were, on average, paying 25 per cent more for their electricity than in first quarter 1989. By the second quarter of 1995, however, the effects of competition were apparent: the average price they were paying was about 16 per cent higher than in second quarter 1989 and 8 per cent lower than in second quarter 1994.

Moderately large and medium-size consumers – which have been in the competitive market from the beginning and had no subsidies to lose – have, as one would expect, fared better over the period as a whole, though they have not experienced such significant recent price declines as larger and smaller consumers. Increases were relatively modest from the beginning: average prices paid by consumers in each group in second quarter 1995 were less than 6 per cent higher than in second quarter 1989 and about 2 1/2 per cent below second quarter 1994.

Outside the competitive market, residential consumers – captives of their local RECs until 1998 – have faced big increases in electricity prices since privatisation. Domestic electricity prices in the second quarter of 1995 were about 42 per cent higher than in the second quarter of 1988 whereas the price of gas (electricity's main competitor in homes) was only 27 per cent higher. Most of the rise in domestic electricity prices took place between 1988 and 1992 since when, eliminating the effect of the imposition of VAT in 1994, prices have fallen slightly.

In general, benefits to consumers (in terms of prices) over the whole period since privatisation seem small when set against the substantial decline in fuel and labour costs. The trend does, however, appear to have changed. Prices no longer inexorably increase from year to year as they did under nationalisation, and prices to most consumers may well

---

[29] Department of Trade and Industry, *Energy Trends*, HMSO (monthly).

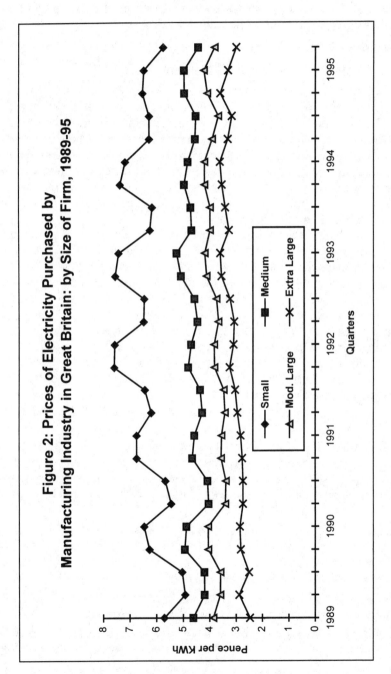

Figure 2: Prices of Electricity Purchased by
Manufacturing Industry in Great Britain: by Size of Firm, 1989-95

fall over the next few years because of increasing supply competition and tighter regulation of distribution charges.[30]

Regulation

The Difficulties of Regulation in Electricity

Regulation of electricity has proved extremely difficult.[31] OFFER has been confronted with a complicated privatisation scheme imposed on a complex industry in which many of the 'new' organisations are based on old ones and old relationships still persist. Two government failures in particular have made life unnecessarily difficult for the regulator: *first*, the failure to isolate naturally monopolistic activities (given present technology) and to regulate only those, and, *second*, the failure to establish conditions in which potentially competitive sectors of electricity would actually be competitive.

In such circumstances, the scope of regulation has been extremely wide,[32] in effect covering the whole industry instead of the network monopoly elements. OFFER, pursuing its pro-competition duty, has been constantly drawn into regulating generation, an activity which could have been highly competitive and which the Government evidently expected would require only minimal attention from the regulator. In other sectors its task has been complicated by the mixture of naturally monopolistic and potentially competitive functions it has had to supervise. Consequently, its resources have been diverted away from the task (difficult enough in itself) of regulating the 'natural monopoly' network of wires.

Regulating Generation

In generation, the sector where some competition was introduced from the beginning, the impact of competitive forces on the incumbents has been muted, as I have explained. Consequently, the regulator has issued five reports on pool prices and related issues.[33] None so far has resulted

---

[30] Reports indicate that many industrial and commercial consumers secured price cuts averaging 4 or 5 per cent for the year beginning April 1995. (See 'Big energy users win price cuts', *The Financial Times*, 31 March 1995.)

[31] Robinson, Manchester Statistical Society, *op. cit.*

[32] Colin Robinson, 'Privatising the Energy Industries: The Lessons to be Learned', *op. cit.*, and 'L'apprentissage de la concurrence', *Le Communicateur*, Paris, Winter 1995.

[33] Office of Electricity Regulation: *Report on Pool Price Inquiry*, December 1991; *Report on Gas Turbine Plant*, June 1992; *Report on Constrained-on Plant*, October 1992; *Pool Price*

in a reference to the MMC, though such references have been threatened.

Following an investigation in February 1994, OFFER placed a temporary two-year cap (until March 1996) on average pool purchase prices at 2·4 pence per kWh time-weighted and 2·55 pence per kWh demand-weighted (both in October 1993 prices), implying a reduction of about 7 per cent compared with the first nine months of 1993-94. It also insisted that National Power and PowerGen 'use all reasonable endeavours' to sell or dispose of 6 GW of coal-fired or oil-fired stations in order to bring into the market other generators with mid-merit or peaking plant. OFFER's report expressed concern that '...the two generators have used their market power to achieve their aims of higher prices'.

Early in 1995, when the surge in pool prices again brought complaints from large industrial users of electricity,[34] the DGES reminded the generators of their undertakings and said he was monitoring their actions: his statement was taken to be an implied threat of an MMC reference.[35] Later in 1995, as PowerGen bid for Midlands Electricity and National Power bid for Southern, both generators announced that sales of the 6GW would be taking place.

The Nuclear Review and Competition in Generation

The most promising recent opportunity for stimulating competition in generation was the review of the nuclear industry conducted by government in 1994/95. Some submissions to the review argued that nuclear power should be privatised in such a way that two powerful new competitors, based on Nuclear Electric and Scottish Nuclear, would be introduced into the market along with a smaller company with Magnox stations; even though the ageing Magnox stations probably could not be privatised, their operation could be contracted out so that they became another competitor in the electricity market.[36]

Statement, July 1993, Birmingham; and *Decision on a Monopolies and Mergers Commission Reference*, February 1994.

[34] In the year to March 1995, the demand-weighted pool price was slightly in excess of the agreed cap. (See 'Power groups face crackdown', *The Financial Times*, 1-2 April 1995.)

[35] 'Setback for Treasury on sale of generators', *The Financial Times*, 28 January 1995; and 'ICI threat of call for electricity price probe', *The Financial Times*, 25 February 1995.

[36] OFFER, *Submission to the Nuclear Review, op. cit.* Colin Robinson, *Privatising Nuclear Power*, evidence for the review of future prospects for nuclear power, September 1994.

The Government published the conclusions of its nuclear review in May 1995.[37] It decided that the industry should be privatised (probably in mid-1996) but that the Magnox stations should remain in state ownership, eventually becoming part of the state fuel services company, British Nuclear Fuels. It did not, however, accept the suggestion that two private nuclear companies should be formed. Instead, the plan is that Nuclear Electric and Scottish Nuclear will merge, becoming subsidiaries of a holding company, British Energy, located in Scotland with one PWR and seven AGRs.

So, if the Government's plans remain unchanged, there will be one large private nuclear company and one small state (Magnox) company, the latter operating for the remaining lives of the Magnox plants. Under these circumstances, despite the formation of the separate Magnox company, it seems that three companies (albeit private rather than government-owned) will continue essentially as a triopoly in the England and Wales market.[38]

The nuclear review was another opportunity missed to enhance competition in generation. The competitive potential of Nuclear Electric and Scottish Nuclear has so far been severely limited because they are state-owned, because of their inability to diversify out of nuclear power, and because of geographical market-sharing arrangements. Despite these constraints, there has been some competition in ideas – demonstrated, for example, in Scottish Nuclear's development of dry storage. Regrettably, such competition in ideas will be suppressed.

It seems a curious scheme which, on privatisation, reduces the number of companies (the small, time-limited Magnox company apart) which used to exist. It is not as though freeing entry to nuclear power is of any advantage at present. No-one wishes to enter the industry, so far as I know: indeed, those in it would like to diversify out. It is entry to the generation industry as a whole which is the issue.

Had Nuclear Electric and Scottish Nuclear been privatised separately and at the same time made more equal in size (by a plant reallocation), and had geographical constraints been removed, they could have

---

[37] *The Prospects for Nuclear Power in the UK: Conclusions of the Government's Nuclear Review*, Cm.2860, Department of Trade and Industry and the Scottish Office, London: HMSO, May 1995.

[38] A criticism of the Government's nuclear privatisation plans is in Colin Robinson, 'Competition before cash in nuclear sale', *The Financial Times*, 5 May 1995.

become formidable competitors for National Power and PowerGen in the pool and the contracts markets. In the course of time, the two companies would have diversified and competed outside the baseload market. It would not have happened quickly (except perhaps by purchase of plant), but the move would have been in the right direction. They would have been rather like new entrants in terms of willingness to compete, but with the incumbent advantages of knowledge of the industry and possession of sites linked into the transmission and distribution systems. I have no doubt that the formation of one nuclear company will, in retrospect, be seen as another example of government failure to seize opportunities to enhance rivalry in generation.

Regulating the Regional Companies, and the Effects of Takeovers

Distribution, a local monopoly within each REC's area, has not surprisingly been more profitable than the supply business where competition has developed for the large consumer (100 kW and above) market. Supply should become very competitive from April 1998 onwards, when all consumers are due to have a choice of supplier, though experience when the monopoly threshold was reduced from 1MW to 100 kW in 1994 suggests that competition will for a time be hampered by metering problems.

The supply price cap for consumers with a demand of less than 100 kW was tightened from RPI-0 to RPI-2 from April 1994.[39] But, of course, distribution charges are of more significance to consumers since, on average, they account for about one-third of residential customers' bills. Consequently, the distribution price reviews have attracted most attention.

The mid-1994 review brought one-off cuts in distribution charges, varying by REC between 11 and 17 per cent, to take effect from April 1995. Subsequently, all such charges would be subject to an X term of - 2: previously X had been zero or positive (up to 2½ per cent).[40] Although the review was accepted by all the RECs without challenge, one of the Scottish companies (Hydro-Electric) appealed to the MMC which carried out an inquiry and reported in June 1995.[41] It used a different methodology from the regulator and came to slightly different conclusions about Hydro-Electric's charges.

---

[39] OFFER, *Annual Report 1993*, p.5.

[40] 'Cuts promised in electricity prices', *The Financial Times*, 11 August 1994.

[41] Monopolies and Mergers Commission, *Scottish Hydro-Electric*, London: HMSO, June 1995.

The 1994 distribution settlement for England and Wales was, however, upset after less than a year when in March 1995 the regulator announced that, though the new distribution charges would stand for the year beginning April 1995, he would reconsider the proposed charges for subsequent years. The trigger for his change of view was evidently a contested bid by Trafalgar House for one of the RECs, Northern Electric, made a few months before REC takeovers became possible on the expiry of the Government's 'golden shares' in March 1995.

According to the regulator, he had already become concerned – because of rising REC share prices and representations made to him by consumers – that his 1994 review might have been too lax.[42] But what convinced him to reconsider was a defence document produced by Northern Electric in response to the Trafalgar House bid which promised big cuts in costs, special payments to shareholders, increased gearing and substantial dividend increases. In other words, the regulator concluded that the bid revealed new information about the costs of one REC and, by implication, all RECs. It seemed that, if pressed, they could reduce costs much more and provide considerably greater benefits to shareholders than had been apparent at the time of the 1994 distribution review. Moreover, they could significantly increase gearing.

Claimed benefits of a price cap régime, with reviews every five years or so, are its stability and the incentive it gives to regulated companies to reduce costs (because, unlike a rate of return system, they can for a time appropriate the cost reductions in terms of increased profits). Despite upsetting that stability and creating uncertainty at a time when the Government was selling its remaining 40 per cent shares in National Power and PowerGen, the regulator decided that the distribution charges he had just set must be revisited.

The new charges, announced early in July 1995,[43] imposed significantly tighter controls on the RECs than the 1994 proposals. Distribution charges were reduced by 10 to 13 per cent in 1996-97 (depending on the REC) and the value of X for the period 1997-2000 was increased to 3 per cent. After the new review, the aggregate

---

[42] Stephen Littlechild, 'Better to grasp the nettle now', *The Financial Times*, 9 March 1995, and OFFER Press Notice, 24 March 1995.

[43] Office of Electricity Regulation, *The Distribution Price Control: Revised Proposals*, July 1995.

reduction in distribution charges for the period 1994-95 to 1999-2000 will vary between 27 and 34 per cent, depending on the REC concerned.

The most interesting aspect of the events of March 1995 and the subsequent re-review of charges is the part played by the market for corporate control. The Government had permitted that market to operate only from March 1995 onwards because of its misguided belief – common to most privatisations – that incumbents require protection from predators for five years or so after privatisation.

In essence, what happened as the end of the golden share period came in sight was that the market for corporate control began to reveal, via a hostile takeover bid, highly relevant information about the RECs. In a regulated industry with monopoly in the product market, a functioning market for corporate control will have beneficial effects not just by imposing efficiency pressures on the companies concerned but indirectly by providing information for the regulator. No matter how assiduous and determined he or she may be, in the absence of a market it is genuinely impossible to determine what costs 'should' be.[44] Even where there is no rivalry in the product market, the market for corporate control helps fill the regulator's information gap.

Although the Trafalgar House bid failed – it was eventually withdrawn in August 1995 – in another sense it was extremely successful. It discovered information which would otherwise have remained hidden, perhaps even to Northern's management. As it was, an incumbent management, under pressure from an alternative management team, found scope for substantial efficiency gains and revealed them to the financial markets.

Subsequently, in the late Summer and Autumn of 1995, there was a flurry of takeover bids for RECs, some agreed and some contested. Six takeovers took place without reference to the MMC (Eastern Electricity by Hanson, SWEB by (US) Southern Electric, Norweb by North West Water, Manweb by Scottish Power, South WalesElectricity by Welsh Water, and Seeboard by Central and South West of Texas). But the Government referred to the MMC the bids by PowerGen for Midlands Electricity and by National Power for Southern (see below). Only four RECs (Northern, Yorkshire, East Midlands and London) remained independent in the Spring of 1996.

---

[44] Colin Robinson, 'Why Electricity Takeovers are Welcome', *The Financial Times*, 3 August 1995.

Price Caps

I will deal very briefly with the criticism to which price cap regulation has been subject. It is difficult to be enthusiastic about price caps: like all aspects of regulation they are unsatisfactory devices. Setting X is an arbitrary business and, since regulators tend to turn to profits as measures of company performance, there is a tendency to revert to rate of return regulation, reducing incentives to introduce profit-enhancing cost savings (because increased profits may lead to increases in X).

Nevertheless, price caps do have some advantages over the main alternative (rate of return) provided that, in practice, they provide stability over a period of years. Furthermore, the problems which have arisen with electricity price caps are essentially a consequence of the initial caps set by government at the time of privatisation. When companies have enjoyed price caps as lax as those which, in retrospect, we can now see governed the RECs in their early years, adjusting them is extremely difficult. Again, I anticipate help from the market for corporate control which is likely over the next few years to set new cost standards for RECs which will help the regulator in future price reviews.

The Benefits of Privatisation

It is only five years since the British electricity supply industry was privatised after many years of state ownership and, prior to that, state regulation. Consequently, there has been little time for the effects of privatisation to appear.

Even at this early stage, however, some lessons emerge – in particular, that most of the problems which have appeared are due to the Government's failure, at the time of privatisation, to make a clearer separation between naturally monopolistic and potentially competitive activities and to ensure that in the potentially competitive sectors the privatisation scheme encouraged a competitive process to begin. Regulation of the industry has been much criticised but it is not so much the regulatory régime *per se* which is at fault. The strains now showing in regulation are symptoms of a more serious underlying problem – that because of the way the industry was privatised, the Government has heaped too many problems on the regulator.

Despite government failure, the new régime has considerable advantages over the old.

- *First,* government has disengaged so that decisions are less politicised and less short-termist.

- *Second,* establishment of an independent regulatory office means that a more open system of regulation prevails than under the old secretive régime when Ministers, officials and industry managers took decisions behind closed doors. It is no longer so easy to sweep the industry's pricing, investment and other problems under the carpet. Moreover, the explicit duty to promote competition helps avoid some of the regulatory problems which have arisen in other regulatory systems. 'Capture' by the industry or by some other pressure group[45] is much less likely if the regulator believes that his or her performance will be judged to a large extent by success in promoting competition.

- *Third,* entry to the industry has become possible instead of being prohibited by the state as it was under nationalisation. New generators and suppliers of electricity can move in, attracted by the expectation of profit, knowing that they can transmit their electricity through a network not owned by generators and distribute it through networks which, though owned by distributors, should not discriminate against them. Consequently, product market competition is increasing. As the competitive market has expanded, companies with a choice of supplier have begun to benefit from lower prices. Prices to residential consumers have fallen a little in the recent past (excluding the effect of imposing VAT): they should gain more from 1998 onwards when they are expected to be able to choose supplier. Indeed, the effects of '1998' may well be profound: providing all consumers with the power of exit is likely to lead to a fundamentally different supplier attitude towards consumers. Whether many consumers actually move supplier is irrelevant. The threat that they may do so should be enough to alter behaviour and competition will be stimulated back down the chain to generators. Consumers should be offered more varied and improved services (including energy management) and price schedules which permit more control over their expenditure on electricity.

---

[45] George J. Stigler, 'The Theory of Economic Regulation', *Bell Journal of Economics and Management,* Spring 1971, and Sam Pelzman, 'Toward a More General Theory of Regulation', *Journal of Law and Economics,* August 1976.

- *Fourth,* the market for corporate control now operates in electricity. There have already been considerable improvements in productive efficiency, especially in the generators, where labour and fuel costs have been greatly reduced compared with the days of nationalisation. Now the RECs have entered the market for corporate control, more efficiency improvements are in prospect.

The fears expressed about the alleged anti-competitive effect of some proposed mergers seem exaggerated. Those economists who think they know exactly how industries should be organised always oppose takeovers unless they are in line with their own views. Some City editors are also opposed even though, until recently, they were among the RECs' greatest critics. They evidently see no inconsistency in now regarding them as great British institutions to be cherished in their present form: foreigners, generators, water companies, Hanson, even other RECs – all are unworthy to take them over.

Given the positive advantages which arise from an active market in corporate control in a regulated industry – both efficiency pressures and more information for the regulator – it seems to me re-organisations of industries which stem from that market should be resisted only for the most powerful anti-monopoly reasons. Taking the case of generator/REC mergers, I would like to have seen a clearer separation of network elements of the industry at the time of privatisation. But it was not done, nor is there any sign that it will be done.

Starting from where we are, rather than where we might like to have been, the argument that such mergers will enhance market power, either in the generation market or the supply market, seems weak. It is not clear to me that consumers who will be able to switch supplier from 1998 onwards can be exploited, except for a very short time. If, as is sometimes claimed, generator-RECs will have a cost advantage over independent RECs, that is a reason for allowing mergers to proceed rather than stopping them. RECs do not have to remain independent: they can merge with generators if thereby they can realise economies. Nor should competition in generation be diminished: indeed, it may be enhanced by the more certain sale of plant by National Power and PowerGen. Regulatory undertakings should surely be capable of dealing with any perceived problems. Other types of merger seem to raise no serious competition issues. Since I have criticised the Government for its many failures in electricity privatisation, I should say that its stance over REC takeovers seems to me admirable – in particular, its refusal to countenance the naïve notion that all mergers should be referred to the MMC so that the 'correct' structure of the industry can be determined.[46]

- *Fifth*, and very important, the electricity supply industry now has the capability to evolve. Provided liberalisation of the market is allowed to proceed, companies will seek out new opportunities and better ways of doing things for the benefit of consumers. Under nationalisation, this form of evolution was impossible (which is another way of saying that one of the worst effects of state ownership is to curb the process of competitive discovery). 1998 will be a particularly important year because various constraints imposed by government at the time of privatisation will come to an end. Not only will consumers gain the power of exit, the present coal contracts with the generators will cease, as will the generators' contracts with the RECs. These changes are likely to lead to much more competitive markets for electricity and for inputs to electricity generation. Detailed prediction of the outcome of such markets is impossible. But it would be surprising if we are not all surprised by the effects.

- *Sixth*, the old protective form of energy policy in Britain, conducted mainly by the support given to nationalised British coal and to nuclear power by the electricity supply industry, could not survive privatisation. Coal protection is now very small (regrettably, the net effect may well be some bias against coal), and support for nuclear power is time-limited. Electricity privatisation, despite its many flaws, was a significant step along the road to a liberalised energy market.

Conclusions

It is a pity more of the potential gains from electricity privatisation could not have been realised in the early years. Nevertheless, it might be argued, a few early problems hardly matter. Creative destruction

---

[46] The proposed mergers of National Power with Southern and PowerGen with Midlands Electricity (see above) were referred to the Monopolies and Mergers Commission in November 1995, just after the lecture on which this paper is based. The MMC report said that they should proceed but, in April 1996, they were blocked by the President of the Board of Trade. (See 'Lang blocks electricity industry bids', *The Financial Times*, 25 April 1996.)

will begin to take over (especially after 1998), more rivalry in product and capital markets will emerge, innovation and entrepreneurship will flourish and consumers will see more and more gains.

I would like to believe that story but I fear that, in practice, the industry's future is more delicately poised. If we could rely on there being little political interference, Schumpeter's gale would indeed blow. But there is a serious danger of a re-politicisation of the industry which would cut short the incipient competitive discovery process. Re-politicisation could stem from London or Brussels, or in the worst case from both.

The present state of disillusionment with privatisation is dangerous, whether the problems are real or imagined. As I have explained, smaller consumers have some reason to feel short-changed by the results of privatisation so far, though they would almost certainly have been much worse off under continued nationalisation. But the constant search by the media for stories about the privatised companies and the regulators, to the neglect of the benefits of privatisation, provides an environment in which politicians are tempted to exploit public concerns and seize control of the industry again. Re-nationalisation is not on the agenda but some form of re-regulation could have much the same consequences. All the apparatus is there. It is only necessary to change the terms of regulation and perhaps some of the regulators in order to produce results more agreeable to politicians.

I have argued that regulation is already too wide in scope, extending well beyond any reasonable definition of 'natural monopoly'. But instead of diminishing, as it would if the market were allowed to evolve, regulation could become wider and deeper.

There is a powerful urge, particularly among the present opposition parties and in the reports of parliamentary committees, to establish committees to examine any and every problem they identify in the privatised utilities or to give present regulators more powers. I am not sure whether those who so favour more regulation by committee or by individual realise where it will lead. Perhaps they do and they like what they foresee.

But regulation is so unsatisfactory that, in my view, it should be avoided wherever possible. The fundamental dilemma is, in principle, exactly the same as in central planning – a regulator must attempt to gather centrally information which is dispersed and which is unlikely to be revealed except by market processes.[47] Or, putting it more succinctly – if there is a market regulators are redundant, and if there is no market regulators do not know what to do. It is one thing having pro-competition regulation designed to decline over time so that, in the end, it covers only genuine natural monopolies (if there are any). It is quite another to embark on extensive regulation on supposed 'market failure' grounds. That route leads to self-perpetuating intervention with no checks and balances which, like other government and quasi-government activities, will grow under its own momentum.

My main fear is that, under governments of whichever party, regulation of the electricity and other privatised utilities will be extended and tightened because politicians with short time-horizons are eager to be seen to be doing something. Although, as I have argued, government failure has been one of the major problems in the privatised electricity market, politicians will always seek out opportunities to fail again because they do not usually bear the consequences.

We are used in Britain to being governed and regulated by the self-styled 'great and the good'. But under increasing regulation, there would soon not be enough of them to go round. Instead we would find ourselves in the hands of the mediocre and the meddlesome. Before long electricity and other privatised utilities would have reverted to a régime not significantly different from nationalisation.

That brings me to Brussels, on which I have time to comment only briefly.[48] The European Commission is trying hard to have an energy chapter inserted in the new version of the Maastricht Treaty.[49] Its Green Paper is worth reading if only as a testament to the power and influence of 'defunct economists'. There are striking similarities to the White Papers on energy policy which British governments used to issue in the 1960s when they still believed in 'indicative planning'. It is about the need for a European energy policy and it produces a range of market failure reasons (in my view spurious) why there should be one. Security of supply, energy conservation, environmental protection, regional

---

[47] Israel M. Kirzner, 'The Perils of Regulation: A Market Process Approach', in his *Discovery and the Capitalist Process*, Chicago: University of Chicago Press, 1985.

[48] Colin Robinson, 'Energy Policy: Back to the Bad Old Days?', in *The UK Energy Experience: A Model or a Warning?*, Imperial College Press, 1996 (forthcoming).

[49] Commission of the European Communities, *For a European Union Energy Policy*, Green Paper, COM (94) 659 final 2, February 1995.

policy all appear as grounds why a European-level policy towards energy is required.

The standard of analysis in the Commission's Green Paper is so poor that instinctively the reader feels it cannot be taken seriously. But that view may well be wrong. Let us not forget the CAP. A CEP (Common Energy Policy) along the lines of the Green Paper would be a disaster. If it were translated into regulatory requirements on the electricity industry, the chances of increasing competition and reducing regulation would disappear. Efforts to continue with energy market liberalisation in Britain would probably be overwhelmed.

The looming prospect of a European energy policy is another good reason for pressing ahead with energy market liberalisation in Britain so that it becomes difficult to undo. It is a reason also for caution in making changes to our regulatory system which make it easier for Brussels to interfere. The Commission has an important task to perform in completing the 'internal market' in energy, which is anything but a market at present because of Continental gas and electricity monopolies. It would be much better occupied in efforts to ensure access to pipelines and wires networks than in airy notions about European-wide energy policies.

To summarise this paper, the prospect of profit has indeed attracted entry to the electricity supply industry since privatisation. The market for corporate control has also begun to operate. Substantial efficiency gains have been realised though so far rivalry in the market has not been sufficiently strong for the bulk of those gains to be passed on to consumers. A genuine discovery process in the electricity market is not yet apparent because of government failures – either of past policy or in the privatisation scheme – but it may not be far off if markets are allowed to work without political interference. The principal issue now is whether or not such interference will occur.

CHAIRMAN'S COMMENTS

Stephen Littlechild
Office of Electricity Regulation

THERE IS A GREAT DEAL that I agree with in Professor Robinson's paper. For example, he sets out well the problems of the industry under nationalisation, the limitations of the initial structure put in place at privatisation and the significant efficiency gains that have been achieved since then. I am also in broad agreement with his six conclusions:

- the rôle of government has been reduced, though evidently not eliminated entirely;
- regulation is far more transparent than government decision-making was under nationalisation;
- new entry is now possible instead of being prohibited, and has taken place on a significant scale in both generation and supply;
- the market for corporate control is now clearly working at least for the RECs, and providing valuable information, albeit better late than never;
- the electricity supply industry has the capability to evolve in terms of structure and contractual arrangements, and is evidently doing so;
- the artificial protection of uneconomic fuels is being significantly reduced. On this last point, where support is being provided, as with renewables, it is being done in an open and explicit way. It allows new entry, it benefits from competition to provide renewables, and does so at the minimum cost to electricity customers. I understand that the system established here has been much praised abroad as being the most economic way of delivering support for renewable technologies.

Competition in the Non-Baseload Sector

One issue that I want to take up is that of competition in the non-baseload sector. Professor Robinson points out that there is only minimal competition in the non-baseload market because the structure of the industry at privatisation gave almost all the mid-merit and peaking plants to National Power and PowerGen, and the take-or-pay gas contracts have meant that new entrant CCGTs have found it most profitable to run at baseload.

This is essentially an accurate characterisation, but I should like to explore his implied suggestion that new entry could have taken place in the mid-merit or peaking parts of the market. That would run contrary to a conventional view that new plants run at baseload, then only move down the merit order as they get older.

There has been a potentially interesting development over the last year or so. Suppose we define baseload as the average level of output in the eight off-peak hours, 11 p.m. to 7 a.m., and non-baseload output as the average output in the 16 peak hours, 7 a.m. to 11 p.m., over and above average off-peak output, then non-baseload accounts for about 14 per cent of total output. (Of course, there are smaller peaks within the off-peak hours, such as the night storage peak, but the above categorisation is nonetheless useful.)

In 1993-94, National Power and PowerGen accounted for about 95 per cent of this non-baseload output. The remaining 5 per cent was mainly from Pumped Storage Business and the interconnectors. But in the 12 months ending September 1995, the share of these other generators nearly doubled to 10 per cent. This reflects a small increase in non-baseload output by the interconnectors, a greater increase by Pumped Storage, but above all, a significant increase by the independents. Their share increased from 0·7 per cent in 1993-94 to 3·5 per cent in the year ending September 1995. This contrasts with an increase in their share of the total market from 6·2 per cent in 1993-94 to 9 per cent in the year ending September 1995. In other words, the independents' share of the total market has increased by about 45 per cent, but their share of the non-baseload market is now five times what it was a year and a half ago. Proportionately, the independents are expanding more in the non-baseload market than in the baseload market.

This should not be taken out of perspective. On average, the independents' level of output during the peak 16 hours is now about 8 per cent higher than during the 8-hour night-time trough. It was only 2½ per cent higher in 1993-94, and Nuclear Electric's peak output is no higher at all than its off-peak output. In contrast, National Power and PowerGen, which can call on additional plant at the peak, have an average output about 40 per cent higher in the peak than during the off-peak. Nonetheless, the expansion of independents in the non-baseload market is an encouraging development.

As to why it is taking place, one possible explanation is the increasingly peaky Pool price. One measure of this is that the average demand-weighted price is now about 11 per cent higher than the average time-weighted price, whereas in 1993-94 it was only 2 per cent higher. Another measure is average peak price compared to average off-peak price – in 1993-94 it was only 40 per cent higher, now it is two and a half times as high. Another possible explanation is the freeing up and development of the gas market, which may enable additional gas to be purchased for use at times of electricity peaks and surplus gas sold at time of troughs in electricity demand. It may be that future gas contracts will be better able to take advantage of such possibilities. It is necessary for the development of competition that National Power and PowerGen complete their disposals of mid-merit and peaking plant to other competitors, but it is also important that there is a constant ability for new competitors to enter the non-baseload market.[1]

The Customer Price Record

An area where I would take issue with Professor Robinson concerns prices to customers. I believe the record is better than he allows. He starts by citing George Yarrow's study in 1992 which suggested that prices in the early privatisation period were considerably higher than might have been expected on the basis of pre-privatisation trends. I welcomed that study as a serious attempt to assess the consequences of privatisation against a counter-factual alternative. However, I disagree about the assumption he made as to how the industry might have developed in the absence of privatisation. I am grateful for the work of my former colleague Sarah Deasley on this topic.

First, Yarrow assumed that the same fall in coal prices would have obtained – about 26 per cent from 1988 to 1991 – in the absence of electricity privatisation. However, privatisation put pressure on the generators to compete against new entrants building CCGT plant and it gave them the ability to import cheap coal. In the absence of privatisation, I doubt whether such pressure could have been put on the

---

[1] Mr John Collings of PowerGen commented in discussion at the lecture that the Vesting coal contracts and associated REC contracts had had the effect of holding down the differential between peak and off-peak prices, and that CCGT plant was technically better suited than coal plant to run on two shifts rather than baseload.

coal industry to deliver such price reductions. By today's post-privatisation standards the coal prices obtained may be remarkably high, but by pre-privatisation standards they were not. If they had fallen by about the same rate as they did from 1982 to 1988 – just under 2 per cent per annum – this would have implied less than 6 per cent over the period 1988 to 1991.

Second, Yarrow assumes that there would be no change in the return on capital in the electricity industry in the absence of privatisation. Some critics, particularly large customers, have viewed the price increases at the time of privatisation as a policy of 'fattening up' the companies for privatisation, that would not otherwise have taken place. In fact, however, a significant change in government policy was under way. The nationalised industries generally had failed to earn adequate returns in recent years, partly as a result of political pressures to hold down nationalised industry prices in the face of inflation. From 1983 to 1985, for example, the electricity industry earned a negative return, and from 1988 to 1989 it achieved a return of 1·8 per cent against a financial target of 3·75 per cent. In April 1989, the Government announced that the required rate of return for nationalised industries would rise from 5 per cent to 8 per cent in real terms before tax. The targets for other nationalised industries were increased – for example, the rate the Post Office was expected to earn was increased from 3·25 per cent for 1986 to 1989 to 6·4 per cent for 1989 to 1992. It seems highly likely that target returns in the electricity industry would have been significantly increased even in the absence of privatisation.

Third, Yarrow makes no mention of the future investment programmes of the industry. In fact, the CEGB had plans for a substantial programme of investments in what are now seen to be extremely expensive coal-fired and nuclear plants, certainly compared to the lower costs of CCGT plants that have since been built.

To summarise, I believe that, in the absence of privatisation, the electricity industry would have had to contend with significantly higher coal costs than Yarrow assumes, a significantly higher return required on capital than he assumes, and a significantly higher capital investment programme on which that return would have to be achieved. All these lead me to believe that, in the absence of privatisation, electricity prices would have been higher than they turned out to be rather than lower.

6

THE FUTURE OF UK UTILITY REGULATION

John Kay
London Business School

Introduction

THE REGULATION OF PRIVATISED UTILITIES IN BRITAIN is widely criticised today. The criticism comes from many quarters. Customers resent their money being handed out in excessive salaries and dividends. Academics are now widely critical of the (RPI-X) formula which was once a proud British innovation. A curious alliance of politicians and senior industry executives is concerned to suggest that the regulatory process is insufficiently accountable.

Much of this criticism of regulators is misconceived. On balance, regulators have done a better job than could reasonably have been expected. The problems of utility regulation are mostly not the fault of the regulators. They arise directly from the failure to address a range of fundamental structural issues about the management of utilities at the time of privatisation. If people are trying to push water up hill, the correct response is not to berate them for incompetence, or to look for ingenious devices to help; it is to point the finger at those who gave them the job to do in the first place. We should address our criticisms to the politicians who devised the framework rather than at the regulators who struggle to operate within it.

The deficiencies of that framework are of three main kinds, and they have been cumulative in their effect. All have a common fundamental cause, which is that the principal concern in all privatisations (with the partial exception of electricity and buses) was to achieve a successful flotation. That was largely perceived as an end in itself. To the extent that the architects of the programme thought beyond that, it was simply assumed that the change in ownership would bring about the desired results.

The *first* weakness is that the terms on which utilities were privatised were much too favourable to firms and their shareholders, and gave insufficient attention to the interests of customers. The *second* is that no explicit mechanism was put in place for securing a substantial share of the expected efficiency gains for customers. Even if – as can be argued – such a mechanism was implicit, the absence of a clear relationship was bound to leave customers dissatisfied. The *third*, and deepest, of the problems is that the privatised utilities lack what political theorists term legitimacy – a popularly acceptable basis for the power they exercise. Much concern has recently been expressed over the accountability of the regulators. The man in the street is not concerned with the accountability of the regulators. He is concerned with the accountability of the companies themselves, and he is right. It is this absence of legitimacy which explains why privatisation remains unpopular with the public even as it has started to deliver benefits to them, in the form of lower prices. It is also why attempts to extend privatisation further, in post and railways, in health and education, have ground to a halt.

This paper develops these propositions and argues that attempts to add bells and whistles, or more accurately balls and chains, to the current regulatory system are certain to fail. They will increase rather than reduce dissatisfaction with the current structure. The right answer is a partial retreat from privatisation. It is an acceptance that the governance structure of the plc is not suitable for the governance of monopoly utilities even if it is appropriate for firms which operate in competitive markets (it is not clear it is appropriate for them either, but that is a matter for another day).

The basic reform proposal developed here is a very simple one, though far-reaching. At present, the conventional view is that the primary duty of corporate boards is to the shareholders of the company, and its obligations to customers arise incidentally to the fulfilment of that obligation.[1] In a competitive market, the interests of shareholders can be achieved only by meeting the expectations of customers. But this is not true for a firm which does not face a competitive market, such as a monopoly utility. For such a company, the legal position should be the other way around. The purpose of a privatised utility

---

[1] The legal duties of directors of privatised utility companies are to some degree imposed by the Companies Act, derive to a larger extent from common law doctrine on the responsibilities of directors, and are also defined by industry-specific statutes. This structure is opaque and potentially contradictory.

should be to serve its customers, and its obligations to shareholders exist only to the extent necessary to ensure that the company can meet that primary purpose. This change would have implications for the appointment and conduct of boards, for the financing of companies, and for the rôle of the regulator.

From my knowledge of the managers of privatised utilities, I believe that this change would reflect the ways in which the vast majority wish to behave and the ways in which they, in the main, do behave. To remove the tension between their aspirations and the expectations of the capital market, would be to the long-run benefit of everyone. Some utility executives will see this as a major erosion of the management freedom which privatisation has given them. The intention, and the effect, would be precisely the reverse. The only hope of maintaining that freedom, and the efficiency gains which have been derived from it, is to find a structure which legitimises it more effectively. Decisions as to what level of renewal investment is necessary, which new activities will benefit customers, how improvements in service quality should be balanced against price increases, are all best taken not by politicians, or regulators, or referenda among customers, but by utility managers themselves. What we need is a framework that both encourages and allows them to make these decisions in an environment which focuses unambiguously on the interests of customers. The alternative, which is already in progress, will be a continued erosion of management autonomy through expansion of the scale and scope of regulation and from increasing direct political intervention.

The Achievements of Privatisation

Before turning to the supposed failures of regulation, it is as well to begin with the successes of privatisation.

There have been substantial improvements in efficiency in all those firms which were publicly owned when the privatisation experiment began in the early 1980s. Most of this improvement, possibly all of it, has come from reductions in manning levels. The most remarkable achievements have been from those formerly state-owned firms operating in a competitive environment: steel, airways, the two electricity generating companies. Telecom and gas were slower to slim their workforce, but have begun to do so as competition has become more effective. The pace of change has been less marked in water and electricity distribution, and in these industries there are probably large improvements yet to come.

In broad terms, these changes have been achieved without loss of output or service levels. To a much greater extent than had been realised, nationalised industries had become employers of large amounts of unnecessary unskilled labour. The CEGB, widely regarded as one of the most efficient of nationalised industries, can now be seen to have been grossly over-manned. Other countries have had similar experiences in the restructuring of their public sectors. It is, however, important to recognise that competition, rather than ownership as such, seems to have been the key element. Not only have changes happened more quickly in competitive environments than in others, but substantial productivity gains have also been made in the same period in other industries, such as the Post Office, which remained in state ownership.

These efficiency gains have revealed clearly the negative effects of traditional 'accountability' which takes the form of detailed supervision of management actions and of firms' investment plans and operating activities. Such accountability had, in practice, undermined the responsibility of the managers of the businesses concerned for the consequences of their actions without effectively transferring it to the supervisory civil servants or politicians. The recent fracas over prison management is an unambiguous reminder of the weaknesses of this structure as a means of organising industrial activities or, for that matter, anything else. Greater freedom to manage has everywhere led to improvements in morale and performance.

Almost all utilities have become more customer focused, in terms of attention to service quality and relationships with customers. British Telecom's redesignation of 'subscribers' as 'customers' is in a sense only symbolic, but represents a real change; customers may now have a choice, and even those utilities which remain monopolies are more inclined to treat customers as if they did have a choice. The influence of employees on British nationalised industries was substantial, but implicit rather than explicit, and hence essentially negative. It operated to prevent change in the structure of organisations, in working practices, and in the range and nature of services provided. There was also an excessive emphasis on technical issues relative to those of marketing and finance, reflecting political love of the grandiose and the wide influence of equipment suppliers. Electricity generation illustrates the nature of change here. The CEGB focussed on large, state-of-the-art generating sets, few of which were ever built to time or budget. Since privatisation, all new capacity (apart from Sizewell B, an overhang from the old days) has taken the form of small, combined cycle gas turbines, which can be built rapidly on well-established principles.

Privatisation has given utilities more investment freedom. The results of this have been more mixed. Most have taken the opportunity to diversify, either internationally, or outside the core business. Since utilities see limited prospects for growth within the core business, internal and external pressures to do this have been substantial. Very few of these diversifications have been in any way successful. Companies have also been able to invest far more in their core businesses, and this has been particularly true in telecoms and in water. Arguably, a systematic bias towards under-investment has been replaced by a systematic bias towards over-investment. And the problem of monitoring investment, and securing effective discipline without depriving consumers of necessary capital expenditure, has been changed in form but not in substance. In water, in particular, the appraisal of investment programmes by the regulator, at once detailed and arbitrary, comes more and more to resemble the methods of Treasury scrutiny and control which were applied in public ownership. No better answers have been found in gas and electricity.

There is a substantial positive balance to be recorded. It is possible that many of the gains which have occurred in the last decade could have been made without privatisation. It is, however, a matter of historical record that they were not made without privatisation, and that they now have been realised. It is also possible that the effect of reducing manpower levels, which is by far the most important consequence of the programme, has been to replace disguised unemployment by actual unemployment. Nevertheless, there is no going back, nor should there be.

Has Regulation Failed?

Criticism of the current regulatory structure comes both from those who applaud the developments described above and from those who remain hostile to privatisation.

One line of attack that unites both is the alleged lack of accountability of the regulators. The various Acts prescribing their duties do so only in rather general terms. The details vary from industry to industry, but the model has substantial common elements. Each utility operates under a licence awarded to it at privatisation. This licence imposes detailed requirements in respect of behaviour and the supply of information to the regulator. Amendment to the licence, or modification or renewal of the cap which limits prices, may be made by agreement with the firm concerned. In the absence of such agreement the Monopolies and Mergers Commission (MMC) adjudicates.

While the appellate rôle of the MMC is confined to major issues involving licence changes, judicial review offers a second mechanism for challenging regulatory decisions. This latter procedure is a common law remedy which has grown explosively since the mid-1970s. Although its scope is in principle confined to 'Wednesbury unreasonableness' – a decision so bizarre that no reasonable person could have reached it – in practice the Courts have shown themselves more and more willing to use judicial review to explore the substantive merits of any decision reached by a public body. One unfortunate effect of judicial review on the regulatory process has been that it has increased the reluctance of regulators to provide detailed rationale for their decisions. It is easier to mount legal challenges to the steps of an argument than to the simple exercise of a general discretion which statute undoubtedly confers on the regulator.

That discretion is itself the subject of criticism. It is easy to sympathise with the argument that what is needed is clarity and transparency of regulatory procedures and formulae, and that management should then be free to operate within the framework so prescribed. But the sought-for clarity and transparency is largely illusory.

Crucial Regulatory Questions and Issues

Consider some of the issues which are central to utility regulation. What is the cost of capital in electricity distribution? When is price discrimination pro-competitive and when is it anti-competitive in effect? What level of efficiency savings can a water company be expected to achieve? Decisions on each of these can only be made by the exercise of informed judgement. It is certainly possible to construct formulae which would, in whole or part, provide answers to these questions by arithmetic rules rather than regulatory discretion. But it is certain that the operation of these formulae would be arbitrary and unfair and that attempts to manipulate the parameters of these formulae would have undesirable effects on the commercial behaviour of the companies affected.

The demand for greater precision and less discretion in regulation is therefore, in substance, a demand for a combination of the more extensive use of these formulae together with a much larger rôle for the Courts in interpreting such statutory requirements as 'the proper financing of the functions' and 'the promotion of effective competition'. The practical issue is therefore whether decisions on the cost of capital, the market consequences of price discrimination, and the reasonableness of efficiency targets, are better made by regulators or by judges.

The balance of argument here seems to me overwhelming. The regulator is specifically appointed for his or her balance of technical expertise and industry knowledge; the judge is not. All experience of the presentation or handling of technical economic and commercial issues of these kinds through formal legal processes suggests that the Anglo-American adversarial procedure, based on the representation of grossly exaggerated and mutually contradictory arguments by each side, succeeds in being at once extremely costly and largely ineffective in identifying and resolving substantive areas of disagreement. It is because most judges themselves perceive this that the Courts have, wisely, been very reluctant to question the exercise of regulatory discretion on matters such as these.

My preference in this paper is for giving discretion and autonomy to informed individuals capable of balancing conflicting duties and interests, rather than for the prescription of detailed rules. This applies both to regulators and to the managers of regulated companies. I am aware that this preference is unfashionable.

Yet it is striking, given the criticisms of accountability and the demands for a more extensive appellate process, how little these procedures have been used. Although the threat has often been present, there has been no successful judicial review of a utility regulator's decision (and only one substantive case). Until 1992 there had been only one MMC reference on utility regulation, and that on a trivial issue. More recently, however, there has been a general review of the gas industry by the MMC, three challenges to price caps, and a further current case in telecommunications.

The central reason for the absence of challenges has been that the firms concerned did not think they would be successful. And given the generous settlements which were made at the time of privatisation, it is not surprising that the firms involved did not expect that the MMC would uphold their case or that the Courts would find that regulatory decisions were Wednesbury unreasonable. Nor does the recent experience of those utilities which have pursued MMC references provide great encouragement to others to take this route. The main reason for the demand for accountability from the utilities themselves is a belief that increased political or judicial supervision of regulatory activities would strengthen their bargaining position against the regulator.

They may be correct in this judgement. They are, however, playing with fire. The other source of demand for greater accountability is from politicians. The substantive interest which politicians have is not with the behaviour of the regulatory agency itself, but with the behaviour of the companies which are regulated. Greater political accountability for the regulator is largely seen as a route to greater accountability of the privatised companies. This demand is not altogether inappropriate, and I discuss below the problem of the legitimacy of privatised utilities, already alluded to in the introduction. But the evident and real danger is that a mechanism of direct political accountability – for example, through supervision of regulators by a Parliamentary Select Committee – would lead quite rapidly to a resumption of superficial and short-term interference in the affairs of these industries. As was true under nationalisation, this undermines the responsibility of managers for their business without effectively transferring that responsibility to anyone else; and the development of clear lines of responsibility has been a primary achievement of privatisation.

Individual or Board as Regulator?

An intermediate mechanism might provide for regulation to be conducted by a board, rather than for the powers to be held by an individual. This is already the case in financial services – where the regulator is Chairman of the Securities and Investments Board rather than Director-General of Securities and Investments – and it seems that the practical difference is very small. There have been three holders of the SIB appointment so far, and the differences among them in the style of regulation has been as great as the differences among successive utility regulators.

All three chairmen have, in different ways, been distinguished figures, and the same has generally been true of utility regulators. Two of these, in particular, have done an outstanding job. Sir Bryan Carsberg of Oftel set the style of British utility regulation. In largely uncharted seas, he managed to steer an intermediate course between the capture by the regulatees, which had too often been characteristic of British regulation (as in transport or sponsoring ministries) and the abrasive style familiar from the USA. Ian Byatt at Ofwat has succeeded in sustaining a relatively tough position while maintaining almost universal respect and admiration in the industry he regulates.

This personalisation of regulation is itself another subject of, largely unjustified, criticism. If able people are to be attracted to regulatory positions, it is likely that they will become well-known public figures, if they are not already; and that they will wish to influence the style and behaviour of the organisations of which they are head. The greater danger by far is that the functions are performed by nonentities. Securing staff of appropriate calibre for regulatory agencies is already a serious problem.

This personalisation has led to differences in style among regulators. Such differences are not necessarily undesirable. In the early stages of UK utility regulation, the adoption of different approaches has helped us to learn about the process of regulation. In the recent reviews in water and electricity distribution, the very detailed requests for operating and capital cost information made by Ofwat, although burdensome, ultimately produced an outcome more satisfactory to all than the more light-handed approach of Offer. Nevertheless, as regulation matures, the case for a single body with greater commonality and consistency of approach becomes stronger. Since a common agency would nevertheless continue to have different sections to deal with different industries, the practical consequence of a merger should not be exaggerated.

And, indeed, the practical consequences of any of the measures or issues discussed in this section should not be exaggerated. The key issues, and the key failings, of the existing structure of utility regulation are not to do with process. They are to do with its substantive context.

RPI-X

The RPI-X formula is the distinctive British contribution to the regulatory debate. The concept behind price cap regulation is that it provides reasonable prices to customers while preserving efficiency incentives for regulated firms. In this it has been contrasted, particularly, with price control based on actual costs plus an allowed rate of return on approved capital investment, the traditional basis of utility regulation in the United States.

The effectiveness of this process depends on the basis on which the price cap is determined. If the price cap is set by reference to the actual costs incurred by the firm concerned on a year-by-year basis, then price cap regulation is identical to rate of return regulation. The price cap is simply the mechanism by which the allowed rate of return is achieved.

So if price cap regulation is to differ from rate of return regulation, it is essential that prices should be based, not on what costs are, but on what they ought to be. The best source for this would be knowledge of what has been achieved by other firms, in the UK or overseas. In practice, almost no use has been made of international comparisons in British regulation, and there is little sign of any sustained attempt to develop them. One fundamental problem, which will emerge further below, is that while broad brush comparisons are possible and instructive, it is very difficult to assemble evidence of a rigorous quality which will survive appeal to the MMC or judicial review.

Another source is the cost levels achieved by other companies. The opportunity for yardstick or comparative competition of this kind provided a specific rationale for the maintenance of 10 separate water and sewerage companies and 12 regional electricity companies. But the failure to make comparative competition effective has been one of the major disappointments of the UK regulatory régime. The agencies have not been successful in developing robust measures of relative performance, and have not been able to get beyond broad qualitative groupings of those above and below average. The MMC has been particularly discouraging, treating the limited attempts to use comparative competition as matters of abstract theory. This further retreat from comparative competition was one of the most important conclusions of its recent reviews of price caps. In *Scottish Hydro-Electric*,[2] the MMC substituted its estimate of the company's actual costs for Offer's calculated figures based on the distribution costs incurred by other electricity suppliers. In *Portsmouth Water*,[3] the MMC explicitly rejected the suggestion that a company with costs substantially below average should earn a higher rate of return as reward for its performance.

In practice, price caps are based on forecast costs adjusted by reference to an efficiency target. Thus they partly relate to actual costs (implying a reversion to rate of return regulation), modified by an estimate of attainable cost savings. This was the essential basis of the recent price reviews in both water and electricity distribution. The incentives established by this régime are not particularly attractive, and in some respects perverse.

The regulator cannot, after the event, distinguish between cost savings which arise because cost forecasts were unduly pessimistic and

---

2   MMC, *Scottish Hydro-Electric plc: a report on a reference under section 12 of the Electricity Act 1989*, London: HMSO, June 1995.

3   MMC, *Portsmouth Water plc: a report on the determination of adjustment factors and infrastructure charges for Portsmouth Water plc*, London: HMSO, July 1995.

those which arise because the firm has done better than could reasonably have been expected. The regulated firm has therefore very strong incentives to pad out its forecasts of operating costs and investment needs. Since the regulator knows less than the company about what is indeed necessary, he or she is inevitably forced to make arbitrary reductions in the levels of cost and capital spending planned by firms, and such reductions will, on average, be justified. But these will affect all firms, not just those which most exaggerated their expected costs; and that means that all firms must play the game of proffering inflated estimates of operating costs and investment needs, even if they would rather be frank and open with the regulator.

The game which results is one the regulator must inevitably lose, because the regulator can never know as well as the company what costs and capital programmes are really required. At the same time, it undermines any rational process of investment evaluation. And it also diminishes incentives to control operating costs. All companies can expect to be set efficiency targets higher than would be achievable if they were already operating at the efficiency frontier. Their rational response is to maintain a reserve of inefficiency, some of which can be eliminated in the aftermath of each regulatory review, hence ensuring that each target can be met or outperformed without either eroding too much the capacity to meet future efficiency targets or encouraging these targets to be set at even more optimistic levels.

These are not theoretical or hypothetical concerns. Elements of this behaviour are apparent from the recent regulatory reviews in water and electricity. Such manoeuvring between regulator and industry is likely to become worse as experience of operating this regulatory system grows. The fundamental problem is that regulator and company management have different objectives, and also different information. However much information the regulatory agency demands – and we can expect that it will demand more and more – it remains at a disadvantage. In the MMC's assessment of South West Water,[4] the firm argued that only the company itself was placed to make decisions about what investment was needed to meet its obligations. The MMC held that within the current regulatory structure, such a claim could not be upheld. But both South West Water and the MMC were right in their contentions. It is impossible, or at least inappropriate, to decide from the regulator's office in Birmingham what investment should be

---

[4]   MMC, *South West Water Services Ltd: a report on the determination of adjustment factors and infrastructure charges for South West Water Services Ltd.*, London: HMSO, July 1995.

undertaken and what not. But it is also inappropriate to allow the shareholders of a private company to invest whatever they choose and levy charges on customers to yield a return on whatever they do choose. That inconsistency between the South West Water and MMC positions demonstrates a fundamental weakness in the existing structure of regulation.

It was always appreciated by most thoughtful commentators on RPI-X that it would, in reality, have many of the characteristics of rate of return regulation, and that much of the regulatory intrusiveness which had become familiar under that régime would arise here also. But there is a further problem, which was not widely recognised at privatisation, and which has become evident as the system has operated in practice. It is that 'success' for a company operating under RPI-X means doing better than the regulator had anticipated when he set the price cap. It inescapably follows that such 'success' appears as a failure of regulation and, worse still, that the more effective the incentives provided by RPI-X the more inadequate the regulatory system appears to be. Customer dissatisfaction is simply inherent in the structure and, paradoxically, the better companies perform in managing it the greater such dissatisfaction is likely to be.

Such dissatisfaction had been building up steadily since privatisation. When the golden shares in electricity and water expired in 1995, the emergence of hostile bids forced companies to be explicit about their success in beating the regulatory system. At that point, dissatisfaction boiled over.

The Problem of Legitimacy

Privatisation is, and has remained, an unpopular policy. One recent opinion poll showed that the proportion of the electorate which disapproved of water privatisation had risen from 71 per cent at flotation to 75 per cent now. In its early stages, the main popular attraction of privatisation was the quick and generally substantial gains which small investors made on the shares and there were few, if any, customer benefits. In electricity and water, the process of preparing the industry for privatisation led to higher prices than would otherwise have been imposed.

With longer experience of privatisation, the combination of efficiency gains by the industries and a tighter regulatory régime has led to significant price reductions. Increases in the x factors in telecoms and gas have led to lower consumer prices in nominal terms in the second five-year phase of price regulation. Competition in electricity generation led rapidly to falling prices, and substantial reductions in distribution charges are now in progress. Although water costs will continue to increase in real terms in the second five-year period, the rise will be much less than in the first quinquennium.

Although these things might have been expected to win more support for the framework of privatisation and regulation, criticism has grown rather than diminished. Coincident developments have not helped. The share options which were awarded at flotation have produced unacceptably large gains for senior executives of privatised utilities. Although the salaries of these executives are not high by the admittedly generous standards of private industry generally, many people still remember that the same jobs were done only a short time ago, often by the same people, for relatively modest remuneration.

The fundamental problem which privatised utilities face is that which political scientists recognise is the issue of legitimacy: 'What gives them the right to do that?'. Legitimacy can stem from many sources: traditional authority, direct election, proper and accepted delegation from those whose authority is itself legitimate. Unsatisfactory though the performance of nationalised industries was in many respects, their legitimacy was not in doubt. But this is not true of their successors. Legitimacy is rarely a problem for institutions which are seen to be doing a good job. But, as Fukuyama puts it, 'The strength of legitimate government is that it enjoys a reserve of goodwill which protects it when things go badly'.[5] The weakness of privatised industries is that they enjoy no such goodwill.

The drought of Summer 1995 illustrated precisely that. No reasonable person could blame either privatisation or the managers of water companies for the absence of rain. Yet the result of water shortages was to unleash a further wave of hostility against the privatised industry. That hostility was not confined to newspapers, or politicians, but widely felt and expressed. In earlier droughts, such as that of 1976, there was a general perception of common cause between water suppliers and their customers. Under the current structure, that perception no longer exists, although the actual behaviour of the suppliers is virtually unchanged.

An instructive demonstration of these issues of legitimacy was provided at the recent annual general meeting of British Gas. An ill-timed announcement of a substantial pay rise for the company's chief executive provoked controversy. The AGM provoked a barrage of

---

[5] F. Fukuyama, *The End of History and the Last Man,* Penguin Books, 1992.

hostile criticism of the company and its management. In the end, the chairman used institutional proxies, overwhelmingly supportive of the management, to defeat all critical resolutions by large majorities.

In a real sense, the institution of the AGM – a meeting of the company's shareholders – was being abused. The representatives of the shareholders included, for example, Ken Livingstone, a left-wing Labour MP purportedly representing an American institutional shareholder. Livingstone was not, in fact, there to express concern for the interests of shareholders, and nor were most of those present at the AGM. He was there to make a political speech on what he considered a matter of public interest.

But it is difficult to argue that Livingstone's interest was not a proper one. It is not a good answer to the criticism levied at the company, and at its relative treatment of its own managers, employees and customers, to say that these things are a private matter between the company and its shareholders. They are not. It is a better answer to say that the regulator is the vehicle through which the public interest in these questions is expressed. But the regulator, correctly, argued that few of the matters in dispute lay within her jurisdiction.

And the vote which vindicated British Gas management turns out, under scrutiny, to be an unsatisfactory affair. The billions of votes which supported the board were in fact cast by a small group – well under one hundred – of City investment managers, who had been assiduously cultivated by the British Gas chairman in the weeks preceding the AGM. These individuals were not themselves beneficial owners of claims against British Gas, and insofar as they had proper authority to act on behalf of those who were, it is not at all clear that such authority extended to matters such as these. It is very likely that the views of the beneficial owners, pensioners and holders of life policies, were closer to those which were expressed at the meeting than to the votes that were cast on their behalf. But even if it were practical to canvass the opinions of those who directly or indirectly owned the shares, no-one can seriously believe that seeking these opinions would be a good way to run the company. The whole procedure might be from *Alice in Wonderland*: nothing is what it seems, no-one is what they say they are.

In the early years of privatisation, it could be argued that the unpopularity of privatised industries was a transitional issue, and that once the structure was properly understood it would be more widely accepted. The moral of the British Gas fiasco is that it is wrong to think that the problem is one of education and explanation. On the contrary, the more closely the structure is studied, the less defensible it becomes.

Incentives for Whom?

One of the advantages generally claimed for price cap regulation is the incentive it offers for greater efficiency in the firms concerned. This argument deserves more careful attention than it has received. The incentives provided under the system are incentives to shareholders. To the extent that firms do better than the efficiency targets set with the price cap régime, earnings will be higher than anticipated.

The importance of incentivising shareholders assumes, however, that shareholders are in a position to bring about improvements in the efficiency of the companies concerned or, alternatively, that unless so incentivised they would wish to obstruct such improvements. There seems to be no reason to believe either proposition. The annual general meetings at which small shareholders are represented are a farce, and almost wholly irrelevant to the operational management of the businesses. If large institutional shareholders have played an active rôle in demanding efficiency improvements in some of the worse run utilities, this rôle has been a very low key one.

The simple, obvious point is that the substantial efficiency improvements described have not been brought about by shareholders, but by managers. If it is necessary and desirable to provide incentives to improve the efficiency of utilities, and it is, then the important people to incentivise are managers, not shareholders. Now the interests of managers and shareholders are to some degree aligned. There are two main elements in this – share options and the threat of take-over.

The Cost of Share Options

It is paradoxical that management share options, which are the most criticised single element of privatisation and its consequences, are also the main mechanism for improving the efficiency of privatised companies. They are not, however, a very good mechanism. If we accept for a moment the widely publicised estimate that the managers of privatised utilities have received £25 million in profits on the exercise of share options, we might observe that this amounts to less than 0·1 per cent of the capital gains made by shareholders since flotation. Put another way, each £1 that is used to incentivise managers costs the company's customers £1,000 to provide. That figure might be easier to defend if there was a clear connection between the incentive and the efficiency improvements. But there is not. There is no correlation whatever between the size of the gains which managers have made from stock options and their assiduity in promoting efficiency. If the executives of some English electricity companies have done particularly well, and the Scottish electricity companies and British Gas relatively badly, it is because of the way the cards fell rather than as a result of the effectiveness with which these managers fulfilled their functions.

Several of the privatised companies – such as BT or British Gas – are in practice immune from take-over. Most of the water and electricity companies were subject to a five-year moratorium on bids which has now lapsed. So far, the record of take-over threat as a spur to efficiency inspires little confidence. In only one of the bids so far made or threatened – that of Scottish Power for Manweb – has the suggestion that an alternative management team could do a better job been a central issue. In others, such as Trafalgar House's offer for Northern Electricity, the bidder has no relevant skills or experience and does not profess them. In most, the bidder has promised – whether credibly or not – that he will not change the operations of the firm he is buying in any material way.

If the objective is to give the managers of utilities incentives to provide better service at lower cost, then the best, simplest and cheapest way to do it is to give them incentives to provide better service at lower cost. If bonuses given to executives were based on performance relative to demanding efficiency targets or, better still, directly tied to reductions in charges to customers and improvements in the quality of services offered, then the indignation which has been provoked by the exercise of share options would largely disappear. The reason there is much less hostility to option schemes in other companies is that profits earned in competitive markets are, at least in broad terms, related to the effectiveness of the company. By contrast, the public thinks that profits are easy to earn in monopoly industries and that profits have often increased for reasons which are unrelated to improvements in efficiency or service. And again, the public is right.

Profit-Sharing

If the considerable efficiency advantages which utility privatisation has brought about are to be maintained, it is essential that the link between firm performance and customer benefit be clearly established. At present, the utility retains all benefits up to the time of the next periodic review, at which time an indeterminate fraction of efficiency gains is passed on to customers. It is essential that the lag be shortened and the connection made explicit.

The most obvious method of achieving this is a mechanism for sharing profits between shareholders and customers. The attraction of a system of profit-sharing is that it represents a relatively modest reform which appears to answer some of the central criticisms of the current régime.

On closer examination, however, the scope of the reform is wider than it appears at first sight, and its effectiveness in defusing customer criticism of the current arrangements more doubtful. The measures adopted by several water companies, and the industry-wide agreement on a programme of leakage control, are examples of voluntary profit-sharing arrangements, and both represent constructive responses to recent customer criticism. But the limitations of voluntary arrangements are obvious. Unless very modest in scale – and the profit-sharing proposals put forward so far have been very modest in scale – they create tensions between companies which choose to behave in this way and those which do not, and they put the managers of companies faced with hostile take-over in an untenable position. Unless very limited in amount, profit-sharing is only possible within the framework of broadly agreed industry parameters.

That leads directly to the need to design a profit-sharing formula. There are two main alternatives. One is sharing relative to the starting level. The other is sharing of profits in excess of the amount projected in the regulator's determination of price caps. Such a formula will also need to prescribe the proportions in which profits are to be shared, and also to define whether its operation is symmetric: do customers face increased charges if profits fall or are below the anticipated level? It is probably not realistic to believe that the mechanism could, in practice, operate symmetrically. But the effect of asymmetric operation is significantly to worsen the risk profile of returns faced by the company, and hence to raise its cost of capital and the overall cost of the company's activities.

The simplest method of profit sharing is to propose that a fraction of all profits in excess of today's level be allocated, not to dividends, but to lower customer charges. The great advantage of such a scheme is its simplicity. One consequence is an effective 'tax' on investment by the regulated company. The source of the difficulty is that reported profit is both a return on capital employed and a return to the effectiveness with which the firm operates. This was the paradox evident in *South West*

Water,[6] where the obligation on the company to re-invest heavily in infrastructure improvements necessarily led, under the mechanism for price-setting, not only to steady and substantial increases in charges but also to steady and substantial rises in charges to customers. It would be possible – indeed necessary – to allow for this in the determination of price caps. There is a substantial element of illusion in this – the obligation on the firm to share profits is compensated for by an offsetting adjustment in the level of profits allowed. But the illusion may nevertheless be helpful.

A more logically coherent approach involves sharing of profits in excess of (or conceivably below) the levels provided for in price-setting. This approach would demand that the regulator be more explicit about the basis of his calculations than has generally been the case in past reviews, where elements of judgement have conditioned the final determination. Some would see this as an advantage. I believe it would be the opposite. Under the present régime, the regulator is able to make qualitative judgements about the efficiency levels achieved by companies and about the extent to which companies are taking advantage of the information asymmetry. The loss of the opportunity to do so would aggravate the gaming behaviour between regulator and regulatee which I have described above. It would also probably increase the incidence of MMC appeal and legal challenge.

Any profit-sharing proposal demands definition of the base of profits. The base should be the profits of the regulated activity. Until now, this has not been entirely clear, and a number of regulatory reviews have taken into account the overall profitability of the enterprise, and not just its profits from regulated functions. The effect of this, however, is to impose an ill-defined tax on the firm's non-core functions. Not only is this undesirable, but the converse implication – that regulated customers should share the losses from unsuccessful diversification – is unacceptable. The game has been further changed, fundamentally, by the acquisition of regulated utilities by conglomerates with a wide spread of operations. There has to be a watertight boundary between Hanson's tobacco business and the activities of Eastern Electricity and this must carry over into distinctions between Eastern's first-tier supply business and its other operations. Any extension of profit-sharing therefore requires ring-fencing arrangements between regulated and non-regulated activities, of a kind which currently exist in water but

---

[6] See above, note 4, p.155.

more loosely, if at all, in other industries. Such ring-fencing inevitably involves regulatory scrutiny of all transactions which cross the ring-fence. These include, in particular, financing transactions and it will become necessary to review, and possible to prescribe, the financial structure of the regulated business with the overall plc. Further measures of these kinds are probably now inevitable, whether or not explicit profit-sharing is introduced, and would best be undertaken on a common basis across regulated industries.

Measuring Profits

The most substantial group of issues to be tackled in implementing profit-sharing is that concerned with the measurement of profits. These problems concern both the base level (however defined) and the figures actually reported. The question is whether current accounting practice and standards are sufficiently robust to allow the difference between base profits and actual profits to bear the importance which it would come to enjoy under an explicit rule-based profit-sharing scheme.

This apparently rather technical question is in fact fundamental. Under almost any profit-sharing formula, the impact of changes even in the timing of reported profitability is likely to have a significant impact on the division of gains between customers and shareholders. Issues such as the treatment of redundancy costs, pension holidays, and expenditure of a quasi-capital nature, such as computer system enhancement, have already been the subject of extended discussion in regulatory reviews. These questions, which are at present no more than relevant background, would instead become central to the functioning of the regulatory mechanism. Worse, firms and their accountants would have every incentive to proliferate issues of this kind. It is difficult to see how a conscientious regulator could, in the final analysis, avoid employing his own auditors; not only for the historic accounts but also for the preparation of projections for the setting of price caps.

The attractions of a general profit-sharing mechanism diminish on closer examination. Such a scheme is likely to aggravate the problem of gaming between regulator and regulatee, and to lead to a significant increase in the intrusiveness of regulation. It is also likely to provide friction and disputes which may take us further from, rather than closer to, the fundamental objective of strengthening customer support for, and involvement in, the present system.

The basic problem is familiar from general experience of non-market-based control formulae, such as the Common Agricultural Policy, British local government finance, or more widely in East

European central planning. A common, and natural, response to criticisms of the simple formula, and the distortions of behaviour created by it, is to modify the formula to meet these specific concerns. Unfortunately, the modifications simply generate new concerns, and increase incentives to sophisticated management of the formula, relative to simple management of the business. The results are ones which continue to fail to meet the underlying objectives while, at the same time, involving ever more frequent intrusion in day-to-day behaviour. This was, as I shall note below, the history of British nationalisation.

The issue is therefore whether the basic objectives – of preserving and enhancing management autonomy while clarifying and increasing commitment to customers – can be achieved by a different path of reform. I now turn to this question.

The Customer Corporation

An alternative mechanism of profit-sharing is one which creates a link between dividends paid to shareholders and charges to customers. The merit of this proposal is that it creates an automatic alignment of the interests of customers, investors and the regulator. The adversarial system described above, in which the regulator's concern for customers is pitched against the company's concern for shareholders, neither generates the quality of information needed for regulation nor provides adequate incentives to efficiency or protection to customers.

But a share whose dividend entitlement depends on charges to customers, rather than on the earnings of the company, is fundamentally different in character from a conventional equity. At this point, the economic question of the shape of the regulatory formula and the political issue of the legitimacy of privatised corporations come directly together.

The conventional view is that a company exists to maximise profits for its shareholders. Of course, a company which considered exclusively the interests of its shareholders would not survive for long. For a firm which operates in a competitive market, the only way in which it can serve the interests of its shareholders is by identifying and meeting the interests of its customers.

But a monopoly utility is different. A firm with a legal or practical monopoly of electricity distribution can do well for its shareholders whether it satisfies its customers or not, and that is why the profits earned by utilities are inevitably a matter of controversy. We therefore suggest that the ordering be reversed. The customer corporation is one whose primary objective is to produce services of the quality demanded by its customers at the lowest possible prices. But since it will operate in a competitive capital market, it will be obliged to consider the interests of investors in doing so.

It is important to understand that putting customers first is the natural instinct of the vast majority of managers of privatised utilities. Few of them leap out of bed looking forward to the prospect of another day enhancing shareholder value; but the motivation to do a good job for customers is generally extremely strong. Many such managers will volunteer that the opportunity to give priority to customer interests, with greater freedom from union influence and political restriction, has been the principal benefit of privatisation.

It is an extraordinary feature of current arrangements that, far from encouraging this emphasis on the consumer, the structure invites managers of utilities to fight against it. It encourages, even requires, that they pursue shareholder value, with the regulator as customer advocate, in the essentially adversarial relationship between companies and regulator described above. It presupposes a priority of shareholder interests which would not necessarily be defended even by the shareholders of these companies themselves. If we truly believed that a water company put the interests of its shareholders ahead of its customers, we would prefer not to have to drink their water.

The companies often do not behave as the model would have them behave, but why do we encourage this futile tension in the first place? The customer corporation leaves managers free to do what they mostly want to do and what we want them to do. It removes an apparent divergence of interest between companies and the public which is quite unnecessary and which has created much of the discontent with the performance of privatisation and regulation.

In advocating customer corporations, I emphatically do not propose either that management should be elected by customers or that customers should 'own' the business. It is essential that these firms are run by teams with common interests, values and identity. Although Yorkshire Water's response was heavy-handed and inept, the election to the Board of Diana Scott (the vocal chair of the company's Customer Service Committee who subsequently sought election to the Board) would not have served the best long-term interests of that company's customers. If the board of a company is not united in purpose and objective, it rarely functions effectively, and the practical consequence is that substantive decisions are made outside it.

The customer interest is likely to be better served by professional managers committed to that interest, and accountable for it, than by representatives of consumers (who are, in the main, rendered unrepresentative by their very willingness to undertake the task). We should learn from the competitive failure of the co-operative movement. Much of the problem was that customers were not, in fact, interested in exercising control, which reverted to employees and politicians. The present method of Board selection and election of public companies generally is considerably less than ideal, but it functions tolerably well in practice, and there is no urgent need to change it. The Board of a customer corporation should, however, be encouraged to be widely representative of the community in which it operates. (Its non-executive directors should not be exclusively businessmen, or exclusively members of any political party, or exclusively anything, for that matter.) Such a requirement should be part of the customer corporation statute.

Activities for Customer Corporations

The following activities are some of those which would be appropriate for customer corporations:

- Water and sewerage services;
- Electricity distribution in England and Wales;
- The National Grid;
- Electricity distribution and transmission in Scotland and Northern Ireland;
- British Gas TransCo ;
- Airport non-trading functions;
- Railtrack;
- The Post Office;
- BT Network Services;
- The BBC.

There is no reason why a customer corporation could not be 'owned' by a plc, in the specific sense that all voting securities of the customer corporation would be owned by the plc. And given the current starting-point, we visualise that most customer corporations would, in fact, be owned by a plc. Thus, Eastern Electricity Customer Corporation might be wholly 'owned' by Hanson plc or by Eastern Group plc. 'Ownership' would, however, relate only to the securities of the customer corporation concerned. The plc would not 'own' the assets or revenue streams of the customer corporation and would not be able to use these assets or revenue streams as security for its own borrowings, although it would, of course, be able to use its shares in the customer corporation and its dividends from them for these purposes. The customer corporation would not be permitted to undertake any activities other than those prescribed in its licence, although a plc which owned it would enjoy the normal freedoms. This would imply ring-fencing the monopoly utility activities of the customer corporation, and any transactions between the customer corporation and its plc parent would be the subject of specific regulatory approval. Arrangements of this kind already exist in the water industry, but would need to be introduced into other utilities.

The Financial Structure of a Customer Corporation

I expect to be told that no-one would invest in a customer corporation, and certainly at first sight it would seem that a move to order interests of customers ahead of shareholders would make it more difficult to raise money from shareholders. This view is superficial. Customer corporations would certainly attract investment, and because of their low-risk character it is likely that they would do so more cheaply than do privatised utilities under the current system of regulation.

The recent regulatory reviews have put the cost of capital to the regulated water and electricity industries at around 6-7 per cent in real terms. The activities concerned are inherently of very low risk – the monopoly supply of electricity and water under a régime which requires the regulator to secure a reasonable rate of return on the assets involved. This return is above what might be expected for such a low-risk activity, since the Government's risk-free debt offers a rate of return of around 3-4 per cent in real terms. The difference is accounted for by the greater insecurity of investment in utility plcs.

Uncertainty about the earnings streams of activities such as water and electricity distribution arises from two main sources. One is the possibility of divergence between the regulator's efficiency target and the actual outcome. The other is uncertainty about the evolution of the regulatory régime itself. If these sources of uncertainty were removed or reduced – as would be true for a customer corporation – then the cost of capital would be reduced correspondingly.

What does this mean in practice for the capital structure of a customer corporation? A customer corporation could be expected to carry considerably more debt in its balance sheet than do the existing utility plcs. Indeed, this is already true of the utility plcs themselves and restructuring to increase gearing is in progress. The debt of these companies might be provided by the parent plc (subject to the regulatory oversight described above) or raised directly by the customer corporation.

Kinds of Equity for Customer Corporations

The equity of customer corporations might take two forms: indexed preferred stock, and ordinary shares. Indexed preferred stock (IPS) would carry a dividend coupon linked to the RPI, but the dividend could be passed in circumstances which would lead the company into loss. It would, in any event, have priority over the payment of any ordinary dividend and the holders would acquire voting rights over the company if dividends were not paid on the due date.

The existing security most similar to the indexed preferred stock of a customer corporation is the permanent interest-bearing shares (PIBS) which are used as subordinated capital by building societies. PIBS offer fixed rather than indexed dividends, and there is no reason why customer corporations could not issue PIBS, but the indexed revenue stream implied by the current regulatory control makes IPS particularly appropriate. PIBS command a premium of 1-2 per cent over equivalent government stock. The security offered by the IPS of a customer corporation would generally be substantially greater than that attached to PIBS, and it seems realistic to believe that IPS could be issued on yields of between 5 and 6 per cent. Anglian Water's indexed loan stock, with greater security, currently yields 4·55 per cent.

That leaves the ordinary securities of the customer corporation. As described above, these might be directly held by individuals and institutions, or wholly owned by a plc whose shares were in turn owned by individuals and institutions. In either case, the ordinary shareholders would enjoy the usual voting rights attached to such shares and would be entitled to a stream of dividends. There are at least three possible ways in which such dividends might be determined.

One possibility is that the ordinary shares might themselves have indexed dividends. In this case they would be further subordinated to IPS. The attraction of this is that it is simple and minimises the need for regulatory oversight. The weakness is that ordinary shareholders have little incentive to take an interest in the company's efficiency. Their concern need not extend beyond ensuring that the company is not in danger of being unable to meet the dividend payments on its equity.

An alternative is that the directors of the customer corporation might set dividends by reference to what they consider reasonable, in all the circumstances and in the light of their statutory duties. If this sounds, and is, vague, it is nevertheless exactly the mechanism by which the dividend policies of plcs are determined today. As the dividend policies of the plc are, in a loose sense, subject to shareholder supervision and, in a formal sense, subject to shareholder approval, so it would seem appropriate for the dividend policies of the customer corporation to be the subject of regulatory oversight. The interests of customers would be protected by the statutory obligations of the company and the ultimate ability of the regulator or of the customers themselves to seek legal enforcement of them. The interests of shareholders would be protected by the company's need to secure continued access to the capital markets.

Would shareholders be willing to hold securities whose rights are thus ill-defined? The evidence of other markets suggests that so long as conventions and competition secure adequate returns, there is little practical problem. In practice, a broad framework for dividend policy could be agreed; for example, real dividend growth might normally be in line with output volume, subject to variation upward or downward for exceptional performance, with that performance judged in relation to customer price and service quality.

Another version would make that relationship explicit. For example, changes in dividend levels might be linked to changes in customer charges, so that dividends would rise when charges fell, and vice versa. Differences between companies in the proposed for charge increases and reductions would be translated into differences in the operating value of equity. It would be necessary to prescribe a formula for measuring charges, and to define how it would be adjusted for variations in service quality. The weakness of this system is that the reliance on a formula re-introduces, although in a much attenuated form, some of the gaming between regulator and company I have criticised above. It is, however, best in allowing companies which believe they can do better for customers to bid for control of the customer corporation, but automatically restricts the class of potential bidders to those who believe they can achieve this (and allows them to profit from the acquisition only to the extent they do).

There are advantages and disadvantages to each of these mechanisms, and no doubt other mechanisms, and other advantages and disadvantages, would emerge over time. Once the general principle is accepted, there is no reason why each company should not find its own distinctive solution.

Regulating the Customer Corporation

The essence of these proposals is that many of the duties of the regulator are taken over by the board of the customer corporation itself. The intention is to replace a régime based on a battle between managers representing shareholders and a regulator representing customers with one in which a customer-oriented management makes the trade-offs for itself. Ideally, this might remove the need for regulation altogether. That would be to go too far. But there are overwhelming advantages from a shift from a relationship between regulator and regulatee which is fundamentally adversarial to one in which both parties are pursuing broadly similar objectives. The result would be a much more light-handed system of regulation than we currently have.

One of the regulator's principal duties would be to assemble and publish information on the comparative performance of firms. There is no good reason why any information about the activities or performance of a customer corporation should be commercially confidential, so that publication would be a key element in promoting performance. In effect, the regulator's job would be to point the finger at firms with poor relative performance – a more informal, but probably more effective, mechanism of comparative competition.

A key function for the regulator would be to police the ring-fence between the customer corporation and the owners of its securities. The objective would be that such transactions would be subject to the same rigorous evaluation that is applied to transactions involving trustees. The regulator would also provide, as to a degree he does today, an important buffer between political influence and operational management of utilities; not eliminating that influence, but preventing it constraining day-to-day management.

Conclusions

On balance, the credit ledger of privatisation far exceeds the debits. The task for the next decade is to find a structure which preserves these gains while meeting the criticisms which are fairly levelled at the existing arrangements.

I have argued that the key to this is to move to a structure which entrenches clear priority for consumer interests in monopoly utilities while maintaining and in general enhancing the freedom of operational management which has been the most valuable product of the last decade of privatisation and regulation. The customer corporation is a vehicle for achieving that.

It recognises fully the consumer interest, while minimising the need for politicians and regulator to second guess what are best taken as managerial decisions. It is less novel than it sounds. It is, in reality, a modernisation of the statutory water company framework, which was by no means unsuccessful in Britain for over a century; the companies were, on average, more efficient than their public sector counterparts but suffered none of the problems of legitimacy which have dogged their privatised successors. There are other historical and institutional parallels. Indeed, one of the attractions of the customer corporation framework is its relevance to schools, hospitals and other state activities for which full privatisation is inconceivable but a dilution of unproductive structures of political and bureaucratic control essential.

CHAIRMAN'S COMMENTS

Rt. Hon. Sir Christopher Chataway
Civil Aviation Authority

PROFESSOR KAY SAYS THAT THE CREDIT LEDGER for privatisation far exceeds the debits. But he has argued with a bold sweep that we must nevertheless beat a 'partial retreat from privatisation' and introduce something new. He has not confined himself to the usual agenda, though he has had some interesting things to say on a number of topical concerns. I agree with him that any reform which lands more substantive issues in the courts is to be avoided. In New Zealand, where there is no industry-specific economic regulation, price disputes affecting Telecom and Wellington Airport have for example taken years to unravel in the courts.

I agree that somewhat greater use of an appeal mechanism to the MMC should be encouraged and it seems to me that there could be provisions in some industries at least for an appeal by consumers. Unlike Profess Kay I come down on the side of Don Cruickshank of Oftel and others who have argued in favour of regulation by a Board rather than an individual. At the CAA the Economic Regulator, Cliff Paice, benefits I believe from the advice and the protection afforded by such a Board. Certainly, if as John Kay envisages, there should one day be just one Economic Regulator it seems to me unthinkable that 'Off – everything' could conceivably just be a he or a she. A powerful Board would be needed if only to withstand the non-stop attempts at interference from government. But these are all issues that are well debated.

Professor Kay's thesis is a more challenging one. He is arguing that the present set-up is beyond repair for three reasons. I think we may wish to probe all of them. The *first* defect he sees is that the terms on which utilities were privatised were much too favourable to firms and their shareholders and gave insufficient attention to customers. But this is just not true of all the utilities. The Gas shareholder, the villain of the moment, or the shareholder in BT, have done no better since privatisation than the FTSE all-share index. Excluding the surge on first day's trading they have in fact generally under-performed the index. In contrast, the Gas customer has seen a domestic price fall of over 20 per cent in real terms and BT's prices overall have of course plummeted. Although there have been steep price increases for water to catch up on years of under-investment, the general picture is of small reductions during the first Government-set price régime and steep falls after that. The immediate jump in share prices on flotation was sometimes excessive, but in criticising the Government and its merchant bank advisers it is easy to forget the mass of political uncertainties surrounding many of those flotations at the time.

The *second* deficiency is the absence of an explicit mechanism for securing a substantial share of expected efficiency gains for customers. To that I would say, first, that unlike their nationalised predecessors, the privatised utilities have delivered enormous efficiency gains and even 25 per cent of a lot is better than 0 per cent of nothing. But I would also argue that the quinquennial price-cap régime has on the whole done better for customers than Professor Kay allows. For example, four years ago we set a régime for BAA of RPI-6. It has delivered those price reductions and generally beaten the profit targets. The customer will gain the full benefit of those additional efficiencies from the start of the new quinquennium. I do not, incidentally, feel that BAA's success in beating targets represents a failure for the CAA as regulator. Without incentives BAA might never have hit the original targets.

But if I have understood Professor Kay right, the real reason for calling it a day with these industries and starting all over again is his *third* perceived deficiency. The privatised utilities apparently lack legitimacy and no amount of tinkering will restore it to them. I remember in the 1960s and 1970s a lot of people saying the same about Parliament. Britain's so-called democracy had, we were told, lost its legitimacy and direct action was the only thing. They may have been right, I suppose. French constitutional reform has often proceeded in that way. And all those who translate their dislike of certain privatised utilities into an assertion of illegitimacy may be right too.

But I am doubtful when I hear the grounds on which this is argued. John Kay cites the AGM of British Gas at which the great battle was fought over Cedric Brown's pay. This was all British farce in the best Brian Rix tradition. Mr Brown's salary had been put up to perhaps a third of the going rate for an enterprise of this size. His salary certainly would not put him among the top 1,000 earners in the City of London. We should never have heard about it, if any reasonably well-known politician had misplaced his trousers during the same week. We would hardly have heard about it if the British Gas Chief Executive had followed at least one previous precedent and announced that he was giving his increase for the year to charity.

The British public is appalled by the vast sums paid to businessmen whenever they are drawn to its attention – taking the view that it is only entertainers and sportsmen who have particular talents that need rewarding. So, for weeks on end, we were treated to the delicious spectacle of eminent columnists with an hourly rate probably higher than Cedric Brown's working themselves into paroxysms of indignation. I really think that whether Mr Brown should go or stay and for how much is a matter for all the shareholders. If the institutions whose managers' pay and future employment depend upon their performance have no confidence in him or think that he is overpaid the Board will soon know. To imply that the whole system lacks legitimacy because private shareholders at the meeting representing 2 or 3 percentage of the vote are unable to get their way seems to me odd.

But what of the 'Consumer Corporation'? My first impression is that it relies rather a lot upon the good nature of management. It is not clear that there are many disciplines or incentives upon them. I rate more highly than John Kay both the disciplines and the incentives of the existing system and doubt whether the huge gains in efficiency would have been achieved without them. A principal purpose of converting the privatised utilities in this way is presumably to reduce the amount of money the shareholders get now and in the future because a lot of the objection is that customers are getting too little of the benefit and shareholders too much. Is the partial retreat from privatisation to go along with partial confiscation? Are the shareholders to be given bits of paper in place of their existing securities which are worth much less? Surely not. For one thing, the regulatory risk would be multiplied by x and the cost of capital for the future would presumably be sky-high. The shareholders are presumably therefore to be compensated by the consumer. Out of vastly increased borrowings perhaps they will be compensated for the drop in value of their holdings. But, if this is what has to happen, it is by no means obvious that the total amount paid by the utilities to providers of capital now and in the future will be in any way diminished.

Privatisations are underway around the world. It would be curious if Britain as a pioneer, and despite the big efficiency improvements achieved, were to put the process in reverse. Privatisation is often unpopular. The big job losses that go with the end of large-scale over-manning are a principal cause. Capitalism itself is never that popular. All that can be said is that nationalisation is probably even more unpopular. I am not yet persuaded that Professor Kay has identified a new, viable middle way but I am sure his paper will provoke much discussion and many questions.

7

PUTTING THE RAILWAYS BACK TOGETHER AGAIN: RAIL PRIVATISATION, FRANCHISING AND REGULATION

Dieter Helm
New College, University of Oxford

Introduction

RAILWAY PRIVATISATION HAS PROVED to be one of the most difficult to complete. Part of the reason lies in the change of political mood. Part lies with the lacuna in transport policy which shows up every day on our roads and rail stations in congestion and pollution. The main reason is, however, the ambitious nature of the restructuring of the industry. Its complexity has only one parallel, that of the electricity industry, and indeed electricity has provided an important model.

The complexity is the natural consequence of the attempt to introduce competition into the industry. Only a major restructuring could allow market forces to enter into it. The break-up of British Rail was therefore a necessary consequence of the adherence to the 'competitive model' for utilities – the structural separation of natural monopoly from potentially competitive elements and the creation of a number of potentially or actually competing firms within the latter arena. But the architects of this privatisation have gone much further. The structural separation has also introduced distinctions between train operators and train owners, and track owners and many supporting services. As with electricity, supply (train operation) is separated from distribution (track operation), and generation (trains) from supply (train operation). The result is that over 70 firms will provide the services which were once provided by the nationalised industry.

Such a system needs a lot of regulation, as has been discovered in electricity. The reason is that there is little which follows the dictates of commercial logic. Electricity companies have chosen vertical integration, and as I shall argue, in the long run, the rail industry is likely to re-integrate. As with electricity, this may be through ownership or – as in the 'transition' to open access in the rail case – through contracts.

To see why this tentative conclusion has some merit, I shall begin my presentation by summarising the structure of the privatised industry and showing how the financial flows link the parties to each other (Section 2). I shall then consider the franchises in the railway industry structure as special kinds of contracts. These franchise contracts introduce an important element of competition (Section 3). The privatisation structure and the form of competition do, however, have drawbacks, and re-integration is to be expected (Section 4). Finally, some tentative conclusions will be presented (Section 5).

The New Structure of the Railway Industry

The restructuring of the railway industry is essentially an exercise in separating out all the main components into separate firms, and then linking them back together by contracts. The structure is set out below in Figure 1.

These new firms do business with each other, and this is facilitated by contracts. There is little 'spot' pricing which characterises 'competitive' markets. In the process of setting up the arrangements, the potential new train operators willing to take up the franchises have faced considerable uncertainty in entering into an untried structure. They have, in consequence, lobbied successfully for contracts which eliminate the risks of short-term competition. Competition will only arrive in the medium term, after a trial period of effective franchise monopoly. The objective of *privatisation* already overwhelmingly dominates that of *competition*, the original rationale for the restructuring. The irony is that if this is the main purpose, then the 'single integrated company' model might have been the best approach.

An additional feature of railway privatisation is that a commercial market would not support the level of service which British Rail has in the past provided. Therefore, *subsidy* is an important element to the system. In Figure 2, the link from government to the railway companies is an important part of the financial jigsaw. In effect, the government pays the train operators who then pay track access fees to Railtrack.

[*continued on p.181*]

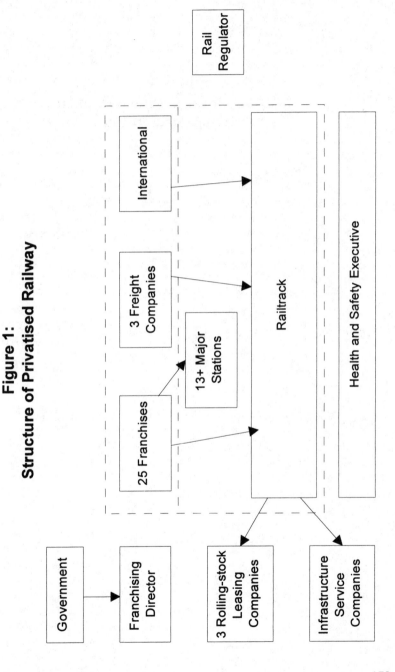

Figure 1:
Structure of Privatised Railway

Figure 2:
Transfers in the British Rail Sector
after Restructuring

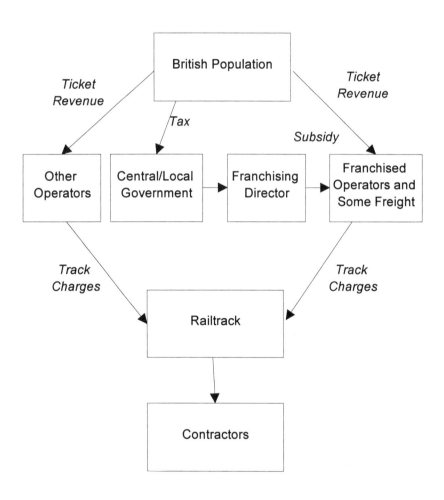

The effect on privatisation is important: Railtrack is, to a limited but important extent, the capitalisation of subsidies paid by government.

Franchises as a Form of Contract

At the heart of the privatised railway structure is a series of franchises, which facilitate the creation of two kinds of monopolies, the train operating companies (TOCs), and the more long-term monopoly (Railtrack). Competition *for* the former has been embedded from the beginning, through a tendering process. The latter will be sold to the public directly.

The franchise concept extends the boundaries of competition. It creates, as Demsetz famously noted,[1] the possibility of competition *for* monopoly. Franchises can be auctioned, realising the highest revenue (or in the railway case, sometimes the lowest subsidy) to the seller (normally the government), or yielding the lowest price to customers. The scope for franchises arises wherever there is a monopoly: for example, at the recent periodic review in electricity distribution, it would have been possible (had periodic franchises been granted) to invite bids for the largest X factor for particular Regional Electricity Company areas. Indeed, the current take-over frenzy in the electricity industry is, in effect, a bidding process for monopoly franchises under a given RPI-X, returning the surpluses to shareholders rather than government or customers.

Franchising therefore can be thought of as a particular way of contracting. In letting such contracts – which is what the franchise director does – an important element of regulation is introduced. Compliance to the terms of the contract and ensuring an open competition when franchises come up for renewal are important regulatory functions. As experience indicates from other industries, winning the initial competition can provide incumbents with major competitive advantages.

The railway franchises are, however, different from the conventional form and therefore add an additional complexity into regulation: they provide for a gradual – and as yet poorly defined – transition to the competitive market. The textbook example of many potential bidders for slots across the system, with Railtrack in the middle, has been at least temporarily put in the 'too difficult' box.

---

[1] H. Demsetz, 'Why Regulate Utilities?', *Journal of Law and Economics*, Vol.1, No.1, 1968, pp.55-67.

It is here that the rail regulator confronts his most difficult problem: how to 'manage' the gradual promotion of competition. As experience from other industries has illustrated, *regulation for competition* is a much more complicated affair than *regulation of monopoly*.

It will be even more demanding in railways than in electricity, since the former requires considerable investment, whilst the latter does not. Competition may be good at promoting operating efficiency, but its effects on capital investment are more ambiguous. Where uncertainty over future markets is placed upon operators, the incentive to invest may be weakened. As I shall argue, the market response may be re-integration.

The investment needs of the industry lie in various parts. The railway infrastructure, controlled largely by Railtrack, has a capital expenditure requirement which can be managed through the traditional RPI-X periodic review framework. It is a regulated franchise, with output targets. The problems here are similar to those in the water industry: Railtrack will in the longer run have the incentive to overstate its capital expenditure requirements ahead of regulatory reviews, and then cut back afterwards. There is to date no generally accepted way of coping with this problem, short of *ad hoc* corrections. The infrastructure problem in the network may, however, be much easier to deal with than that of rolling stock and trains – at least in principle. Separating rolling stock from TOCs provides many of the incentives which are apparent to drivers of company-owned cars. Train builders will look for contracts which recover their capital costs. The operators will be looking to their cash flow. Put simply, the short-term needs to generate cash out of existing stock may dominate the long-term needs to renew that stock. But the extent of this problem is far from clear.

Re-integrating the Structure

Left to market forces – as is being currently demonstrated in the electricity industry – the neat divisions set up in the initial structure would probably rapidly collapse. Faced with potential competition, commercial firms may seek greater control. Re-integration might follow. The implication is of critical importance to regulation: *the current structure may only survive as long as regulators and governments insist upon it.* Furthermore, because re-integration may be the natural commercial step, the companies may well, in any event, strive to reproduce many of the features of integration through contracts. In electricity, the regional electricity companies sought 10-15 year back-to-back contracts with so-called independent power producers, who in turn entered take-or-pay contracts with gas producers. This was *de facto* vertical integration. In rail, the new operators may well try to gain ownership (or at least contractual control) over track and even equipment supply. In addition, they may seek horizontal integration with buses (indeed, some bidders for franchises already fall into this category).

The regulator and the Government will need to consider their responses to these pressures. It may be attractive to a Labour government to allow the market to put the bits so carefully separated back together again. The Conservatives have (to an extent) proved willing to go down this route in electricity, and may succumb in railways after the election, if they are still in power.

From a public interest perspective, re-integration may also be desirable. The choice between a market transaction and an internal one is a matter of balancing the costs of the two forms of organisation. As Williamson pointed out[2] a long time ago, the matter is an empirical one. The new system of structural regulation certainly has high transactions costs. It remains to be seen whether these are less than the efficiency gains from a more open structure and whether the new fragmented industry will result in better investment quality and a lower cost of capital. The evidence from the electricity industry, the closest comparator in many respects, is at present far from encouraging.

Conclusions

I have argued that the new railway structure places considerable emphasis on the effectiveness of structural regulation. The concept of franchising has much to commend it, but the particular form of the railway franchises may not be sustainable in the longer term. From a public interest perspective, the investment issues are significant in railways and it is far from obvious that the new structure gives sufficient attention to them.

A possible response from the new companies is to seek to re-integrate, either through take-overs and mergers, or – if this is blocked by regulation – through contracts which reproduce many of the features of vertical and horizontal integration. If Labour wins the general election, the re-integration may simply come about faster than under the current government. However, as recently witnessed in electricity, initial privatisation structures are not sacred cows.

---

[2] O.E. Williamson, *Markets and Hierarchies: Analysis and Antitrust Implications*, New York: Free Press, 1975.

CHAIRMAN'S COMMENTS

John Swift, QC

Office of the Rail Regulator

LET ME START WITH A LITTLE ANECDOTE. In early 1993 I was appointed Special Adviser to the Secretary of State and Regulator Designate. As often happens with first meetings with civil servants, they try to bounce one. We were looking at the Railways Bill 1993, and I was asked for my views.

I said that, as I understood it, one of my duties was to promote competition in the supply of railway services. I addressed this question to the Permanent Secretary. He said: 'Yes that's perfectly correct'. I said that, as I understood it, you are setting up Railtrack as a monopoly, and you are proposing to moderate competition in respect of the first set of franchises, so Railtrack will be supplying track access services to franchisees who will themselves be protected from competition. I asked: 'How, in those circumstances, am I supposed to promote competition?' There was a pause, and the Permanent Secretary said: 'That is a perfectly good question, I will ask the Deputy Secretary to answer that.'

So the Deputy Secretary looked at the Permanent Secretary and said: 'John has identified a possible tension in the development of our policies, but I will ask the Under Secretary to give the full answer.' He turned to the Under Secretary, who then sought to explain that it was all really a question of time and that one might engage in a process of moderation of competition in the short term in order to develop competitive structures on a sound basis in the longer term. And there I saw immediately that Railtrack privatisation, the privatisation of the passenger train operations, and the privatisation of the freight train operations would not be completed in a nice, simple manner within an easily definable term.

I think Dieter is absolutely right: the structure that was prepared on the blackboard of Marsham Street[1] has proved to be more complex, more difficult, and more costly to implement than those textbook designers and blackboard designers thought in the first place. That is

---

[1]   Editor's note: Marsham Street in London is the address of the Department of Transport.

not to say they are wrong, but the costs of 'conversion', if I can use an expression familiar to my economist friends, from a single public sector corporation which has been under state control for 47 years into a set of 70 companies, all of which have to be related to each other through contracts, themselves supported by the state, in an industry which still requires a subsidy of £1·8 billion a year, has taxed the taxpayer more than might have been contemplated by the theory. The costs of conversion have been very significant.

Whether the long-term costs to the industry, and thus to the taxpayer and to the user, will be greater as a result of the process of privatisation, I think remains to be seen. A great deal will depend upon success in the first target in Dieter's conclusions, which is the emphasis on operating cost efficiency. This is not a question of just shaking the tree of British Rail, which would have happened had there been privatisation of British Rail as a whole. It is shaking the tree of 70 separate organisations (as is happening at the moment) to see what fruits fall. Without giving too much to the Austrian School, inevitably a discovery mechanism is involved, because one does not know the extent of inefficiencies that have been hidden within British Rail.

I do not say that British Rail is an inefficient company, but it has priced in a monopolistic manner; all decisions have been governed by 47 years of state control; and three-year PES[2] rail negotiations. That is the situation which is now being revolutionised.

In terms of competition, one has, of course, to remember that three freight companies have been established. Three rolling stock companies have been established, as have more than 10 companies responsible for infrastructure service maintenance. It remains to be seen whether or not, in due course, there will be rationalisation and merger as between those companies. Of course, we intend to concentrate our efforts on the passenger train operators and the franchising system, but there are other sets of outputs and inputs which will themselves contribute to the efficiency of those operations. A very useful way of testing a blackboard structure is to see what is happening on the ground. I have found in my many trips around the track that the passenger train operators are already adjusting to a situation in which they control the operation of their trains from A to B. That is, they have established effective working relationships with Railtrack, with the

---

2   Editor's note: The annual budgeting round conducted by the Treasury. Three years is the period for which bids are invited.

rolling stock companies and with others involved in that process. Now, I cannot test that against any theory of economic efficiency. What I can say is that those elements of the re-structuring appear to be working reasonably well.

There have, of course, been publicity disasters in the operation of the railways which those who are opponents of the present structure will almost certainly attribute to the process of re-structuring, whether it is the great British time-table which needs its third supplement, whether it is the fares, whether it is the so-called regulated sponsored routeing guide which takes two men to carry into a ticket office – or any number of those. They have also served to provide public relations disasters for those protagonists of the re-structuring process and a windfall for the Labour and SDP politicians who are determined to do down privatisation.

However, the system is working. There is a momentum, but we will not see the full benefits in operating costs efficiency in the course of this financial year. Rather, I think, we are talking about the next two or three years. I certainly expect to see the market leading on questions of re-structuring. I think Dieter is right when he said that it will be the market which drives. One has to distinguish, therefore, between those solutions which are market-driven in the sense they contribute to increased efficiency, and those market solutions which are seeking the acquisition of a dominant position or the knock-on effects of seeking to shelter oneself from new positions which are being developed initially in the market-place.

It does not take me to remind you of the huge inefficiencies which were created as a result of vertical integration in the milling and baking industries in the early 1970s as a result of a desperate need by the millers to buy into baking. As a result of it, massive inefficiencies were incurred by the industry which took years to eradicate, precisely because they were seeking to develop an oligopolistic structure based on vertical integration. I, as a regulator, have to be extremely careful to ensure that I use my powers to increase the likelihood of efficient outcomes, and to remove the possibility of the second kind of outcomes. This will continue to be a major job, affecting not just my office but also the Franchising Director, because he has to decide who are going to be the successful bidders for the franchises, and the Government.

Two final words. First, Dieter finishes with the conclusion that Labour may speed up this process and the process may include speeding up my exit from this job, I suppose. On the other hand, at a conference which I was invited to address last week, which was hosted by Dieter at Oxera, the Labour spokesman for Trade and Industry and for Transport (Mr Brian Wilson) did not think I would have much to do, in the sense of regulating privatised railway firms. When Labour gets into power, he could offer me the buses. Those of you who are familiar with the IPPR Study[3] will know that Labour, at least in principle, favours the idea of regulation by industry sector; so it is perfectly possible that we will not be Ofrail, but Oftransport, by 1997. So our eyes are already on the CAA for airports; London Underground is just around the corner, and we already have the railways. Not, in any sense, you will understand, is this grandiose power-seeking by the regulator or his office!

In conclusion, this process of re-structuring has at its heart an industry which continues to get state subsidy and state funding. Dieter has quite rightly pointed out the idea of state contracts. Enterprises created out of the new railways industry will depend, in the short or the long term, on major structural decisions by the Government as to the kind of rail industry it wants, and the costs it is prepared to incur in order to support the industry. There is regulatory uncertainty, and there are uncertainties arising out of the reconstructed industry. But the biggest uncertainty of all remains the lack of a bi-partisan policy involving both the Conservative Party and the Labour Party, on the kind of railway system they want for the future. We are going through a short-term reconstruction which has long-term implications for users and taxpayers in this country.

Speaking personally, it is a fascinating process to be engaged in. I cannot wipe the blackboard clean. I have to work with the structures we have, but I can assure you we are not here to preserve blackboard solutions into the 21st century. We are here to adopt a pragmatic solution and accept market-led structural change. It is essential to increase benefits to the users for whom this complex and radical legislation has been passed.

---

[3] Dan Corry, David Souter and Michael Waterson, *Regulating Our Utilities*, London: Institute for Public Policy Research, 1994.

8

LESSONS FOR UK REGULATION FROM RECENT US EXPERIENCE

Irwin M. Stelzer

American Enterprise Institute

Introduction

I HAVE THREE REASONS for approaching this paper with great trepidation. *First*, it is daunting to be among so distinguished a group of contributors to regulatory theory and practice. *Second*, it is awkward for an American to suggest ways in which British institutions might be improved – by being more like those in America! *Third*, my assignment is fraught with peril: I am asked to extract from recent American experience with regulation some 'Lessons for UK Regulation'. This assignment rests on two rather dubious assumptions:

1. It assumes that a foreigner can understand just what is going on in Britain's regulatory arena. That is an heroic assumption, since the regulatory process here is not as transparent as the one in my country, a point to which I shall return in a moment. In his wonderful book on your country's constitution, Peter Hennessy refers to '... this curious compound of custom and precedent, law and convention, rigidity and malleability concealed beneath layers of opacity and mystery ...'[1] I will not go so far as to argue that Britain's regulatory process is as opaque and mysterious as its constitution. But I will suggest – by way of exculpation for any errors I am about to make – that an outside observer such as myself does not always find the published decisions of the regulators, the competition authorities, and the Department of Trade and Industry a

---

[1] Peter Hennessy, *The Hidden Wiring: Unearthing the British Constitution*, London: Victor Gollancz, 1995, p.7.

crystal-clear guide as to what really went on, what was really decided, and what, in apparently similar circumstances, might be decided in the future.

2. A second, and even more problematic assumption underlying my topic, 'Lessons For UK Regulation From Recent US Experience', is that it assumes that someone in Britain believes that it is indeed possible to learn from American experience. Experience teaches me, however, that an American imprimatur does not guarantee that an idea or product will be well received here: it is not the equivalent of a royal warrant. Indeed, it has been my experience that my British friends very often succeed in scuppering an idea they find disagreeable by the simple expedient of labelling it 'American-style', as in the phrase, 'American-style fast-food'. Thus, when the debate about aviation policy was raging here, anyone who suggested that American experience with free and open competition might contain lessons for Britain was accused of proposing 'American-style deregulation', code words for anarchy and chaos. And when the various 'OFFs' – wat, gas, er and tel – were being established, any suggestion that procedures be adopted to make the regulatory process transparent and accessible to all affected parties was derided as an invitation to 'American-style litigation', a fate that would eventually doom regulators to be harassed by (a) silly consumers who presumed to know when they were receiving poor service and when they were being held to ransom, and (b) potential new entrants who thought that a willingness to risk their capital somehow gave them the right to compete with incumbent service providers.

True, 'the litigious nature of the American [cost-plus] system ... might have posed less acute problems in the more secretive British framework', as one leading British academic has argued.[2] But it was, nevertheless, to be avoided.[3]

Indeed, so great was, and is, the fear of 'American-style litigation' that one would think that acceptance of the American procedural model would doom Britain to a situation in which it would be impossible for

---

[2]   Catherine Price, 'Economic Regulation of Privatised Monopolies', in Peter M. Jackson and Catherine M. Price, *Privatisation and Regulation: A Review of the Issues*, London: Longman Group, 1994, p.82.

[3]   I am not here arguing in favour of a full-employment act for lawyers, or even for economists, although such legislation would have one major advantage: economists involved in regulatory proceedings would have less time to unburden themselves of economic forecasts.

ambulance drivers to respond to emergency calls lest they run down the horde of fee-crazed lawyers that would be spawned as the American disease spread from the offices of the regulatory bodies onto the streets of Britain's cities and towns like some noxious plague.

Drawbacks of the British Approach to Regulation

This decision to establish a decision-making process that, for all intents and purposes, excluded consumers from participation, relied on the very English notion that responsible chaps know what is best for the public. So the Government established a régime in which the director general of this or that 'OFF' would sit down with his counterpart in the regulated company and come to a mutually agreeable determination of just where the public interest lies. This had – and still has – two serious drawbacks. *First*, it severely limits the range of inputs available to the regulator. *Second*, it denies to the regulators' decisions the credibility that only open systems can provide.

Another error was to rely on a single decision-maker, the Director General. This tends to personalise the regulatory process, producing a stream of 'Look what Bryan Carsberg has done now in his mad effort to inject competition'; 'How could Professor Littlechild be so unworldly as to suggest he might review regulatory policy when such a review might move markets?'; 'Look how much Ms. Spottiswoode is being paid'; and 'Why is Don Cruickshank trying to wreck BT?'. A good example of this personalisation is reflected in a report on page one of *The Financial Times* (24 November 1995): 'The war of words' between Don Cruickshank, Director-General of Oftel, and Sir Ian Vallance, Chairman of BT, said the paper, escalated as Sir Ian wondered 'What lies behind the director-general's ambitions?' and Mr Cruickshank questioned BT's business ethics. Policy becomes obscured by personality.

This personalisation of the regulatory process might have been avoided had the Government looked to US experience and chosen either one of the two alternative regulatory formats available to it. It could have set up multi-member commissions to monitor each of the regulated industries, or it could have established a single, multi-member regulatory body to monitor them all. Consider, for a moment, the advantages of the latter structure, one which is used in almost all states in America.

RPI-X

The problems facing regulators in the gas, electricity and telecoms industries have much in common – water, I believe, may be a special case. Each of these industries is regulated so that the prices it charges change in line with the Retail Price Index (RPI) minus some X factor to account for productivity improvements. Initially, X was of necessity set quite arbitrarily. As Professors Beesley and Littlechild so elegantly put it, 'There is nothing unique, optimal, or mechanical about the initial choice of X'.[4] After all, who could tell just how much fat had accumulated on the bones of the publicly owned utilities during their long, slothful period of inactivity in the public sector? And who could tell just how much improvement in productivity it would be possible to obtain?

But as time passed, the staffs of the regulatory agencies should have been able to move to more reasoned determinations of X. They became familiar with various studies of total factor productivity, and of the advantages and limits of using benchmarks, perhaps even benchmarks derived from international data of the sort recently used by Oftel to raise questions about BT's efficiency. The underlying techniques involved in doing such productivity studies are quite the same, whether one is dealing with the electricity industry, the gas industry or the telecoms industry. Surely there must be advantages to having one regulatory body perform these analyses for all of the regulated industries.

Access

So, too, with questions of access. The competition policy and other economic issues involved in determining the terms of access to the telecoms, gas and electricity networks are certainly not identical. But they have sufficient similarities so that there are economies of scale in the process of learning how to deal with them – a regulator who has confronted the problem in one industry has moved up the learning curve sufficiently to have a head start when he confronts it in another.

In the event, the Government decided that the American procedural model – open hearings, multi-member regulatory bodies, an overall OFREG, instead of OFTEL, OFGAS, and OFFER – was not to be adopted in Britain. It decided, too, that the American method of setting prices on the basis of cost-plus-a-reasonable-return was not acceptable, and that it was preferable to develop a system in which the prices charged by the newly privatised utilities would be related to the rate of

---

4 M.E. Beesley and S.C. Littlechild, 'The Regulation of Privatised Monopolies in the United Kingdom', in Cento Veljanovski (ed.), *Regulators and the Market*, IEA Readings No.35, London: Institute of Economic Affairs, 1991, p.35.

inflation with adjustments for projected improvements in productivity. The reasons for rejecting cost-of-service regulation were two: a fear that cost-plus pricing provides no incentive to efficient operation, and a feeling that the 'plus' – that is, the cost of capital – could not be determined with acceptable precision.

'Regulatory Lag'

The first of these fears has some basis in fact – but only some. For it gives no weight to what is known as 'regulatory lag'. Outside observers see the sometimes leisurely pace of America's regulatory proceedings as an unambiguous evil. They miss an important point: regulatory lag provides the incentive to efficient operation that would be absent were cost-of-service regulation instantaneous. For regulated companies know that if they succeed in lowering their costs it will be some time before the regulator will initiate hearings, and even longer before he concludes them. During that time, the increased profits resulting from the lower costs will flow through to the bottom line and to the shareholder. Similarly, if the companies allow costs to rise, it may be some time before the procedure for obtaining relief is concluded, during which time profits will fall.

Thus does regulatory lag provide an incentive to efficiency that would otherwise be absent from a cost-based regulatory system. In short, cost-of-service regulation provides some of the advantages that British policy-makers thought inhered only in the RPI-X formula. And it avoids the problem created by a lack of explicit attention to the possibility of monopoly profits.

Cost of Capital

The second factor that led to the rejection of a cost-based regulatory scheme was the perception that it would be difficult to determine the rate of return investors should be allowed to earn on the capital prudently committed to the business. That important conceptual and data problems face anyone charged with the responsibility for determining what is known as a fair rate of return there can be no question, as both Alfred Kahn,[5] in my country, and John Vickers, in yours, have pointed out, the latter calling profit measures 'subjective, open to manipulation, and prone to an inherent problem of circularity'.[6]

[5] Alfred E. Kahn, *The Economics of Regulation: Principles and Institutions*, Vol.1, New York: John Wiley & Sons, 1970, pp.45-54.

[6] Colin Mayer and John Vickers, 'Profit-Sharing Regulation – An Economic Appraisal', September 1995, mimeo, p.11.

But neither can there be any question that the theoretical and data problems facing anyone attempting to determine the appropriate rate of anticipated productivity improvement, X, make those faced by a seeker-after the cost of capital, k, seem trivial by comparison. In part this is because the resources-rich financial community has long had a stake in sharpening the analytical tools with which to measure the cost of capital and such of its components as the financial and other risks faced by investors. In part, too, it is due to the fact that generations of regulatory hearings in the United States have invited those with different theories of cost-of-capital measurement to thrash out their differences, while efforts to measure such concepts as total factor productivity are a relatively new element of regulatory proceedings.

Problem of Productivity Gains

But there is a more fundamental and enduring reason why it will always be more problematic to determine X than k. There are real transactions involving real money in real, competitive financial markets to guide us towards at least reasonable approximations of what any regulated firm must pay to attract capital. But when we turn to X we set sail on a sea of doubt. We are trying to capture the cost reductions that will occur naturally, as the result of exogenous forces and the intrinsic character of the industry under examination, and without any particularly distinguished management effort. That natural or automatic portion of any improvement in productivity will go to customers in the form of lower prices. (I leave aside, as requiring a separate paper, the question of which customers should be selected by the regulator as beneficiaries of this natural rate of productivity improvement.) Any productivity gain in excess of the natural rate is assumed – and I do mean assumed – to be attributable to some extraordinary skill and effort on the part of management, and therefore flows through to shareholders – after, of course, the managers appropriate a modest portion for themselves by way of self-congratulation.

Unfortunately for the British consumer, it was impossible for anyone in authority to imagine just how inefficient the public sector utilities had become. As John Reynolds, electricity analyst with James Capel, has pointed out, '... everyone underestimated the inefficiency of nationalised industry'.[7] That is not surprising, since the wild over-manning, egregious insensitivity to consumer wants, and inflated prices

---

[7] *Financial Mail on Sunday*, 26 November 1995, p.2.

had all occurred under the supposedly watchful eyes of the very Ministers who were now setting up the regulatory system under which X would be determined; they could hardly be expected to recognise the full extent of the inefficiencies accumulated on their watch. Of course, it was conceded, the monopoly electricity service had chosen a capital-wasting means of generating electricity; true, the chaps at British Telecom had taken on a bit too much staff; and there could be no denying that the management of British Gas so intimidated Ministers that they dared not question the gas monopoly-monopsonist's decisions. But these minor excesses would surely disappear as the newly liberated managers pursued the incentives provided by that wondrous regulatory tool, RPI-X.

Or so everyone thought. In fact, the public sector companies were so bloated, so inefficient, so unconcerned with that annoying creature, the customer, that it was what teenagers now call a 'no-brainer' for managers to increase efficiency at a far more rapid rate than any propounder of a specific X could imagine, with consequences I shall discuss in a moment.

Add to that the Government's political calculation that Tory rule would be assured well into the next century if it could create a nation of shareholders, or at least a nation in which there were more shareholders than trade union members. This prompted it to sell off British Gas as a vertically integrated monopolist-monopsonist; to protect British Telecom from all save peripheral competition with its duopoly policy and a cable television franchising system guaranteed to prevent vigorous competition for the right to provide alternatives to BT; and to moderate the pace at which competition could be introduced into the electricity supply business.

This, despite warnings and complaints from Colin Robinson,[8] George Yarrow,[9] John Vickers[10] and a host of others. I well recall joining

---

[8] 'The ... privatisation programme ... has degenerated into an exercise ... with little regard for the liberalisation of product and factor markets.' ('Privatising the Energy Industries', in Cento Veljanovski (ed.), *Privatisation & Competition: A Market Prospectus*, Hobart Paperback No.28, London: Institute of Economic Affairs, 1989, p.113.) (Hereinafter referred to as *Privatisation*.)

[9] '... Government policy has been distinctly less pro-competitive than would have been desirable, and regulatory policies and structures contain many weaknesses'. ('Does Ownership Matter?', in Veljanovski, *Privatisation* , p.69.)

[10] 'In several important respects, the regime in which BT and Mercury are to operate is by no means liberal – for example, the refusal to license more public networks, and the prohibition

Ralph Harris in a visit to the appropriate Minister to plead that the gas industry be restructured before it was privatised and turned loose on an unsuspecting public. I recall, too, being told that the goals of privatisation were to (1) maximise the number of shareholders, (2) to give 'Sid' a good run for his money, and (3) to be sure not to antagonise British Gas's management. Effective regulation was notably absent from the list. All three goals were, indeed, achieved, although the last only temporarily.

Weaknesses of UK Regulatory System

These interrelated errors – closed procedures, single regulators, refusal to control profits – have now come back to haunt the Government in the following ways:

1. By rejecting America's open procedural model in favour of what Professor Price calls 'the more secretive British framework', the Government has denied the regulatory process the public credibility on which its success and acceptance crucially depend.

2. By rejecting the American multi-person commission in favour of a single regulator, policy-makers have personalised the regulatory process, causing issues to be fought out in the atmosphere of 'High Noon'.

3. By rejecting the use of profit controls, and relying on necessarily wild and, in the event, incorrect guesses as to attainable productivity improvements, the creators of Britain's regulatory system have permitted the utilities to earn monopoly profits and to overpay executives, all of whom had somehow managed to avoid having international recruiters pound on their doors during their tenures in the public sector.

4. By avoiding restructuring, the Government created a tangle of regulatory and competition policy problems that have been the subject of some of the earlier lectures in this series, and to which I now turn, with special reference to recent American experience in the electricity industry.

---

of 'resale'. These are major restrictions on competition. ...[T]here was no attempt to restructure BT to promote competition.' (John Vickers and George Yarrow, 'Telecommunications: Liberalisation and the Privatisation of British Telecom', in John Kay, Colin Mayer and David Thompson, *Privatisation and Regulation – the UK Experience*, Oxford: Clarendon Press, 1986, p.222.)

US Experience

In my country, as in yours, we are on the verge of an era in which it should be possible for all electricity customers to shop for supplies, mercifully reducing the need for direct regulation, at least in the generation sector. Entry into the generation business is now technically possible, especially in this era in which low-priced natural gas combines with new technologies to make a nonsense of old arguments that there are overwhelming economies of scale in power generation. And, perhaps after some irritating delays of the sort you seem to be facing here, billing and other arrangements will be sorted out.

So natural barriers to entry and customer-billing problems are not barriers to competition in electricity supply. In my country, the principal barriers are four:

Stranded Assets

Ours is an industry characterised by vertically integrated suppliers operating pursuant to monopoly franchises in specified geographic areas known as service territories. All utilities have an obligation to serve all comers, pursuant to which they built expensive plants in anticipation of demand which, in many cases, did not materialise. So long as the utility operates under the protection of its monopoly franchise, it can charge prices high enough to permit it to recoup its investments, and a reasonable return thereon, assuming, of course, that the investments were prudently made – again, a subject for another paper.

Allow competitors to enter, offering prices based on low-cost, gas-burning generating equipment, and the incumbents will have what has come to be called 'stranded assets' – to the tune of billions of dollars. And they will also be burdened with still more unrecoverable costs in the form of high-priced power purchase contracts, often signed at the insistence of the regulators. To force them to swallow these costs, argue the incumbent utilities, would be unfair, since the now-excess capacity was built pursuant to a social contract between regulator and regulated: you invest enough to serve all possible customers, and we will allow you a reasonable return on your investment.

I have elsewhere analysed the economic and equity issues surrounding the arguments about 'stranded investment'.[11] What is relevant here is that the presence of this stranded investment is the source of American utilities' bitter fight to delay the introduction of

---

[11] Irwin Stelzer, 'Stranded Investment: Who Pays the Bill?', remarks delivered at the Southeastern Electric Exchange, 30 March 1994, mimeo.

competition in retail markets. And with good reason. The mere consideration of a competitive model by California's regulators caused a 20-30 per cent sell-off in the shares of the state's utilities. Indeed, if the generating assets of electric utilities were marked to market – valued at what they would be worth if the power they produce were sold at competitive prices – many US utilities would have negative book values.

Vertical Integration

The second barrier to competition is the vertically integrated structure of the electric utility industry. New entrants into power generation must move their electricity over transmission and distribution wires owned by the very utilities with which they aim to compete. With reason, they worry that the terms and conditions of access might be so stringent as to make it impossible for them to compete, even though they are more efficient at generating electricity. As Harvard Professor William Hogan, who has studied this problem more intensely and intelligently than any American observer, noted in a privately circulated but not confidential memorandum, 'Competition in generation can be sensitive to the transmission and pricing rules'. In recognition of that fact, the Federal Energy Regulatory Commission, which regulates the interstate transmission of power, has hit upon the rule of 'comparability'. Broadly stated, this means that any vertically integrated utility that comes before the Commission to have a merger approved, or for almost any reason, must agree to move the power of any competitor on terms comparable with those on which it transmits the power produced by its own generating stations.

This is a solution that might commend itself to your Monopolies and Mergers Commission when it examines the proposed re-integrating mergers now before it. It certainly has considerable support in many segments of the American industry and in the regulatory community. But I would urge the MMC to consider, too, the possibility that comparability is unattainable. The dimensions of wires service are complex; the owners of the wires have a strong incentive to manipulate the terms of access when they also own generation facilities; and, as John Vickers reminded us:

> 'A vertically integrated firm that dominates one level of production has an obvious profit incentive to distort downstream competition by raising rivals' costs and discriminating in favour of its own downstream unit'.[12]

---

[12] John Vickers, 'Competition and Regulation: The UK Experience', Chapter 4 in this *Readings*, quotation cited from p.97.

Professor Vickers went on to note: 'If conduct regulations were perfect and costless, the anti-competitive behaviour problem could be solved without resort to structural remedies. But it is not so.' And this is not to criticise the regulators. Information asymmetry disadvantages them; as does an enormous difference between the resources available to the regulated and those at the disposal of the regulator; as does the inherent difficulty of defining the service that is being regulated, costed and priced. In the end, if emerging competition at the retail level is not be strangled at birth, structural separation of the generating and wires businesses will probably prove necessary where there is substantial market power at either vertical level. And just such separation has been proposed by several American utilities as part of a 'grand bargain', the *quid pro quo* being permission to recover their stranded investment.

So, too, in the telephone industry. So long as BT controls the telecoms network, two problems, both insoluble, will bedevil the regulators. The first is the terms on which competitors should be granted access. The second is determining the dividing line between fair and unfair competition, between vigorous competition and predation, between practices that protect a market position and those that erect unreasonable barriers to entry. Don Cruickshank's willingness to seize the poisoned chalice of monitoring BT's competitive behaviour is admirable, but it represents, I fear, the triumph of hope over experience – experience with efforts to regulate vertically integrated companies.

The Greens

The third barrier to emerging competition in America's electricity supply industry is the political clout of the environmental movement. So long as each utility had a monopoly of its service territory, it could acquiesce in the demands of environmentalists for a host of economically inefficient conservation arrangements, and for wider use of environmentally benign but high-cost power supply technologies. After all, the costs could be passed on to captive customers. But times have changed. Competition from new, low-cost producers makes continuation of the anti-consumer, utility/environmentalist alliance impossible. So the environmentalists have enlisted in the anti-competition cause, or at minimum are demanding that a 'green surcharge' be added to prices imposed on new power producers for the use of transmission and distribution wires. I believe you will find similar pressures developing in Britain if competition forces incumbent suppliers to cut back on environmental expenditures.

State Regulators

The fourth barrier to competition is the state regulator. These regulators, many elected to office, worry that competition will benefit only large, industrial customers, who can threaten to move their plants or expand in some other state; lower rates to these customers, they worry, will force utilities to recoup lost revenues from the small householder who does not have much bargaining power. So, in many states regulators have specifically rejected the idea of subjecting the utilities they regulate to competition from outside suppliers.

Despite these obstacles, competition is breaking out all over. Large customers have begun shopping for power supplies, and are being offered substantial discounts. Some regulators are considering how to develop more competition in wholesale markets, with California serving as the battleground for those who would force all generators to sell into, and all customers to buy from, a pool, and those who would allow bilateral deals between customers, producers, brokers and aggregators.

This dispute, of course, is simply a specific variant of the old, general argument about the virtues of co-ordination versus competition, with co-ordination advocates having the advantage of seeming to be able to predict the consequences of their proposals, whilst market advocates cannot. But, in my view, that is precisely why market advocates should prevail: their inability to predict the results of competition stems from the fact that those results will be determined by consumers expressing their price and quality preferences in unpredictable ways. It is they who will decide how much power is needed, where, at what prices, and in what combination of firm and interruptible supplies. Central planners need not apply.

Questions of how to apply competition policy have not yet arisen, but will soon: the Antitrust Division of the Department of Justice has only now begun to take a serious interest in the electric utility industry. That interest has been reflected, *first*, in a greater inclination to examine the competitive impact of the mergers that are occurring in the utility industry. It is reflected, *second*, in queries about the operation of some of the regional power pools, and in particular the terms on which the co-operating competitors who are members of the pool are willing to make transmission and other services available to non-members. Remember: in America the Federal Energy Regulatory Commission and state regulatory bodies have, in a sense, primary jurisdiction in these matters. But the heightened interest of the competition authorities should increase the weight given to competitive impacts by the regulators.

Summary: Five Lessons from US Experience

Let me now summarise the five lessons to be gleaned from American regulatory experience:[13]

Structure Matters

Business historian Thomas McCraw put it well in his sagacious study of regulation and regulators: 'More than any other single factor ... underlying structure of the particular industry being regulated has defined the context in which regulatory agencies have operated'.[14] Both British and American experience suggest that a vertically integrated monopoly is the most difficult of all beasts to regulate: integrated companies can use the natural monopoly of their transmission grids – gas pipelines, electricity transmission lines, the telephone network – to deter entry into other strata of the business.

Competition Matters

Even limited competition provides regulators with some benchmarks against which to measure the performance of a dominant firm; gives consumers some alternatives; spurs the dominant firm to reduce costs, improve service, and innovate.

People Matter

In the regulatory game, people matter. While regulators are limited by the economic forces at work at any time, their biases, intellects, and perseverance can affect the regulatory process in important ways. In America, Alfred Kahn's penchant for economically sensible pricing was a powerful force for rate restructuring in the electricity business, and his preference for competition hastened the demise of airline regulation. In Britain, Sir Bryan Carsberg rose above his training as an accountant to adopt an economist's attitude towards such concepts as cost. So far, Britain has managed to find a set of quite able, fair-minded regulators. Americans have little to offer by way of suggestions for improvement.

---

[13] In this connection, see my 'Two Styles of Regulatory Reform', *The American Enterprise*, March/April 1990, pp.70-77.

[14] Thomas K. McCraw, *Prophets of Regulation*, Cambridge, Mass.: The Belknap Press of Harvard University, 1984.

Procedure Matters

Open processes add credibility to the result, and give regulators access to varying points of view. Expedition at the expense of a full presentation of all viewpoints is very dearly bought.

Profits Matter

A regulatory formula that ignores the profit levels it produces cannot survive politically. Nor should it, for a formula that produces profits that are inadequate to attract capital will result in a derogation of service, and one that produces monopoly profits will unduly enrich shareholders and managers at the expense of customers. This may be why Britain's regulators have been driven to an explicit examination of the cost of capital in determining a proper figure for X. But this obscure and merely tangential use of profits in the regulatory formula still leaves regulators open to the charge of condoning excess profits – a not unreasonable reaction from a public untutored in the arcane niceties of regulatory computations.

Competition Policy Lessons

Finally, I would like to touch briefly on competition policy, since I believe there are important lessons to be learned from US experience. These are:

- Competition policy functions best when it is not overlaid with other objectives. If a practice is anti-competitive it should not be condoned because, for example, it creates jobs, since such jobs will exist at consumer expense and will in the long run make the economy less competitive in world markets. Nor should mergers that create dominant firms be justified on the basis of a need to create 'national champions' to compete in world markets. If such 'champions' cannot compete at home, they will not in the long run be able to compete abroad.

- Competition is desirable in and of itself, and not only because it produces an efficient allocation of resources, or because multiple players, particularly in industries subject to rapid technological change, are likely to produce a greater variety of products and services, at lower cost, than is a single, all-dominant firm. It is desirable, too, because
    (a) it eliminates the need for government to set prices and otherwise involve itself in business matters;

(b) it diffuses private economic power and creates an atmosphere that encourages entrepreneurs to take the risk of challenging incumbents, whom they know will be restricted only to responses stemming from their efficiency, rather than their sheer power; and

(c) it produces enough players to minimise the political power of the largest firm.

- Certainty is not attainable, at least not if competition policy is to remain a flexible instrument. A few *per se* rules are possible, the outlawing of conspiracies to fix prices being the most notable. But attempts to limit market shares penalise success, and attempts to ban certain competitive practices, without inquiring into their competitive impact, stifle competition. In the end there is no avoiding a careful analysis of competitive impact, on a case-by-case basis.

- A modicum of predictability is attainable. This necessarily means that a body of precedent must be developed to provide some guide to businessmen and their counsel, some means of separating acceptable from unacceptable behaviour. The deliverers of such decisions carry the burden of being clear and explicit, of carefully setting forth their reasons for rejecting this argument, for adopting that one, for defining a market one way and not another. A simple recitation of each party's contentions, followed by unexplained conclusory paragraphs, is not enough.

*   *   *

I hope these few remarks have not offended you: it is always difficult for an outsider to be in the position of telling an audience that 'we do it differently, and better, where I come from'. That has not been my intention. Indeed, it is we who have borrowed from you the notion of introducing more incentives into the regulatory system, and we who are trying to benefit from your experience with a power pool as we restructure our own electric utility industry. So my goal was merely to offer you a few bits from the American system by way of reciprocation. I hope that I have succeeded, at least in small part.

CHAIRMAN'S COMMENTS

M.E. Beesley
London Business School

FIRST, LET ME COMMENT ON THE ORIGINS OF RPI-X. Keeping the lawyers at arm's length was certainly a concern among the founders of the system. But this did not mean neglecting the need for checks and balances. We learned from the USA that 'regulatory capture' was likely to occur, so several devices were thought up to stop the Regulator doing a cosy act with the regulated, to the latter's advantage. For example, many of the concerns of existing anti-monopoly law were incorporated in the Acts, and the licensing régime provided a considerable re-inforcement of these. The relationship was meant to engender opposition between the regulator and the regulated, with the MMC as the arbiter on the critical issue of the money involved. Conflict between the two, even in public, which we have certainly experienced, can be to the good. I think of Sir James McKinnon's invention of the device of negotiating with British Gas through announcements via morning television! This was thought by many to indicate a very stressed relationship between the two, but no-one now doubts that his campaign to make regulation in gas more effective was successful. Sir Denis Rooke's masterful defence of gas tradition in the 1986 privatisation has not yet been negated, but much progress has been made.

On the points raised in the paper about the British regulatory system as a whole:

- Irwin argues that a commission would be better at predicting productivity, bench marking, and so on, than a single regulator now is. I find it hard to believe in economies of scale in intellectual work, and I wonder whether Irwin's own experience in organising consultancies supports that idea?

- In effect, he argues that the American process copes with the inefficiencies often said to be one of its drawbacks by pointing out that it, too, has built-in regulatory lags. I have a small but perhaps crucial point in this connection. It seems to imply US regulators can initiate the price revision procedure, so that the length of the lag is not, as we had originally supposed, in the gift of the regulated.

- Overarching commissions may be good for the USA, but the USA never had to privatise – rather, regulation was imposed on private industry. For that reason, among many, we could not start by proposing 'leisurely' American regulatory proceedings, as he describes them.

- Privatisation was and is very much a learning process, and we have learned to discount the special pleading Irwin correctly notes in his remarks on the gas privatisation. My own paper in this volume,[1] and other remarks, attest to the naïveté of what should perhaps have been sophisticated financial advice in the early days. The important question seems to be how much is being learned, and is it to good effect?

On the points about electricity:

- I do not feel much sympathy when incumbents plead 'stranded assets'. *My* objective in entering is to strand *your* assets. The problem arises from expectations derived from regulation, which in turn reflect protective devices inherited from the past. The history of UK regulation can be seen as devising means to relinquish these burdens, and has, I think, been innovatory in doing so.

- On vertical integration – of course, generation was separated from the wires business right from the start. The big problem for us is the integration of distribution with much of supply. Proposals to re-merge wires and generation have to be viewed, *inter alia*, in terms of their impact on this. It is to be hoped that Irwin's insistence on the importance of structure in dealing with competitive issues will be listened to carefully.

- Irwin tells us that, in the USA, competition is breaking out, despite the best efforts of the regulatory authorities which have been superimposed on the basic American anti-trust laws. His account causes me to be thankful we avoided such regulation. But Irwin's

---

[1]   M.E. Beesley, 'RPI-X: Principles and Their Application to Gas', Chapter 9 in this volume, pp.207-222.

point about the rising interest of American anti-trust in electricity is most interesting. Anti-trust grinds exceeding slow, but often has an influence far outweighing other regulators' in the end – witness the early discomfiture of FCC (Federal Communications Commission) in trying to resist MCI's (Microwave Communications Inc.) bid to expand, in the Execunet decision (1977), and later, in the 1982 divestiture. It will be fascinating to see anti-trust law further muscling in on traditional utility regulation and to observe further reactions by the regulators thus implicitly criticised. Of greatest interest, perhaps, will be how intra-State regulation fares. Here the conflict between opening up to competition and inherited consumer positions is perhaps at its strongest, and we would wish to learn much more from US experience in the similar difficult issues now being tackled in the UK.

9

RPI-X: PRINCIPLES AND THEIR APPLICATION TO GAS[1]

M.E. Beesley
London Business School

Introduction

As ONE OF THOSE WHO HELPED TO PUT THE RPI-X SYSTEM INTO PLACE, what strikes me about current debates is the unwillingness to see it as a major change in the modes of influencing utilities. Technically, RPI-X is an incentive system for motivating utility managements. Its essence is in the forward-looking targeting of prices for a period ahead sufficient to give inducements for companies to better the targets. Privatisation's essential contribution was the break from old forces shaping the motivations of incumbent managements. Exposure to capital markets and potential competition among managements for control plus the personal gains in prospect no doubt has tended, over time, to replace the incumbent management culture.

But the fundamental shift, in my opinion, is in *ex post* and *ex ante* influences on incumbent conduct. By this I mean that before privatisation, conduct was bounded by the very limited forward look permitted by Treasury control, and, much more, by criticism *ex post*, via House of Commons committee, MMC 1980 Act inquiries and the like. To attempt to set price limits in advance, leaving room for unexpected efficiency gains, was a very big undertaking indeed. I notice that critics do not wish to give up the incentive properties of RPI-X. The problem is that they sharply underestimate what was and is *still* involved in the change.

My plan for the lecture is first to remind ourselves of what the regulatory task of creating the necessary conditions to mount a

---

[1]   The views expressed here are not those to which other Economic Advisers to Ofgas would necessarily subscribe; neither do they represent the view of Ofgas.

successful incentive system was on privatisation; to review progress in the essential tasks to date and to draw some perhaps not fully appreciated consequences of adopting the required approach to deriving relevant information. I will then comment on the current problem of fixing British Gas's TransCo prices. Finally, I shall reflect briefly on the implications for proposed reforms of RPI-X such as profit sharing.

The Inheritance

Regulators inherited a poor information base for their emerging tasks. The nationalised industries simply did not need, or have, commercially-driven information systems. Evidence on this is necessarily anecdotal, but those of us actually engaged in the process were acutely aware of the deficiencies.

My experience includes the following. When conducting my original telecoms inquiry on competition in 1980, one main issue was prospective damage to BT's net cash flow that resale on leased BT lines would entail. Even then, a central issue was BT's ability in the future to sustain the large elements of cross-subsidy implicit in continued response to social obligations. I expected, naturally, that this would be approached by BT's considering what large business accounts were in danger, since obviously large businesses with substantial telephone bills would be first in line. To my asking 'What was your total business with ICI last year?', BT's response was one of astonishment. To paraphrase their response, this was a wholly unreasonable request. ICI could be any of at least 4,000 local accounts, and, even if these could be totalled for a customer, which they never had been, there were many other ways – for example, leasing itself – in which BT collected revenue from ICI. Of course, BT said, it would be possible to do this when local exchanges were fully digitalised, then expected at about 2003. There I learnt the first lesson: that the information for regulation meant very great changes *in the subject firms*, not likely to be achieved overnight.

The second memory is the widely fluctuating estimates from companies of the capex consequences of adhering, belatedly, to European water standards, suddenly required because Brussels could now refuse to sign off on the Water Bill. At one point, X's of up to 12 per cent or more a year looked quite possible. Of course, some order was brought to this, and the wilder estimates revised. The moral here, however, was that 10-year planning of options for meeting standards had to be initiated virtually from scratch.

Again, as late as the MMC Gas inquiry of 1992/93, the MMC was told that it was impossible for British Gas to estimate, even very crudely, what the cash likely to be needed or generated would be beyond the four years then remaining in the price control. Since privatisation the companies have developed relevant commercial information and the regulators have increasingly developed the ability to use it. But we should not over-estimate the speed that was, and still is, possible.

Information has to be interpreted, indeed defined, in some conceptual framework. At privatisation this was weak too. I recall that, in contemplating floating BT in 1983, solemn advice from the merchant bank advisors was that if 100 per cent of shares were to be floated at once, the Gilt market would be affected for six months! So much, then, for the influence of business school finance departments at that time. The Capital Asset Pricing Model (CAPM) and reference to perfect capital markets did not command the respect they do now. Today, something like a consensus is emerging on the intellectual issues in this area, for example, the approach to the required cost of capital, to no little extent prompted by regulators' needs when price controls loom.

My first point is, then, that the basis for laying a practical incentive system of control, expressed in RPI-X as a particular form, takes time and mutual effort on each side of the regulatory relationship. The general opinion now is that the Government imposed too lax X factors in the first periods of price control, for several imputed motives. However that might be, my own experience suggests that the basis for anything which would remotely satisfy present critics was simply not there. In effect, the present methods of supporting an *ex ante* view of prices – a critique of company plans based on comparators and/or simulation of what is judged to be an efficient company's cash needs – have had to evolve, and the pace has not been even across utilities. The principal focus of this forward-looking effort has to be expenditure (cash-flow) orientated, for reasons I will spell out shortly.

However, another necessary building block has had to be formed from the initial hand the regulators were dealt. This stems from the fact that effective regulation, UK style, depends on separation of contestable from non-contestable activities (or potentially competitive or natural monopoly elements, if you prefer). Unless price controls can be effectively confined to the latter, regulators have difficulty in clarifying what the RPI-X 'bargain' – the target efficiency level – is, to say nothing of the tactical advantage to incumbents in bargaining when the frontiers for inter-company transactions are fuzzy. This is a quite general requirement, whatever the form incentive pricing takes. The ideal standard of separation and reportage this implies is in effect a ring-fenced natural monopoly where there is at least a shadow stand-alone company, with its balance sheet, capital structure, and reporting within the company to cash reconciliation level.

With very hesitant steps, the utilities have progressed differentially towards this ideal. In telecoms, the ideal seems still remote. In later privatisations, the Government did indeed pursue separation, but perhaps with more concern to meet critics on implications for competition, rather than to pay closer attention to price regulation needs. In electricity, having 12-14 'comparators' is and was useful, and should be preserved; but there is still Scottish integration, and no structural separation of RECs' businesses in supply and distribution. Even in water, where the issues were more clearly seen, there is still regulatory mileage in separating water supply from sewage in big companies. In gas, most progress has arguably been made, thanks to the restructuring after the MMC report. But it took until 1993 for this to happen, well into the second price control period.

So far, then, I have in effect been addressing the case for saying 'Do not expect a regulatory system to perform well until it has been given the time needed to construct the tools'. One corollary is, of course, that it is foolish to attempt a sophisticated incentive tango before one has learned, and is able to perform, the basic steps.

The Forward-Looking Expenditure Approach

I wish to turn next to supporting my assertion that the centre-piece of effective incentive regulation is the forward-looking expenditure as seen in future cash flow. As is apt for an incentive mechanism, it fixes the target. It is the necessary focus for appraisals for three reasons. *First*, for a practical reason. Outputs from models, however derived, of what needs to be spent have to focus on evidence about actual past cash outlays, then consider how they may trend in the future. The issues involved in assessment are largely economic. The application of economic reasoning to costs must be forward-looking. In economics, bygones are bygones. Economists' conclusions are always to do with options *now* available; however fancy the econometric work on past data has been, the application has to be translated to future conditions. Hence an emphasis on 'avoidable' costs. In practice, this means forecasting cash flows.

Second, in practical regulatory affairs, there is a need to underpin principles for price structures with appropriate cash estimates. The principles should involve attribution of costs and, with joint costs, mark-ups. This need is common to both sides of regulation work, price controls and encouraging competition. In the natural monopoly areas, the influence of price fixing goes through to final prices, and the incidence of costs in consumption for various consumer groups has to be recognised. In competitive areas, rules for competition and dealing with conflict will have to incorporate views of costs, for example, as triggers for detecting 'too low' or 'too high' prices offered by incumbents and entrants.[2] Consistency in the measurement of costs between the two areas of regulatory work is essential if regulators are to be effective. In other words, the forward-looking expenditure approach in both is required. Moreover, the main incumbent is typically a conglomerate. Insofar as it is necessary to predict effects of regulatory decisions on total company welfare, the adding up process can only feasibly be done if all sub-businesses are looked at in a common currency. This is the cash flow which will be involved.

Third, whatever method is used to establish the target trend in productivity underlying 'X', the tests have to be translated to actual prospective expenditure. The principal need at a price review is to set the scene sufficiently far ahead to make sense of the main trade-offs occurring in utilities, namely the timing of capex (capital expenditure) and its substitution by opex (operational expenditure). Hypotheses about their effects must be formulated in response to economic views of costs, though it will typically be engineers who propose feasible technical means to explore options.

Cash flows should, therefore, be the chief organising principle of a regulator's activities. There has been a need for parallel development, internally, in companies since privatisation. Businesses newly exposed to capital markets and other market forces have to develop their own information systems, various forms of management accounts and testing for commercial change. As the company gets better informed, so the potential relevant information for regulators increases.

But the corollaries of a forward-looking expenditure approach do not fall comfortably on certain ears. First, the approach down-plays distinctions between different forms of outlays. In a forward-looking context, lumpy outlays (capex) are just a dated cash outflow. The consequence is that 'assets' (embodied capex) have no special

---

2 In practice this centres on 'predation', for which both attributable avoidable costs and 'stand-alone' costs are relevant, again necessarily forward-looking.

significance either. Assets in balance sheets are necessary, of course, to translate the effects of cash-flow movements into financial accounts for company reporting, and so on. But the tendency to identify 'assets' with the 'shareholders' interest' has not been happy in the regulatory context.

Accountants are extremely uncomfortable with the notion that the shareholders' pay-out is not necessarily connected with what the books happen to say about 'assets'. Fundamentally, what shareholders subscribed to on privatisation was to own a company which had rights to generate net income in a utility; they did not invest in 'assets'. The capital markets assess companies on their future capabilities to throw off dividends (cash) and add to the share price, convertible into cash by shareholders via the market. Trying to stuff shareholders' interests into the 'assets' strait-jacket has caused much diversion, but little enlightenment. This strait-jacket is particularly unhelpful in situations where 'assets' are in any case of much less importance, compared to operating expenditure, as in supply price controls.

The implication is that a price control fixing episode is an exercise in forming and assessing a financial project, just as is the assessment of any business opportunity. So long as a compatible set of prices is selected to match the present value of outlays the company can be said to be 'financially viable', as required by all Privatisation Acts. But this is insufficient, for several reasons.

First, it ignores what shareholders have already put up. From their perspective, mere ability to finance future flows implies that they are going to commit sums in future (the outlays) which will earn at the required rate. They will justifiably argue that they have money already committed up to the present. Moreover, punters rarely invest in a financial project simply to get their opportunity cost of capital, duly adjusted in risk terms. The idea of using an externally derived required rate in a financial project is to help investors select from options. These are standardised in a manner ensuring that different risks are recognised (for example, by the CAPM). Projects giving greatest net present values in excess of 0 are selected, with NPV = 0 as the rejection point. Stock market prices (which, by definition, refer to surviving companies) have a strong element of quasi-rents, values in excess of the minimum financing level required. Something must be added to the allowed revenue stream.

There is another important reason to do this, namely its possible effects on incentives which will, hopefully, increase the size of the pot which both shareholders and consumers can share. A regulator having the temerity to push prices sharply towards levels indicated by future financing requirements alone without reference to the shareholders' existing position, would be ignoring how incentives work in practice. Economists, because necessarily forward-looking in their arguments, would normally say that such behaviour would indicate an increase in perceived regulatory risk, having effects on the future required cost of capital. No-one has ever quantified change in 'regulatory risk' on required rates. This is a useful project for a university finance department, difficult as event analysis is. My own belief is that a far more important effect is psychological.

A workable incentive system which is entirely forward-looking is an impossibility. Motivation to do well is destroyed by rewarding 'success', by snatching away the prize. Hence the principle of 'no clawback' is rightly stressed. Of course, this also implies attempting to measure the 'prize' to be preserved. In the RPI-X context, it is the gain, if any, made in the last period by unanticipated cost improvements (that is, not already defined in the previous 'X') which company managements have been responsible for. Here is another question to which regulators were not handed the solution on taking office. I add some ideas of my own about this later (below, p.220). That the art is not yet very sophisticated does not mean that regulators and regulated cannot agree on what is a reasonable approach and judgements are in effect made now in the exchange between the two.

Unexpected Efficiency Gains and Regulatory Uncertainty

The parallel question is over what period unexpected efficiency gains should be transferred to customers. Something of a consensus among regulators seems to be emerging that this should be done so that gains in the last period are exhausted by the end of the next. This seems a sensible approach. I note that in making the two projections – attainable productivity gains able to be made by a competent management in the future, plus some rent of past efficiency which will continue – redefines the meaning of a favourite maxim – that regulators do (or should) 'mimic competition'. The competition which is being 'mimicked' is not neo-classical competition, but Schumpeterian. The regulator is playing both the rôle of creating the possibility of earning innovatory gains and that of the 'perennial gale' of competition which tends to blow them away over time.

When the question of what to add to the cash flow to respond to the incentive needs is settled, there remains the final problem of how to settle the remaining zero-sum game. Some degree of freedom remains.

Consumers can benefit if shareholders get less. Deciding on the final trade-off between consumers and shareholders is an unenviable, and unavoidable, task for regulators. To that extent, they do 'fix' market values of shares. But the process I have described cannot be said justly to be 'circular'. It is designed to set rationalised limits to the regulators' discretion. This is inevitable once real competitive forces are absent, as they are here, by definition. In practice, regulators value continuity, and increasingly emphasise predictable processes, openness and interaction with parties, all calculated to reduce regulatory uncertainty.[3]

In deciding this final trade-off the history of how consumers, on the one hand, and shareholders, on the other, have fared is certainly relevant. Price trends and stock market experience will enter the scales. Here again, development of techniques will serve to narrow down areas of contention. Development is mainly needed on measuring shareholders' experience, to cope with the fact that 'the shareholder' is such an abstraction. One thought on this: Would the concept of a 'random' shareholder help? – that is, measured gains and losses made by shareholders over whatever periods they could have held the shares? Then one could at least argue from some idea of total experience to date.

But a sense of proportion about the effects on consumer prices of these debates must be maintained. Regulators can affect prices through the forward assessment of proposed outlays far more than they can by varying shareholders' returns. This is why I have emphasised the organisational aspects of cash flow. Like the rest of us, however, regulators do not altogether relish playing the rôle of arbiter between consumer and shareholder. I sometimes think that the persistence of debate about this or that approach to 'asset valuation' is implicitly a search for the 'just regulatory price', to be given externally, to the relief of regulators.

---

3 An important aspect of reducing regulatory uncertainty is the fact that, because utilities in practice have no foreseeable limit on their lives, the forward-looking cash flow approach must imply some recognition of funding needs beyond the forthcoming price control period. This requires an understanding on both sides about the future incidence of capital expenditure and its possible substitutes, within which the expenditures for the forthcoming control period can be set. In effect, this in turn requires a model to deal with such trade-offs in time, a technical matter to be argued between regulator and regulated. When the judgement is made, uncertainty about regulatory attitudes five years hence can be bounded by recognising the amounts allowed in the forthcoming control and those still to be funded afterwards. The regulator can never be bound absolutely to previous estimates, but transparency about the basis of the current review decision will then be an established part of the argument next time round.

To summarise my argument so far: Establishing a forward-looking expenditure base is the lynch-pin of incentive regulation. For regulators who deal with incumbents with interests in both contestable and non-contestable areas, even where clearly structured, it is essential to use cash as the process for adding up the likely financial effects on the group as a whole. Equally essential, it enables consistent views about pricing structure issues in both areas which can be founded in standard economic arguments about costs and mark-ups.

Reporting in accounting terms is essentially secondary in the sense that it is required cash which should drive the results, not accounting conventions. If necessary, these decisions, based on cash, can lead to revisions in accounting methods, to avoid the charge of being inconsistent – as was levied against MMC in its refusal to make 'arcane adjustments' in the 1993 report.[4] So long as the cash-flow focus is maintained, how one expresses the question of what to allow the shareholders is secondary. One can, as is suggested in the Ofgas Consultation Document,[5] look at it as writing another cash line, along with future capex, and so on. This merely makes explicit what is otherwise implicit. Moreover, it focuses the question of the trade-off between consumer and shareholder at the margin. Or one can translate the cash outcomes into accounting conventions, as the Consultation Document also suggests. The important point is the process by which the outcome is decided.

Price Control for TransCo and the 1993 MMC Report

What I have said is relevant to the current consultations set off by the Consultation Document.

The issues I have been concerned with arise largely in Section 5 of the document, 'Calculating TransCo's Required Revenue'. The starting point is suggested as a long-term NPV calculation, perhaps covering 25 years, within which special attention is given to satisfying 'reasonable expectations' of British Gas's shareholders, and the difficulty of acquiring data on costs the further ahead one looks in time. A further concern is added, about the implications of particular anticipated profiles of capex spent or revenue allowed during a forthcoming

---

4   *Gas*, Vol. 1 of Report under the Fair Trading Act 1973, Cm. 2314, London: HMSO, August 1993.

5   Ofgas Price Control Review: *British Gas' Transportation and Storage: A Consultation Document*, June 1995.

period, the first of which TransCo now faces. Were allowed prices closely to reflect the anticipated incidence within a given period they would show a perhaps unacceptably uneven profile through time. This is an independent choice for the regulator, because a long-range NPV calculation of expenditure is neutral as to when the revenues occur, so long as the NPV derived is the same.

Alternative ways of calculating the shareholders' interest consistent with an NPV calculation are presented. The first is to form a 'regulatory value' for the assets to be entered as an expenditure at the start of a period. The second is to assess a dividend stream to be added to cash flow on the revenue side over the years. These are discussed as to their respective methods of computation. The implication, from my remarks, is that the same underlying issues of incentives and distributive justice will have to be addressed whichever mode is adopted. There is no reason why the outcome, in cash terms, will be different, unless conformity with the regulatory precedents is recognised as an independent factor which should influence the results.

Most interest of course centres on TransCo's own response, in July 1995.[6] A notable feature of this is that whereas, in commenting on the other sections of the Ofgas document, TransCo could find much to agree with, the case is different when it comes to Section 5. TransCo does not attack directly the issue of whether forward-looking cash flows should be the lynch-pin. But there is much in the discussion which suggests they would be unhappy with such an emphasis. TransCo summarises its approach in the area in five points. Of these three are non-controversial, and incorporated in a forward-looking expenditure approach. Allowed revenue should:

- Provide sufficient funds to finance TransCo's operating costs.

- Provide a rate of return at least equal to the cost of capital.

- Be based on a realistic forward projection of expected efficiency gains over the period of the next Formula.

I would, of course, argue, as I have done, that the last point requires cash flow as the centre-piece. TransCo also says that allowed revenue should

- Reflect the regulatory asset value established by the MMC and properly roll it forward to the start of the formula.

---

6 TransCo, *Response to Ofgas Price Control Document*, July 1995.

This is one form of calculating the shareholders' interests, and is obviously an option. The underlying assessment needs remain.

The real crunch comes with the third point in the list, namely, 'to recognise CCA depreciation as a cost of consuming assets'. This cuts across the very purpose of setting up the expenditure approach, the essence of which is to provide a means of evaluating actual capex and other needs in the future and not to accept what is in the balance sheet. Past depreciation is certainly useful evidence about what may be needed in the future. But, to aim to 'recover the real cost of both past and future investment' (p.8), and, specifically, to reject using an estimate of future investment instead of the depreciation charge, as at page 8, is to substitute company for regulatory judgement.

My misgivings are reinforced by the way TransCo quotes the MMC 1993 Gas report. In order to support its view that 'recognition of CCA depreciation as a cost of assets' would 'build on the conclusions of the 1993 report', it quotes a passage (para. 7.76) in which MMC is dealing with the question of how to express its approach in accounting terms. The important statement is made at paragraph 7.80, the summary of that section of the Gas Report:

> ' For the purpose of assessing the appropriate level of the price cap, we prefer to concentrate on two simple criteria: whether the future cash flows are adequate to sustain the business, and whether the marginal rate of profit is sufficient to induce the desirable level of investment, during the period for which the cap is set.'

That is not a unique position for MMC to take. In MMC's South West Water Report[7] (July 1995), much of its work centred on re-appraising the 10-year forward cash outlays, including re-running Ofwat's analysis of efficiency (Appendix 8.3).

> 'Regulation of water undertakers is, as with other privatised utilities in the UK, based on the setting of a price cap [which] provides companies with the incentive to improve profitability by reducing costs.' (para. 2.59)

It continues:

> '...The price cap approach cannot however be divorced from consideration of the rate of return on new investment, or, although this involves different issues, on existing capital. ...The prices have to be sufficient to enable a rate

---

[7] MMC, *Report on the Determination of Adjustment Factors and Charges for South West Water*, July 1995.

of return which will attract sufficient finance for new investment. It is also necessary to consider what is a reasonable rate of return on existing assets and thus to shareholders, itself relevant in ensuring that capital for future investment can be attracted, assuming reasonable levels of efficiency.'

As to depreciation, referring to Ofwat's common approach in this to water companies, '...in the context of our more detailed examinations...we based depreciation projections on investment levels and programmes we felt reasonable' (para. 2.78). 'Depreciation' thus follows, not dictates, allowed cash outlays. This also seems to accord better with Ofgas's approach than with TransCo's.

Release of Information

The question of using MMC's reports to support regulatory arguments raises what is in many ways a more important issue, about publication of material relevant to a price control decision. Despite the MMC's Gas reports having emphasised the importance it attached to the forward-looking cash needs, and regretted the inability of British Gas at the time to foresee its cash position more than four years ahead, the forward-looking emphasis did not get the prominence in discussion afterwards that it merited. I think a cogent reason for this is that critics had very little to go on to substantiate the concern.

All future impacts on cash flows, even for the four years admitted to be possible, and (equally important) BG's own business plan forecasts, were deleted in the published version of the Report on the grounds of commercial confidence. The only quantified clue as to MMC's concerns appear at Appendix 6.5, dealing with BG's accounting treatment of a replacement expenditure, which contains the estimates for 1993 to 1997 of replacement and CCA depreciation referred to in Ofgas's Consultative Document.

Dearth of information about future choices is by no means confined to the 1993 report. It has been repeated in MMC publications in regulatory matters, as with all references. This raises acute problems of public interest. I think the cloak of 'commercial confidence' is far too freely used. The problem has worsened over the years. In a natural monopoly context it is inconsistent with the increasing ability of the public to criticise both regulators' and firms' positions which I have noted as a major gain for privatisation.

Moreover, regulators have rightly become increasingly concerned over the years that there should be informed debate, involving all interests, at a price review. The implication of my emphasis on the importance of forward-looking estimates of expenditures is that disclosure of information during a review consultation period should go beyond predictions about possible effects on accounting rates of return to the underlying projected expenditures. They should be given in sufficient detail to enable informed views to be taken and counter-views expressed. This is particularly important where competitors have a keen interest in how the computations affecting the future of competition over the pipes and wires are to be made, and so affect them and their integrated incumbent competitor. The issue will, I hope, be dealt with in the current gas discussions.

Revising RPI-X

After the two summers of discontent about shareholders' and others' gains in utilities it is understandable, and quite appropriate, to consider revisions to RPI-X. For Ofgas to raise the question in its TransCo Consultation Document is a welcome initiative. I shall not pass judgement directly on whether some form of sliding scale or profit-sharing is desirable, but try to draw out some implications for these from my remarks so far.

Ofgas proposes to build on the existing framework of RPI-X. It is common ground amongst all parties that the incentive properties of price control must be preserved. That means the reforms, if any, must be accommodated in the forward-looking calculations. I have already said enough, perhaps, to indicate that much needs to be done to secure the basis for these. But I am also concerned about the fact that the stimulus for reforms was perceived gain by the company, not improvements in RPI-X.

A Windfall Tax?

This has given rise to demands for a one-off utility tax, to be applied some time in the future. This has merit perhaps as a money-raising device, but will certainly not improve regulation. Even as a proposal intended to mete out justice, it will fail. It cannot unscramble take-over deals, in which the sellers will retain their gains, leaving the buyers, who are always liable to give away too much to gain control, licking their wounds. If suspected of becoming a regular feature of UK utility operation, it will not necessarily dampen down efficiency-seeking, but it will raise the cost of capital. Moreover, I think it possible that eventually some regulator is going to make a 'mistake' in the downwards direction. If so, there will be pressure to even things out by allowing claw-back from the consumer. This would amount to engaging consumers in directly reducing companies' risks, which seems to negate the point of trying to enlist private capital into utility operation.

Sliding-Scale Regulation

However, on the issue of improving RPI-X, the basic idea of the proposals is to anticipate net gains made by the regulated firm as a target, directed to an expected productivity/efficiency performance, presumably rather as now. Deviations upwards in the event will be limited, giving consumers more; deviations downwards will be limited also because prices will remain as set. This, it is thought, will dampen down, but not eliminate, the incentive properties of RPI-X.

To decide on what to allow for unanticipated efficiency gains is now performed by setting the regulated companies' experience in some norm of achieved efficiency gains and then, as I have explained, to make the gain into a quasi-rent to be passed on over a future period. The essential task is to sort out what has been attributable to management by eliminating the irrelevant noise thrown up in the last period. Regulators so far have done this as best they can, and would not seek to justify their answers to an econometric jury. It is understood that this is part and parcel of bargaining at review time, and companies of course look at the total 'deal' represented in the proposed 'X', not just the efficiency aspect.

To make an unanticipated efficiency gain the subject of a sharing scheme set in advance, would place far more demands on the precise definition of the models to detect it. I think the main problem would be handling of the system as it will evolve over the price period. Logically, the regulator would be involved in a continuous re-running year by year of *ex ante* scenarios to eliminate the factors irrelevant to management action, a very tall order. But to move the debate forward, I have two suggestions.

First, the 'deal' should be struck in cash-flow terms. This is a necessary requirement to link to the forward-looking estimates of expenditures. It would also do much to avoid the opportunism involved in reporting in profit terms.

Second, a practical way forward may be to make 'unanticipated' gain the subject of measurement at the time of a price review. One would seek to agree a set of indicators to reflect specific items involved in productivity changes. These would be derived first from physical measures which the industry and the particular regulated company have in common, and which can be given an anticipated cash-flow interpretation in industry-wide terms. A predicted physical interpretation of this would be set up for each regulated company. Thereafter, how each firm does can be interpreted in cash terms, against the progress of its individual physical 'norm'. This will separate the unrealised efficiency arguments from all the other unforeseen impacts on a company's experience.

But Stephen Glaister's warning,[8] of the influence of quality in utilities' performance, is well taken. The issue is, at base, the question of trading company expenditures against consumer benefit, and he reminded us of the difficulties for measurement which different consumer valuations of quality imply. This has wider ramifications, not least in approaching the question of how to deal with failure on the part of regulated companies to spend the capex allowed for in the control. To pursue this would take us too far afield on this occasion. But I believe the priority of translating academic ideas into regulatory practice lies in this area, of evaluation of quality, rather than in devising ever more ingenious schemes which gloss over information problems.

Summary and Conclusion

My argument has run as follows. The RPI-X incentive approach marks a fundamental change in the way the control of utilities is approached. The basic economic tool – the forward-looking estimates of required cash flow in separated uncontestable activities – has had to be constructed from a very imperfect start at privatisation. This has required information development on both sides of the regulatory interface (companies and regulators). Substantial progress has been made, but much remains to be done to achieve a better system. Whatever position critics take, they wish to preserve the incentive properties of the controls. I have indicated important and needed developments in techniques, notably the detection of unexpected efficiency gains and rationalising their dispersal to customers to preserve incentives, in which behavioural effects, as well as forward-looking inducements, are important.

I drew out some implications of the fact that the regulators' task on this view is to evaluate a financial project when proposing an 'X'.

---

[8] In Glaister, 'Incentives in Natural Monopoly: The Case of Water', Chapter 2 in this volume, above, pp.27-62.

Accounts must be the servants, not the masters, of computation of allowed revenues. In the current exchanges between Ofgas and TransCo on the price control, I detected what I thought would be a difficulty, namely, the acceptance of forward-looking expenditures as the 'organising principle for regulatory review', as I put it. I have also argued that useful debate will involve a much greater willingness to disclose information. On the question of modifying RPI-X, I argued the case for learning how to run with the present system rather than to set up more elaborate systems. However, the debate is well worth pursuing and I have suggested some ways forward.

Finally, because I have been dubbed the 'Austrian godfather' of UK regulation, perhaps I should end by indicating where I think Austrian insights *are* essential to regulation, UK-style. Underpinning both sides of the regulatory tasks, price control and competition, is the Schumpeterian understanding of how profits are made and are dispersed and, particularly for the competitive side, the Hayekian insistence that it is competition – that is, entry, in the current case – which creates the information which both regulators and regulated have to use. Marrying these to neo-classical views of what is meant by costs is the main intellectual challenge now facing regulators.

CHAIRMAN'S COMMENTS

Clare Spottiswoode
Office of Gas Supply

I AGREE WITH A GREAT DEAL of what Michael Beesley has said. I would like to draw out some of those areas where I agree strongly and then note slight differences of emphasis in other areas.

One of the really key issues that we are facing is information. Information is a very important issue which we would have liked to have seen addressed more substantially in the new Gas Act. It is quite clear that we are not going to get, particularly from TransCo, and probably from British Gas Trading also, the figures that we would like to have to be able to set the price control.

Much of this has to do with where British Gas has come from. Because of the quality of information now it will take many years to obtain the right kinds of figures for regulators to be able to use effectively. Having these figures would be to the benefit of both our regulated companies and ourselves. The other key area concerning information, as Michael also emphasised, is what we can publish. We have fought long and hard with British Gas to put information into the public domain. We should not need to do that. We did try to get the DTI to make much clearer what information could be published; and certainly we feel very strongly that any information that belongs to a monopoly should be put in the public domain, unless there are very good reasons for it not to be. The current law, frankly, is too strongly biased against disclosure, but it is also very confused. Issues about information come up in five or six different parts of the Gas Act and also in the Licences; they all say slightly different things. Finding out what one can actually do in law is difficult in many areas. Getting on the wrong side of the line is a criminal offence for which I could be put in jail, so one tends to be rather conservative when interpreting those particular parts of the law!

I also very much agree with Michael about the whole issue of cash-flows. I think it is not just economists but business people who know that bygones are bygones, and that what is done is done. One has to look to the future. There is absolutely no point in crying over spilt milk if you have made a mistake. Conversely, you can revel in the money made by good investments. We will need cash flow information in order to set out price control cash-flows. We will get it from British Gas; or we will have to assess it for ourselves. But one way or another, we will have to have the information. We will obviously also look at such things as the value of British Gas to a predator and gearing issues, and we shall also be looking at the more traditional approaches to price control.

I think we ought to have slightly more emphasis on accounting figures than Michael said. We need to able to show how you move from accounting figures to economic analysis, if only to explain what is happening, so that people have some yardstick by which to judge what we are doing. Of course, if we put in a price control that has a form of profit sharing or sliding scale, such a control would need to have accounting figures.

Speaking very personally, because we have not yet come to a conclusion in Ofgas about this, I am not convinced that the balance of risks in the current RPI-X formula is absolutely right. Now, a lot of the risks that are currently there are partly because we have a very simple form of price control. One route can be to make it more sophisticated. For example, as the volumes of gas rise either through weather effects, or through general growth of gas use, profits rise more than proportionately, so clearly a coefficient of one, as we have in the current formula, is not right. Now, whether we can do better than that remains to be seen, but it is clearly a feature we must improve.

There are many other areas where we can make the formula more sophisticated. Any such change will change the value of the risk factor and may get rid of many of the present risks. But also we do not want to make the formula too complex, because then we will be chasing our own tails. Whatever we do has to be kept simple. So a balance has to be struck. But as I said, whatever we do choose in the end, I still want to have a look at what it will mean for the balance of risks. I am personally not completely convinced that a straightforward RPI-X without any error correction is necessarily the right balance of risk between consumers and the company.

Going on to another topic, there was a big furore about the Schedule when the Gas Bill was going through the House of Commons which relates to the assets the Trading company is to have in order to back up the take-or-pay contracts with the producers. Michael pointed out the importance of ring-fencing. Now this scheme to transfer assets within British Gas is going to be very important for ring-fencing. There are major regulatory issues in what happens.

The form the Trading company takes will affect the way in which we can ring-fence the future companies. For example, if all Trading's assets were held in BG plc, so that all BG trading activities had to be via rents or through contracts or whatever, the licence and commercial contracts between the trading company and BG plc pose a problem. To ring-fence all those contracts and to ensure what is done is fair and at arm's length will be difficult.

Once the Secretary of State has set the transfer scheme, it is let loose on the world. We need to ensure, in that case, that there can be changes in licences to ensure that we have proper regulatory control over what happens to the Trading company.

I rather suspect there is going to be a large amount of interest from the producers about what this transfer scheme contains. So I sincerely hope it is to be made public as soon as the information is available, so that it can be accessible to interested parties which can then assess it. There are legal issues about what can be made public. But precisely what that transfer scheme says is going to be very important to the industry.

Markets and the Media
Competition, Regulation and the Interests of Consumers

Governments, faced with problems which elicit public concern, are all too ready to pass restrictive legislation, establish supervisory committees and commissions, or pass difficult issues to regulators of particular sectors of the economy. In the course of time, the probable outcome is a huge regulatory edifice, involving massive compliance costs for firms and individuals, and striking at the roots of economic change by severely hindering entrepreneurship.

The 'media' industries in all their forms are favoured candidates for regulation. Governments seem unwilling to let markets in media work, claiming 'imperfections' and 'failures' which require regulation.

But what substance is there in these claims? To what extent is regulation feasible, given that technological advance is blurring the dividing lines among different forms of media? And are there such problems in the media – for example, concentrations of power through dominant owners – that market processes cannot be trusted to protect consumers?

IEA Readings 43, edited by Michael Beesley, explores such questions. Professor Beesley introduces the volume, summarising and commenting on the views of the other contributors. The following four chapters deal with specific issues in media regulation – copyright by Dan Goyder, digital technology and its implications by Malcolm Matson, the future of public service broadcasting by David Sawers, and concentration and diversity by William Shew and Irwin Stelzer.

Contents

ISBN: 0-255 36378-8

IEA Readings 43

£16.50
incl. p&p

The Institute of Economic Affairs
2 Lord North Street, Westminster
London SW1P 3LB
Telephone and sales: 0171 799 3745
Fax: 0171 799 2137

Trouble in Store?
UK Retailing in the 1990s
TERRY BURKE AND J.R. SHACKLETON

1. Retailing is a dynamic and highly successful sector of the economy, generating approximately 10 per cent of GDP and employing around 2½ million people – many of them individuals who would otherwise have difficulty finding employment.

2. Nevertheless, retailing has always attracted a good deal of suspicion from the public, leading to a variety of different forms of regulation.

3. Retailing has also been wrongly criticised as being in some way inferior to other forms of economic activity.

4. Concentration in retailing has increased in recent years. Grocery retailing in particular is dominated by the larger multiples.

5. However, competition persists in a variety of forms and there is no evidence that the current degree of concentration is detrimental to the public interest.

6. UK retailing is ahead of most of its competitors in the use of information technology, and is set to benefit from movements towards electronic shopping.

7. The recent trend to out-of-town shopping has been widely criticised for its impact on the high street, and the current Government is supporting new restrictions. The grounds on which this increased regulation is justified are not, however, unassailable.

8. Attempts to restrict new retailing development serve to protect other retailers from competition and frustrate individual choice.

9. The environmental impact of out-of-town shopping on local neighbourhoods, increased road use, excessive packaging and retail sourcing has been criticised. These criticisms are exaggerated and the critics' policy proposals are likely to be inappropriate and ineffective.

10. There is no economic case for significant further regulation of retailing. New theoretical developments, indeed, suggest that much existing regulation (in consumer protection, for instance) may be unnecessary.

ISBN 0-255 36374-5

Hobart Paper 130

The Institute of Economic Affairs
2 Lord North Street, Westminster
London SW1P 3LB
Telephone and sales: 0171 799 3745
Fax: 0171 799 2137

£9.00
incl. p&p